FRIENDS OF FRIENDS
Networks, Manipulators and Coalitions

FRIENDS OF FRIENDS

Networks, Manipulators and Coalitions

JEREMY BOISSEVAIN

University of Amsterdam

PAVILION SERIES

SOCIAL ANTHROPOLOGY

OXFORD
BASIL BLACKWELL

ISBN 0 631 14970 8 Cloth bound edition
ISBN 0 631 14980 5 Paper bound edition

Printed in Great Britain by
Western Printing Services Ltd, Bristol
and bound by Kemp Hall Bindery, Oxford

To
INGA,
IENEKE, LIETJE, MARIA and ANNA

Preface

This book is a personal document in many senses; but no one works alone. I have tried to indicate all the published sources of ideas that have been important to me. The most important influences, however, have been from discussions with members of my personal network, and they are many and diverse. Some agree with the ideas presented here, but many do not.

The book started as a series of four lectures given at the University of Sussex in March 1968. These were expanded before different groups at the University of Amsterdam during the following two years. Drafts of the chapters were then presented as weekly papers to graduate students, who criticized some sections severely and constructively. The following pages consequently reflect the ideas of many students, too many to mention individually. But I must thank Jojada Verrips, Carla Jonker and Emmy Brunt for particularly helpful comments.

Many others have contributed ideas and helped in various ways. Research I carried out in Malta, Sicily and Montreal between 1960 and 1969 forms the experience on which much of the book is based, and for this I have to thank the British Colonial Social Science Research Council, Salvinus Duynstee, Terry Spens, the American Philosophical Society, the Cooperative for American Relief to Everywhere (CARE), the Canadian Royal Commission for Bilingualism and

Biculturalism, the Social Science Research Council of the United States, the Wenner-Gren Foundation for Anthropological Research, the Netherlands Association for Pure Scientific Research (ZWO), and the University of Michigan Project on Mediterranean Networks directed by Eric Wolf. The first draft was rewritten in the hospitable isolation of the Pauwhof, Wassenaar, during three weeks 'leave' that students and colleagues kindly gave me early in 1972.

Rudo Niemeijer provided technical assistance on matters statistical and supervised the processing of data for chapter 5. He also carried out library research and read parts of the manuscript critically, as did Jolanthe van Opzeeland-De Tempe, who roughed out many of the diagrams, which H. M. van Groos kindly prepared. She also prepared the index. I am most grateful to the University of Amsterdam for making their help available, and also that of Carolien Prakke, who skilfully typed and retyped various versions of the manuscript from drafts and tapes. Mrs. M. A. Jansen-Moesenbroeck kindly helped type the final draft and Hanny Hoekstra the index.

Freddy Bailey, the book's patient editor, Bruce Kapferer and Bonno Thoden van Velzen read the entire first draft and provided many useful suggestions, some of which I have adopted. Mart Bax, Ioan Lewis, Clyde Mitchell, Julian Pitt Rivers, Peter Storey, Norman Schwartz and Klaas van der Veen gave me helpful criticism on the sections they read. Francis Mizzi, Anthony Cuschieri and Arturo Xibilia provided essential assistance and many insights, and Wim Heinemeyer, Herman van der Wusten and Leo van den Berg gave valuable bibliographic advice. Discussions with Anton Blok over the past few years have helped enormously to tighten the argument.

Sections of several chapters, as indicated in footnotes, have appeared elsewhere. The original version of chapter 8 was written as a contribution to a *Festschrift* for Lucy Mair, my supervisor at the London School of Economics. I shall remain grateful to her for many things, and especially for the many hours she spent trying to teach me to write. (Publication of the *Festschrift*, edited by John Davis, has unfortunately been delayed.) I am indebted to Bruce Kapferer, to the Institute of Social Research in the University of Zambia, and to Manchester University Press for permission to publish extracts of the case discussed in chapter 3.

Inga, my wife, delicately straightened twisted sentences and helped correct the proofs; Ieneke, our eldest daughter, arranged the bibliography. I am grateful to my entire family for putting up with my many absences, both mental and physical, during the writing of the book. A book like this, written alongside many and varied duties in a growing university undergoing rapid change, comes out of the time that otherwise would be spent with family and friends. It is thus also a modest monument to a form of exploitation that is rarely mentioned: the exploitation by universities of the private lives of their members, who are expected to do research and write, yet are given little or no time to do so. In gratitude for their help and support I have dedicated the book to the five members of my family.

Bussum, The Netherlands   Jeremy Boissevain
June 1972

Acknowledgement

The quotation on pages 53, 54 and 55 from Bruce Kapferer's 'Norms and the Manipulation of Relationships in a Work Context', from J. G. Mitchell (ed.). *Social Networks in Urban Situations* (1969), is made by kind permission of the author, the editor, University Publications of the University of Zambia in Lusaka and Manchester University Press.

Contents

1
Introduction

A POINT OF VIEW

I can think of no better way to begin than by describing one
of the episodes which prompted me to write this book. In a
sense I am merely beginning at the beginning.

One Sunday morning in March 1963 *Professore* Volpe discussed certain personal problems as we strolled slowly back
and forth across the principal square of Leone, a Sicilian
town in which I was then carrying out research. He had been
having difficulties over the education of his eldest son, and
both the problems and their solutions are rather Sicilian. He
suspected that a colleague at the secondary school in the
neighbouring town where he taught, and where his son was a
pupil, was trying to fail the son and thus block his entrance
to the University. This would have damaged the family's
position as an important member of the professional class in
Leone. So Volpe arranged, whenever his enemy passed
through Leone on his way to the provincial capital or Palermo,
to have him followed by certain of his own clients and those
of his brother, an important notary in Palermo. He was proud
that this brother, who lived on the other side of Sicily, but
'who has friends everywhere', even managed to get reports
of conversations held by the suspect at the latter's social club.
Both the conversation overheard and the contacts which his
enemy was seen to make in Palermo seemed to confirm his

B

suspicion. *Professore* Volpe's brother then moved swiftly to apply counter-measures through a nameless important person in Palermo. This person placed pressure on the men who would decide the boy's admission to University and who had been previously contacted by the patron of *Professore* Volpe's enemy. As the two brothers between them boasted a wider range of contacts and a more powerful protection than their rival, they were able to resolve the affair to their satisfaction. The son was admitted to the University.

It is quite possible that the entire plot to dishonour the family was a figment of *Professore* Volpe's imagination, for it was all based upon intuition and indirect evidence. The suggestions by his brother to his influential friend in Palermo were most certainly couched in allegory and allusion, as was his recital to me in which no names or specific accusations were mentioned. But *Professore* Volpe believed it to be true, and acted accordingly.

The story continues. Several months after his son was admitted to the University, *Professore* Volpe was insulted in front of most of his fellow-teachers by his old enemy. He told me that he was so angry that he had to leave the common room, but before slamming the door he had shouted at his enemy that he would have his apology. He had returned to Leone and during his evening stroll the same day met '*uno dei quelli*' ('one of them', an expression often used to allude to a *mafioso*). In telling me this, he pulled his cap down over one eye to indicate to me a *mafioso* in Sicilian sign language. This person was one of those who had helped keep his enemy under observation two months before when he passed through Leone on his way to the provincial capital and Palermo. He mentioned the insult he had received, and his friend, the *mafioso*, said, '*Ci penso io*', 'I'll see to it'. His friend apparently went to the neighbouring town late one evening soon after and knocked on his enemy's door. In a courteous but tough voice—which *Professore* Volpe imitated for me—he informed the enemy that it would be better to apologize or there might be unpleasantness. Two days later *Professore* Volpe got a short note of apology by post. When I asked how much he had had to pay his friend for all his help, he smiled and replied, 'Nothing, of course', and explained that the friend was the son of a man whom his own father, an important notary, had helped to keep out of prison forty years before. 'He helped me for *amicizia*, for friendship. Because of our father we have friends all over Sicily. They are not criminals. They are men who make themselves respected. They will help you when you need it, but . . . when they turn to you for help, you give it or . . .', and he made the chopping motion that means the application of violence. 'You help them and they help you. They give and you give.'

Professore Volpe ended by saying that his son is doing well at the University and thus justified his faith in his ability and intelligence. 'But his younger brother is lazy and not very bright,' he observed. 'He will probably fail this year. My enemies are busy again. I must see what can be done.' And muttering about the many responsibilities of fatherhood, he went off to lunch.[1]

Most Sicilians seem to spend a very large part of their time making arrangements similar to those of *Professore* Volpe. In fact, most of us do the same, although we do not have such extreme educational and status problems as my friend Volpe, nor do we employ such elaborate means to resolve those we have. Nonetheless, the means must not be examined in isolation from the problems, for extreme problems demand extreme solutions. The difference is but one of degree: all of us have problems which we at least attempt to resolve via friends and friends-of-friends with whom we may even form temporary alliances. This basic form of social behaviour provides the central focus of this book.

My discussion thus concentrates on the way in which inter-personal relations are structured and influenced, on the way individuals seen as social entrepreneurs seek to manipulate these to attain goals and solve problems, and in the organization and dynamism of the coalitions they construct to achieve their ends. The subject matter is familiar: the network of friends, relatives and work mates; the visiting, bargaining, gossiping and manoeuvring that goes on between them; the impact on these of promotion, ideology, and conflict; the steps an ambitious man takes to build up his fund of credit among useful relations; and the operation of neighbourhood and workplace cliques and factions. These are processes and situations with which we are all involved and they are the basic stuff of social life. Nevertheless I found it difficult and often impossible to reconcile these observations and experiences with the model of society which—like most social anthropologists of my generation (I obtained my Ph.D. in 1962)—I had been trained to employ. Very briefly, sociologists and social anthropologists were, and very many still are, largely concerned with the study of society as an enduring system of groups, composed of statuses and roles, supported by values and connected sanctions which operate to maintain the system in equilibrium. This is the so-called structural-functional view of social behaviour and society: it has dominated sociology, social anthropology and to a considerable extent political science since the 1930s.

In various research situations as well as in my personal life I have encountered a shifting environment of social relations which individuals construct and which cannot be adequately described only in terms of norms.[2] Many interactions were transactions, which are not the same as the morally sanctioned reciprocal exchange of rights and obligations about which structural-functionalists write. Role relations seemed in perpetual flux, the expectations of each actor varying according to the situation and the other relationships he maintained. People fenced with values, modifying and selecting them to excuse or explain more venal personal motives. Empirically, informants seemed to ask themselves the questions: 'What is the best for me and my family?' 'From what possibility will I derive the greatest benefit?' 'How much can I get away with?' as often as they did the typical structuralist questions: 'What is expected of me in this situation?' 'What is best for my group?' Persons in conflict with others won not so much because they were 'right', that is, had morally the most telling argument or defended more important values than their opponents, but because they had access to influential allies who could bring pressure on their rivals and their allies. Moreover, certain persons seemed to wield great power not because of their formal roles, but thanks to their carefully cultivated but constantly shifting sets of contacts. Furthermore, many informants invested enormous amounts of time, energy and other forms of social capital in shifting alliances of persons—patron-client relations, cliques and factions. Such alliances were temporary, and they were not the perpetual 'corporate' groups I had been trained to believe were the key to the social structure, though some could and did become enduring. Yet these temporary coalitions seemed to play an extraordinarily important part not only in political and economic activities, but also in the daily round of social relations.

In short, it has become clear to me, as it has to others, that the static, structural-functional model of society does not work at the level at which real people interact.[3] That is, it cannot be used to explain the behaviour of real people and the patterns and forms it assumes nor, as a consequence, to predict it.[4] It is not enough for students of social behaviour to ask: 'What is the pattern of social relations?' and 'How is this pattern maintained?' the two fundamental questions with which structuralists concern themselves. They must also try to explain the system in terms of something besides the system. That is, they must also ask: '*How do such patterns emerge?*' and '*How are they changing?*' It seems to me that these are the essential questions, for if we can answer them we can explain not only the patterns of behaviour we observe, but also their genesis and development. We must be able to explain the *is*, the *being* and the *becoming* of social institutions. To do this it is necessary to examine other influences besides those of custom, coercion and the moral order.

Patterns emerge, or emerged in the past—for we inherit many institutions—because persons make similar decisions in the face of similar influences. These influences may range from culturally defined directives for behaviour, through the demands made by relations, friends and associates, to the limits imposed by the physical environment. Within the social, cultural and ecological framework so established, people decide their course of action on the basis of what is best for themselves, and not only, as structural-functionalists would have us believe, on the basis of the accepted and sanctioned norms of behaviour. Man is thus also a manipulator, a self-interested operator, as well as a moral being. That is, he is constantly trying to better or to maintain his position by choosing between alternative courses of action. But since he is dependent on others, it is impossible for him to achieve his own self-interest unless he takes others into account and can demonstrate that his action in some way benefits or does not harm them. Naked motives of crude self-interest can never be brought forward to justify action to others. Pragmatic action is dressed up in normative clothes to make it acceptable. A Sicilian who wants to be elected mayor so that he can plunder the town's resources campaigns for office by explaining how he is motivated by a desire to help obtain running water, paved roads and a community centre for his fellow villagers. On a more pragmatic level, he can even argue that he must get his hand into the municipal till so that he can help his needy relatives.[5]

The study of the 'true' motives of social action is a difficult problem and one in which I would rather not become entangled at this stage. Nonetheless, I think it is clear that the view that man is also a self-interested operator opens up important lines of investigation. Instead of trying to answer the question 'Why did he do that?' with only the structural-functional questions 'What are the rules of behaviour in such a case?' (or, as so often happens, 'Why did he say he did it?' which usually amounts to the same thing) I suggest it is equally important to ask 'What is he getting out of it.' In the final analysis he will probably advance the most convenient for himself of several possible 'rules' to justify action from which he is the prime beneficiary. While I agree that people often act in terms of the moral values and rules of their society because they truly believe in them, a sociological model which suggests that people normally act in this way is naive.[6] The assumption that man, in addition to being a moral being, also is out for himself, is useful for generating testable propositions and examining the kind of problems in which I am interested.[7] Essentially it is no more than a common sense model.[8]

The starting point of the book is thus the failure of existing theory to take into account the range of social forms usually dismissed as informal organization.[9] Instead of looking at man as a member of groups and institutional complexes passively obedient to their norms and pressures, it is important to try to see him as an entrepreneur who tries to manipulate norms and relationships for his own social and psychological benefit. I begin therefore by taking a closer look at our immediate social environment, the network of relations into which a person is born and which he constructs, tries to manipulate and through which he is manipulated. This network is not only the source of many of his social problems, it also forms the raw material with which as it were he must solve these problems. In chapter 2 I set out some structural features of this personal social network and demonstrate how its structure influences and constrains behaviour. The discussion is illustrated in chapter 3 by means of an extended example of a conflict in a Zambian factory. Chapter 4 is concerned with the way in which biological, physical, cultural and social factors influence the structure of this micro-environment of personal relations, the influences of this on personality, and the reciprocal influence of the two on each other. A detailed examination in chapter 5 of the personal networks of two Maltese informants illustrates some of the points. The discussion then moves on in chapter 6 to show how persons intent on the pursuit of power and prestige attempt to manipulate their networks of relations to achieve their goals and in doing so construct coalitions of persons to assist them. Chapter 7 explores the nature and internal dynamics of some of these coalitions, in particular of cliques, gangs, action-sets and factions. The discussion in chapter 8 demonstrates the process whereby rival coalitions become transformed into permanent institutions and indicates how the structure and inherent dynamism of conflict groups reflect and lead to cultural and social change.

Throughout the discussion I have, on purpose, placed the accent rather heavily on the notion of individuals choosing between sets of socially prescribed alternatives, yet acting primarily in accord with what they consider is best for themselves, rather than what is best for their neighbours, their groups or their society. I stress again that the two points of view are related, for most persons are also moral beings. That is, in addition to pragmatic motives, a person also acts in terms of values which are important to him because he forms part of certain groups and takes part in institutionalized activities with their own internal value systems to which he subscribes. In short, a person does or does not do certain things not because he believes that he will be rewarded or punished for doing so, but because he believes that it is morally right or wrong to do so. These moral values as well as his social, cultural and physical environment form the constraints within which he acts.

If I have suggested that we look at interacting individuals primarily as self-interested entrepreneurs rather than as faceless objects of the pressure of groups and society, I must make it quite clear that I am not positing a polarity between the individual and the group or society, and opting for the first. Of course social pressure is exerted on individuals, but this is not the pressure of an impersonal society or group. It is pressure from other individuals caught up in a pattern of interdependencies. I am suggesting that social configurations such as coalitions, groups, institutions and society must be seen as networks of choice-making persons competing for scarce and valued resources. Neither interdependent individuals nor the particular configurations which they form can be considered separately from each other. The interrelation between the two is dynamic, and forms a process with an inherent momentum or development of its own.[10] Pattern, process and momentum must be viewed as the cumulative result of decisions made by persons interacting with each other who are faced by similar constraints. These can be analysed.

This book suggests some of the ways that the interdependence of individuals may be approached. In doing so it seeks to reintroduce people into sociological analysis, from where they have been banished since Durkheim. This is of more than just theoretical interest, for I believe that the insights into social life which can be gained this way can provide valuable leads to those interested in psychiatric and development work. It is not, however, my object to provide a tightly-formulated theory, but only to suggest a series of questions about particular social patterns and processes and indicate some of the concepts needed to answer them.

In the remainder of this chapter I discuss some of the reasons which explain why the questions asked in this book are not yet an established part of social anthropology.

STRUCTURAL-FUNCTIONALISM, MYTH AND
MIGHT IN ACADEME

1. *The structural-functional model, or what happens to Jack and Jill*

The structural-functional view of society as a system of enduring groups composed of statuses and roles supported by a set of values and related sanctions which maintain the system in equilibrium flows logically from the questions social anthropologists and sociologists ask about the world around them. The central question is still, in most cases, the same one asked by Hobbes: considering that man is basically out for himself, *what makes social order possible?* This central problem of sociological theory has been answered in ways that have given rise to two basic models of society: the 'consensus' or 'integration' model, and the 'coercion' or 'conflict' model.[11] Briefly the first model attributes to social systems the characteristics of solidarity, cohesion, consensus, co-operation, reciprocity, stability; the other attributes to it the characteristics of division, coercion, dissensus, conflict, and change. Nonetheless these two views of society do not require revision of the accepted theoretical apparatus used by social scientists. The models are not genuine alternatives.[12] Their congruence should not surprise us, for the advocates of both start with the same basic questions: Why does society exist? What brings about the social order we perceive around us? Some answer that we accept the values that underlie this order voluntarily; others argue that they are forced upon us by those who have a vested interest in maintaining the *status quo*. There is nonetheless a difference in emphasis that has direct consequences for the type of problems the researcher examines.

This difference in accent is quite possibly derived partly from the conservative or radical ideology of their respective advocates. In fact an interesting political application of the consensus model is that of the corporate state introduced by Mussolini, Franco and Salazar. In Italy, Spain and Portugal, the regimes were or still are based on a concept of social order that assumes that 'capital and labour, or owners of the means of production and workers, do not have conflicting interests to be expressed in syndical or political strife, but complementary interests to be dealt with harmoniously'.[13] Those who support consensus theory are not all conservative, but it is interesting that the corporate state was adopted at the same time as functional social theory.

It is also interesting that social anthropologists have subscribed almost wholly to the consensus model. This in itself is not surprising, considering that most anthropological research until the late 1950s took place in colonial territories and was financed by colonial powers. These were of course pleased to learn that the native and minority populations accepted the imposed social order voluntarily and that conflict was abnormal.[14] This theoretical orientation, coupled with intensive participant observation at close quarters with the object of study, which is the anthropologist's primary research instrument, has produced a flood of detailed monographs on literally hundreds of societies. Most display a remarkably uniform approach. The researcher sets himself the task of describing the *social structure*. This is viewed as an arrangement of persons in institutionally controlled or defined relationships, such as that of chief and subject, or that of brother and sister, or as the relations between groups of persons within a system of groups.[15] The basic assumption is that there is thus a social structure that can be isolated and, eventually, compared with other social structures. A second assumption is that this can be done through isolating the institutionally controlled relationships. These then are for the most part relations between, or which derive from, membership in groups. For as Radcliffe-Brown, one of the founding fathers of the structural-functional approach, has noted, 'A continuing social structure requires the aggregation of individuals into distinct separated groups, each with its own solidarity, every person belonging to one group of any set.'[16] Elsewhere he noted that science, in contrast to history or biography, is not concerned with the particular, the unique, but only with the general. That is, with kinds and events which recur. 'The actual relations of Tom, Dick and Harry,' he wrote, 'or the behaviour of Jack and Jill may go down in our field notebooks and may provide illustrations for a general description. But what we need for scientific purposes is an account of the form of the structure.'[17]

We are presented monographs which set out in admirable detail what the social structure is, how it is maintained, how various institutions are interrelated to form a system of relationships. We are then shown how the value system supports this structure. All loose ends are neatly tied up: behaviour that does not conform to the normative picture presented is ignored or explained away as 'deviant' or 'exceptional'. Yet that does not solve the problem, for this exceptional behaviour takes place within the same social system that is being studied; it must be explained by factors which operate there. In short, we are presented with a model of how the anthropologist thinks (and all too often how the latter's informants would like him to think) the system *should* work. The trouble is that *ideal* systems are presented. Jack and Jill are dismissed as exceptions at best or deviants at worst. Yet Jack and Jill are real, and the system but a model. What we end up with is a set of generalized role relations: nameless husbands and wives, rulers and subjects, and so forth. Examples, if provided, are carefully selected to illustrate this. Real people making choices between conflicting norms and manipulating these for their own benefit are almost totally absent. Jack and Jill have disappeared.[18]

In short, according to the structural-functional model, behaviour is explained in terms of the system. It should follow from this that behaviour can be predicted once the norms of behaviour and the underlying values and sanctions that maintain these have been delineated by the investigator. Man is a moral being who acts in accordance with the dominant values that support the system. It is a nice, simple model: but it does not work. It is incomplete.[19] If the individual behaviour of real people has been systematically eliminated from the data used to construct a model, the model so constructed can obviously not be used to explain their behaviour. Yet this model is often put forward and used as a device which will explain behaviour.[20] What has been constructed is in fact a model of an ideal system that has the same relation to what actually happens as myth does to history.

The eccentric behaviour of Jack and Jill does not fit into the structural-functional model. Neither do the transitory and often highly individual systems of social relations which they and others build and manipulate to solve their problems, the networks and coalitions with which this book is concerned. Moreover, the model in its pure form misleads the researcher and reader alike, and poses grave problems, especially to those interested in politics and the distribution and manipulation of power.[21]

2. *Immaculate social conception*

Another of the many problems of social anthropologists and sociologists that must be seen as a legacy of structural-functionalism is their failure to come to grips with social change. They study the *status quo* and seek to explain it in terms of the *status quo*: they rarely attempt to explain the genesis or development of the institutions they study. The explanation of the development of this static social theory is fascinating. It is largely an overreaction to nineteenth-century evolutionary theories brought about by the shift in power relations within and between the societies of which social scientists form part.[22] The simultaneous rise of fascism and structural-functionalism are reactions to the shift in the balance of power away from the industrial, agrarian, bureaucratic and military bourgeoisie in favour of the workers, native peoples and other subjugated persons. Both fascism and structural-functionalism venerate and thus protect the old order against changes which threaten it.

This reaction, combined with the difficulties of studying the history of illiterate peoples, has enabled anthropologists to rationalize away the need for a historical dimension in favour of purely synchronic studies. They thus have rarely sought to explain how and why the institutions they studied came into being in the first place. It is almost as though social anthropologists and sociologists believed in a doctrine of immaculate social conception. It is strange to find this in the works of people for whom the evolutionary theories of Darwin are basic beliefs. Although the teleological elements inherent in structural-functionalism may be viewed as the working of the evolutionary process of the survival of the fittest—only those institutions persist which are best suited for society— again no explanation is provided of how the institutions were generated.

3. *The model tested*

Some of the analytical problems raised by the structural-functionalist approach may be illustrated in one of its classics, Evans-Pritchard's superb analysis, *The Nuer*.

The Nuer are a semi-nomadic, cattle-owning people who live in the swamps and open savannah along the banks of the Nile and its tributaries in the Sudan. They migrate between their small villages or hamlets perched atop hillocks, where they live when the rainy season turns the savannah into a marsh, and the larger cattle camps near the river and water holes, to which they are forced to move by the total absence of water inland during the long dry summer. They are—or were when Evans-Pritchard studied them in the 1930s—a proud, independent people, quick to take offence and prepared to defend with violence their honour and cattle against neighbour and outsider. In spite of their warlike nature, they have no formal leaders, though there are certain ritual experts, and each wet season village appears to have a central figure—the *tut* (bull)—around whom the others are clustered. This man is supposed to be a member of the dominant clan of the tribal segment in which the village is located. The essential question with which Evans-Pritchard was concerned was how these 200,000 people manage to live reasonably peacefully together in spite of their warlike nature and lack of formal political structure. His answer is that this is made possible by the complementary opposition which is inherent in their principle of reckoning membership in their kinship groups—the clans and, at a lower level, the lineages—through males. This patrilineal (or agnatic) ideology provides the principle which ensures order; it is the basis of the social structure.

In cases of tension, the descendants of brothers co-operate against those of first cousins, brothers and first cousins unite against second cousins, rival tribal segments join with each other against outsiders, and so on. As men must marry outside their clans, the membership rules of the descent groups are fairly straightforward, and a person's allies in the event of tension are clear-cut. Conflict in fact brings the political structure into relief. Order is ensured by the constant opposition and co-operation between the same persons in different situations: fission and fusion according to circumstances and in conformity with the patrilineal principles of descent. It is a beautifully constructed model.

Problems arise when this model—which I have, of course, simplified to be brief—is used to explain actual behaviour and to predict what Nuer will do when confronted with real life situations. Considering the prominence given to their patrilineal ideology, their combativeness and their residential problems, many readers attempting to use the model will conclude that Nuer related patrilineally will unite to fight more distant relatives if called on to do so, and, among other things, that villages will be composed of patrilineal kinsmen. Yet what actually happens is occasionally rather different.

As illustration of the way political segments are supposed to unite against genealogically more distant segments Evans-Pritchard gives the following example.[23] This example is extremely important for it is one of the very few he gives. In a particular conflict in Nuerland, segment *C* (*Thiang*) sought and found protection with neutral segment *A* (*Leng*), the dominant lineage of which stood, via ancestors, in the relation of brother's son to segment *B* (*Yol*), the enemy from which *C* was seeking protection. In spite of the warnings of *B*, their patrilineal relatives, *A* gave asylum to *C* on the grounds that the ancestor of *A* was the maternal uncle of the ancestor of *C*, and that they could not refuse protection to their sisters' sons. Thus in this example, close patrilineal relatives (brother's sons) did not combine against an outside lineage (sisters' sons), as the reader had been led to believe would occur according to the model presented. Nor is their failure to do so ever made clear to the reader. He can only conclude therefore that something rather basic is missing from Evans-Pritchard's elegant model of the Nuer political system.

The primacy of the patrilineal principle is also rendered questionable by the way in which people are grouped on the ground. Though the inhabitants of the wet season villages can all trace some sort of genealogical relationship to the chief man, the *tut*, and hence to each other, the surprising thing is that patrilineal relationships appear to be insignificant in doing so. In fact, in one village of 100, Konye, the ten homesteads clustered around the *tut*, Rue-Wor, are, genealogically speaking, a thoroughly mixed lot. They include some of his mother's relatives, some of the in-laws of his wives and of his brother, sister and son, to mention but a few categories. But they *do not include one patrilineal relative.* Moreover, Rue-Wor is not even a member of the dominant clan in that tribe, though several members of it do live in the village.[24] Surprising? Evans-Pritchard explains this deviation from his model as completely consistent with it:

> *It is the clear, consistent and deeply rooted lineage structure of the Nuer which permits persons and families to move about and attach themselves so freely, for shorter or longer periods, to whatever community they choose by whatever . . . tie they find it convenient to emphasize; . . .* it is on account of the firm values of the structure that this flux does not cause confusion or bring about social disintegration. It would seem it may be partly just because the

agnatic principle is unchallenged in Nuer society that the tracing of descent through women is so prominent and matrilocality so prevalent. *However much the actual configurations of kinship clusters may vary and change, the lineage structure is invariable and stable.*[25]

Is this a scientific statement or a declaration of faith? If the term 'faith in God', or 'family' or 'capitalism' or 'socialism' or 'constitution' were substituted for 'lineage structure' (of the Nuer)', the statement would explain just as much or as little. People in Malta move about, as they do in Montreal and Amsterdam or any other place in the world without lineage structures, attaching themselves freely to groups, big men, business houses, government departments, women, villages, guided tours and what have you by 'whatever tie they find it convenient to emphasize'. The point is that they do this without a deeply rooted lineage structure. Is it surprising then that Edmund Leach has exclaimed: 'The structural anthropologist, like the theologian, will only persuade those who already wish to believe!'[26]

4. *Confrontation with reality*

When I set out to conduct field research for the first time, I also wished to believe. Consequently I set out to discover the groups to which people belonged, the enduring role relations which derived from these, the norms which guided role performance and the moral constraints which supported these, so that I could grasp the social structure. The disproportionate amount of time I spent making the rounds of village associations and participating in their activities, even though their members represented but a fraction of the total population of the village and the political role of many of the associations was minimal, can be attributed partly to my misconceptions about the nature of society. I saw these associations as the formal groups which I had been trained to think

C

would provide the key to the social structure. They did not.
But it has taken me a long time to escape from the simplistic,
group-dominated functionalist model I used as my primary
analytical tool in 1960.[27] Yet ten years later there are still
monographic field studies being produced which set out in
exquisite detail how the Bongo-Bongo or the goat herding
nomads of the Urgubad highlands are *supposed* to behave.
They do not explain how the people studied actually behave
or why they behave the way they do. They are essentially
rule books about the ideal behaviour of the non-existent,
generalized 'average man'. Moreover, many students are still
setting out with the same research programme derived from
the same basic structural-functional concern with structure
and order. They are thus headed for the same mistakes I
made in their desire to produce rule books. The social reality
I encountered, as will these young researchers, is not quite
this simple. They, as I was, will be confronted with real life
situations which can only be built into the structuralist model
by an act of faith.

Yet, structural-functionalism still prevails. In spite of the
loud and often abrasive clarion calls of Leach and Jarvie to
social anthropologists to join in battle against structural-
functionalism, relatively few have done so explicitly.[28]
Increasing numbers, however, have indicated a certain dissatisfaction with the classical structural-functional model.[29]
But others indicate implicitly[30] or explicitly that the structural-
functional model 'does, indeed, take one a long way in the
description and analysis of societies which are small, homogeneous and relatively static. In the study of large, complex
and changing societies, however, this approach is faced with
certain limitations'.[31] I have suggested above that the model
does not work very well either for small, homogeneous
societies such as the Nuer.

Well removed in his Bergen niche from the highly interconnected network of British social anthropologists, Fredrik
Barth has been one of the few social anthropologists to react

positively to the none too gentle kicks Edmund Leach has been giving established theory since 1954. Barth argues that social anthropologists should be concerned with exploring the ways in which social forms are generated. To do this he develops the concept of the transacting individual. This provides 'a model whereby one may *generate* forms according to the rules of strategy, given the parameters of value'.[32] In brief, his point of departure is 'to explore the extent to which patterns of social form can be explained if we assume that they are the cumulative result of a number of separate choices and decisions made by people acting *vis-à-vis* another'.[33]

Though it need not detain us very long, it is interesting to speculate why, in spite of its demonstrated inadequacies, structural-functionalism has still not passed into history.

5. *Some thoughts on the persistence of a myth*

Why has the structural-functional model of society persisted for so long and the common sense complement of man as a self-interested transactor found relatively little support?

The most obvious reason is that structural-functionalism provided a scientific belief system which was most congenial to the colonial commitments of the countries in which social anthropologists were employed. Since nearly all social anthropological research is government financed, and social anthropologists are generally rather poorly paid academics who need large sums of money periodically to do research, it would indeed have been surprising if they had bitten the hand that fed them. I know from my own experience in two government financed research projects that, not surprisingly, the grant applications were formulated to evoke a generous response.[34] Once formulated, such research proposals tend to become self-fulfilling.

Secondly, the structural-functional approach provides a tried and simple recipe for research which the inexperienced researcher can use with relative safety. He locates key informants who can set out the rules of the social structure. These can then be illustrated by means of apt cases and tables. As noted, exceptions, i.e. not apt illustrative data, tend to be left out. In short, it is an appealing technique, a simple model which is quite safe to use since most of the great names in social anthropology have used it. It provides a simple analytical framework for often complex data. Since the research design was constructed to elicit the sort of data which would fit into this analytical framework, there is also little danger of other data disturbing the picture, for the data collected reflect the questions asked and thus the theory which articulates them. Even if the researcher begins to have doubts about the validity of his structural model during his writing-up period, there is usually not much he can do about it, for he lacks the data to back up his doubts, having failed to collect them while in the field.

Another reason for the persistence of structural-functionalism is that it is a belief system in which those with the greatest resources at their disposal have vested interests. They use these resources often unconsciously to defend their pet theories. Unquestionably those who have helped shape this theory and carried out their initial research under its influence hold, or held until recently, the senior university chairs in their profession. Now the academic profession, in spite of the lip-service it pays to merit, integrity and universalistic values, displays many of the particularistic characteristics of a feudal society: it has lords (deans, department chairmen and full professors), vassals (associate professors and lecturers) and serfs or body servants (teaching assistants). Power, in the form of control over degrees, research funds, recommendations for jobs, research leave, and so on, tends to be found at the top. Those at the top are also those who have been if not the architects, then the chief builders of structural-functionalism. An open challenge on strictly scientific grounds to the theory on which the life work of one's teacher/chairman/patron is based is viewed as disloyal, reckless and probably dangerous to career prospects. Hence the challenge is not made, or if made, is perhaps squashed before it is made public. Most persons who monopolize these resources would not use them consciously to protect their vested theoretical interests. Nonetheless, the *fear* that they might do so, or in other ways take offence, tends to inhibit criticism. Moreover, if criticism of the pet theory of an established authority is made, it tends to unleash a counter torrent of vigorous rhetoric which can be rather unsettling for the self-assurance if not the reputation of the target.

Consider the implications of the following exerpt from a letter I once received from a clever and very self-assured assistant-professor:

> Enclosed is a recent paper I have just completed with a colleague. The paper is out of the more usual style but is intended as an oblique attack on Radcliffe-Brownian structural-functionalism using a symbolic interactionist line. We gave it as a paper to the University X seminar. Went down like a lead balloon. XXX [his department chairman, a charismatic and persuasive defender of his own ideas—J.B.] was upset that we didn't feed ourselves into the University of X genealogy. Possibly it is a bit out of key and slightly risky but it was sure good fun trying.

If a self-confident man so obviously felt the disapproving hand of his academic patron and considered it 'out of key' and 'risky' to put forward ideas outside the particular structural-functional genealogy sired by his Professor, the ideas of a more timid person might well remain private thoughts.

There are also the polemic exchanges in the journals to serve as examples to the would-be critic. An excellent example, to which I have referred elsewhere, was recently provided by Gluckman's reply to Paine's article on gossip.[35] Here Gluckman assumes the role of a slightly annoyed, and at times puzzled structural-functionalist vigorously defending the place of group-centred analysis and a pet theory—at times with the majestic (or functionalist?) first person plural of established tradition which brooks no disagreement—against a younger anthropologist seeking to place the manipulating individual at the centre of his analysis.[36]

Considering the pressures which operate in Academe to inhibit criticism of vested theories, and I have personally observed their operation in Canada, Britain and the Netherlands, and have every reason to assume that the same is true in other countries, I think it is no coincidence that criticism often comes from outsiders. Barth and Harris, for example, who have questioned some of the basic assumptions of British social anthropologists, are non-British and criticize from abroad. Their social and geographic distance give them perspective; it also ensures that they are less vulnerable to counter pressures. Those who criticize from within the system are rugged individualists like Leach and Van Velsen, or angry young men like Jarvie.

Furthermore, those at the top also have the greatest voice in planning the teaching programmes designed to prepare students for the examination questions, which, naturally, have been set by themselves and, not surprisingly, reflect their views. In short, a theory, once it is established within the academic community, tends to be self-perpetuating.

Moreover, the dogma of structural-functionalism expresses a belief in the system *as it is*. This belief can be used, knowingly or subconsciously, to buttress one's own belief that one is right: A is a functionalist. A has reached the top of his profession. Structural-functionalism teaches that the system has a moral force. A is an integral part of the system. A must be right, because he is at the top, and the system continues. Therefore B, who is junior and who challenges A's theory, must be wrong, because A must be right, and so on. Their scientific belief supports their establishment role. This is circular, of course, for being part of the establishment, as I try to demonstrate in chapter 8, generates a conservative ideology (something that many senior academics fail to realize). Those who contest their view will tend to belong to the ideological opposition of the establishment to which the structural-functionalists belong. They will also belong to a younger generation in political as well as in educational/scientific terms. It would indeed be interesting to learn how many of the anthropologists who teach, and therefore must believe in, the moral force of society, have resisted the often legitimate requests for changes from within their own community, the university in which they work. I suggest that structural-functionalists oppose change. Their whole theoretical orientation is behind their conviction that their university system is morally right, and that, therefore, change must be resisted. There has been a great deal of debate in recent years over the influences of political ideology on scientific research. The reverse is equally relevant: scientific theoretical orientation influences political behaviour. Marx, after all, was also a sociologist.

Entrenched power hierarchies in the scientific community thus inhibit the development of scientific theory.[37] Nonetheless, the long term prognosis is favourable. The gradual shift in the balance of power in most universities away from the traditional university establishment of deans, chairmen and tenured professors towards younger staff members and students is helping to dislodge obsolete theories, as the power domains of those who established them begin to crumble. Thus increasing student power, which is reducing the differences in relative power within the universities, may well bring about not, as those who fear it proclaim, the end of the university as a community of scientists, but a more rapid development of scientific theory.

2

Networks: Interaction and Structure

NETWORKS

The social relations in which every individual is embedded may be viewed as a network.[1] This social network may, at one level of abstraction, be looked upon as a scattering of points connected by lines. The points, of course, are persons, and the lines are social relations. Each person can thus be viewed as a star from which lines radiate to points, some of which are connected to each other. These form his first order or primary network zone. But these persons are also in contact with others whom our central person does not know, but with whom he could come into contact via members of his first order zone. These are the often important friends-of-friends. They form what might be called his second order zone. This process can be carried out at still further removes so that we can theoretically speak not only of a person's second, but also of his third, fourth and Nth order zones (see Diagram 2.1). In fact, all of society can be viewed as a network, and via links in his various zones, an individual, in theory, can eventually get in touch with every other person. When I use the term network here, however, I use it chiefly in an egocentric sense, as the chains of persons with whom a given person is in actual contact, and their interconnection. This egocentric, personal network is of course unique for every individual.

The concept of personal network thus provides us with a

way of viewing social relations. It is not a theory of society, though the builders of theories will have to take such networks into account more than they have hitherto done. It offers a concept or social dimension intermediate between relationship and social system (or society), between local level and national level.[2] Diagrammatically, a network is similar to a communication circuit: it indicates that certain persons are in touch with each other, but in its simplest form, it says nothing about *how* they are in touch. That is, by isolating an individual's first order zone, the researcher has done nothing more than plot a series of links between a given person and a number of others, some of whom are also in touch with each other. These links are thus *potential* communication channels, but it must be established empirically that messages do in fact flow along them, and what kind of messages do so. As will be seen later, the nature of the messages and their volume depend on the nature of the individual link, and this, in turn, is partly affected by other links in the network, thus by its structure. Nonetheless, once the diagrammatic structure of the network is established, and the nature of the links determined, we are in possession of a model of how a given individual can in theory receive messages and, conversely, how he can send messages, and to whom as well as through whom he can do so. It is obvious that the number of persons an individual can send messages to is far greater than the number of persons he actually knows—those located in his first order zone—because each of these, potentially at least, can act as a relay to place him in touch with many others (see Diagram 2.1).

A social network is more than a communication network, for the messages are in fact *transactions*. By transaction I mean an interaction between two actors that is governed by the principle that the value gained from the interaction must be equal to or greater than the cost (value lost).[3] If the transaction is reciprocated in the sense that goods and services are returned, and thus flow in both directions, it is then useful to

speak of exchange. Exchange is thus reciprocal while a transaction may be only unilateral, such as the conscious spreading
of a rumour by a person to damage the reputation of a rival.
Over a time however the pattern of transactions may usually
be viewed as a relation of exchange, for messages, goods and
services move in both directions. It will be evident that
asymmetry can very easily creep into relations: person A

DIAGRAM 2.1

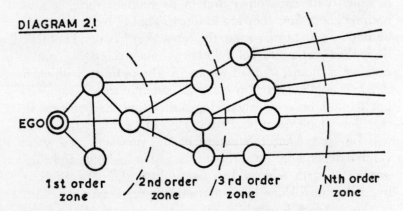

1st order zone   2nd order zone   3rd order zone   Nth order zone

provides more socially valued services to B than the latter is
able to reciprocate and is thus obligated to A. This provides
A with a certain hold over B: it gives him the power that, in
some measure, enables him to have his own way in spite of
B's resistance. Thus differences in power arise out of the
transactional process itself, and not only from the prior status
of the actors or the resources they control, although these
very often are related. These exchange relations and the
relative differences in power are thus properties which emerge
from sets of transactions.[4] Pursued this notion leads to a concept of society as a process rather than as a static, self-
regulating system. For if interaction in the sense of exchange
between people is continuous, so is the creation of these
imbalances of power which are used to influence the social
and physical environment of persons and groups. Social relations are not static, but dynamic. They form a shifting pattern

of power relations between persons and groups trying to gain freedom from social and physical constraints in order to pursue their goals. To do this they must obtain power. Hence the transactional element present in social relations.

A person's network thus forms a social environment from and through which pressure is exerted to influence his behaviour; but it is also an environment through which he can exert pressure to affect the behaviour of others. It is the reservoir of social relations from and through which he recruits support to counter his rivals and mobilizes support to attain his goals.

A first question we must try to answer is whether such networks can be said to have a structure in the sense of some sort of patterned relation of constituent parts. If so, does this influence behaviour, or, conversely, a person's ability to attain certain goals? Finally, if such networks do display variations in structure, what are the factors which influence these? Throughout the next few sections we shall thus examine more closely the immediate environment of social relations and the factors which affect it. It is well to note at the outset that this social environment is partly ascribed and partly achieved. That is, by virtue of his position in society—birth, rank, job, race—part of a person's environment is given to him gratis; and part he constructs, sometimes carefully but often haphazardly, to suit his purposes and personality. His interaction with this social environment is neither wholly self-determined, nor wholly predetermined. He is not only constrained and manipulated by his environment, he also manipulates it to suit his interests.

One could begin the analysis of social networks by viewing them as a series of points and interconnected lines without ascribing any different value to the lines.[5] In graph theory these are called 'undirected graphs'. But when dealing with social networks we are dealing with lines which have varying values; thus with 'directed graphs'. It is appropriate therefore to begin a discussion of the characteristics of networks by pointing to the heterogeneity of their links. This is a characteristic which is obscured in the commonsense usage of the network metaphor, which suggests linkages of equal weight (and thus an undirected graph).[6] We shall thus begin with content rather than form. The nature of this content lies at the root of the assumptions concerning the way in which personal networks, behaviour and institutions are related.

INTERACTIONAL CRITERIA

The linkages between persons in a network may be examined in terms of their structural diversity, the goods and services exchanged, the direction in which these move, and, finally, the frequency of interaction. These criteria make it possible to plot various exchange circuits either within the universe of a person's total personal network, or more usually within selected segments, or *partial networks*, isolated from the total network by means of the application of some criterion such as friendship, religious affiliation, place of work or residence.[7]

1. *Diversity of linkages: multiplexity*

Perhaps the most important characteristic of a personal network is that it is composed of persons linked in a large variety of ways. The social relations that link people derive from the many different activity fields in which each participates. They are in fact role relations. The concept of role is borrowed from the theatre. When sociologists speak of role, they mean the norms and expectations that apply to the occupant of a particular position.[8] Each person plays many different roles: neighbour, husband, employee, football club member, and so on. By virtue of each he comes in contact with particular sets of people who share with him a particular activity or interest.

The concept of role is an abstraction from reality, for it presupposes that we can isolate various institutional systems or activity fields composed of positions which individuals occupy. If we take this step, and I think it is legitimate to do so, a person's social network is seen as composed of a diversity of individuals recruited from the various activity fields in which he plays roles. The image I have is that of a many bladed Japanese or Chinese hand fan, each blade representing an activity field, but all converging at one point, the person at the centre of this network. Each blade may be viewed as a partial network consisting of sets of persons who actually or potentially have a relation in common by virtue of their role in that activity field. The network of interconnected roles in any given activity field, from ego's view point, is virtually unbounded.

DIAGRAM 2.2

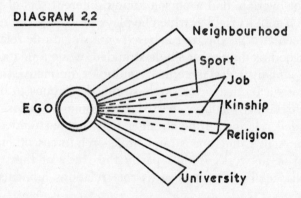

Many of the people in a given activity field also play roles in other activity fields. Each is thus sometimes in touch with the same people in different capacities. A person may know his brother as a neighbour, member of the same religious association, fellow employee, and supporter of the same political party. This is very often the case in relatively isolated communities. It also happens, however, that people, especially from open (non-isolated) communities, such as cities and villages in industrialized societies, are in touch with certain persons in only one of the many roles they play. Through individuals who play diverse roles, many institutional fields overlap; that is, they share in part the same personnel. The integration of communities, groups and institutions into the whole which we call society takes place via the personal networks of the individuals which constitute them. This measure of overlap is one of the ways in which societies differ. Certain, small-scale, isolated societies or communities (the kind traditionally studied by anthropologists) possess a high degree of overlap: people are in touch with the same persons in many different roles. In terms of the metaphor used above, we may say that the Japanese fan representing the activity fields is almost closed, the blades resting one upon the other. But in other societies, often characterized as large-scale, complex, industrialized, the fan is fully extended; the blades of the fan do not overlap, and a person knows different sets of people in each activity field in which he plays a role. A social relation between two people that is based on a single role relation is described as uniplex or single-stranded, while a relation that covers many roles is termed multiplex or many-stranded. There is a tendency for single-stranded relations to become many-stranded if they persist over time, and for many-stranded relations to be stronger than single-stranded ones, in the sense that one strand—role—reinforces others. The study of networks is thus partly the study of the ways in which social relations seen as role relations influence each other.

Once an attempt is made, however, to give the role a more specific content one soon discovers that the norms and expectations which apply to the occupant of a role vary enormously. Not only are the norms themselves vague, their relevance is determined by the degree to which they are perceived and by the sanctions available to enforce them. Expectations and norms are also a function (in the mathematical sense) of the degree to which information is exchanged between the actors (itself, as will be seen, a function of their respective network structures). It is thus possible for the two actors of social relation A/B each to hold different expectations about their role relation, which, in turn, may be at variance with the expectations of their audience. Furthermore, these expectations are influenced by other roles they play, by their cultural, physical and biological environment—expectations shift with age and sex—and by their own temperament. The way roles are played and the way they interact on each other is highly complex.

Nonetheless one of the basic assumptions underlying social anthropological analysis is that the diverse roles an individual plays can (1) be isolated analytically and (2) influence each other. This has implications for network analysis. In the many-stranded relation A/B, role relation X affects the behaviour of A and B in role relation Y. Stated simply, though an individual wears different hats on different occasions he is still the same person. A few illustrations will make the implications of this assumption clear.

Pietru Cardona, a Maltese informant, gets on well with his brother-in-law, who lives near him. They get on well as relatives (role X) and also as economic partners (role Y), hence help each other cultivate their plots of agricultural land (see Diagram 2.3). Pietru, on the other hand, the last time I visited him in his village, was not on good terms with a certain Maria, a member of the same *festa* (Maltese for *fiesta*) faction (role X, see Diagram 2.4). The reason was that Pietru had helped the parish priest at a fund-raising fair though the band club committee of the festa faction had decided to boycott the fair because of a disagreement with the parish priest.[9] Pietru, though an ardent partisan of the patron of the festa faction, thought the boycott nonsense. Hence Maria, a fanatic about festa affairs, refused to speak to him. After two weeks of glowering silence, Maria became friendly again. The reason for the sudden change was that Pietru in his capacity of tutor of Maria's daughter (role Y) had helped her to pass the stiff government secondary school entrance examination.

Clearly in a many-stranded relation between two persons it is impossible to characterize the relation in terms of any single role. It is for this reason that one of the hypotheses underlying the network approach to behaviour, but which is usually treated as an assumption, is that *where a many-stranded relationship exists between two persons, there is greater accessibility, and thus response to pressure, than is the case in a single-stranded relation.*

DIAGRAM 2.3

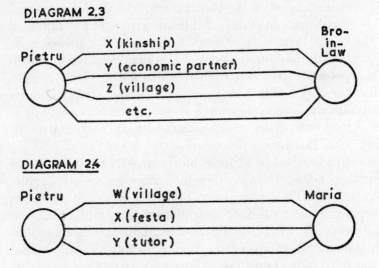

Another important hypothesis that is not always made explicit is that *where multiplex relations exist they will be more intimate (in the sense of friendly and confidential) than single-stranded relations.* These assumptions must be made explicit for what they are: hypotheses that can and must be tested. People sometimes detest persons to whom they are bound by multiplex relations, and are more intimate with persons to whom they are only lightly or even fleetingly bound (think of the confidences exchanged with a fellow passenger on plane or train). The transactional content of a relation must be measured and not merely assumed, as it so often is. An index for the degree of multiplexity can be obtained by dividing the number of multiplex relationships by the total number of all relevant relationships.

2. *Transactional content*

By transactional content I mean the material and non-material elements which are exchanged between two actors in a particular role relation or situation.[10] The elements transacted depend in part upon the role, but also on the way in which it is played by the actors. Normally, the husband/wife relation includes cash, affection, miscellaneous gifts and sex, to mention but a few of the elements exchanged in this complex role. Now it will be apparent that not all these items are always exchanged between all husbands and all wives. Nor are they transacted in the role relation brother/sister or neighbour, though, of course, they sometimes are. It is thus possible for a role relation to be given a more specific content by tabulating the elements exchanged. Kapferer recorded five items exchanged by the fourteen men in the work situation he studied, and which we examine in the following chapter: conversation, joking behaviour, job assistance, personal service, and cash assistance. I noted if two Maltese informants exchanged greetings, civilities, conversation/ information, and visits (see Tables 5.6, 5.7 and 5.8 in chapter 5). By recording this information both Kapferer and I were able to weight, albeit very crudely, the content of each relation in the networks we were studying. The transactional content of a relation thus gives a crude measure of its quality. The nature of the items transacted indicates not only the investment of the actors in it, but, especially, their anticipated benefits from it, and hence its importance as compared to other relations.

3. *Directional flow*

By directional flow I refer to the direction in which the elements exchanged move. It will be apparent that the flow of elements exchanged may be equal, complementary or unequal. The directional flow of these transactions can be

D

plotted, and provides an index of the relative investment of each of the actors in the relation, and thus of its relative importance. Equality or complementarity in the flow of items exchanged is an indication of equality in terms of power or prestige between the actors. Where there is asymmetry in the flow over time, there is very often a difference in status and power between the actors. This transactional account, in bookkeeping terms, is thus an important measure of the quality of a link in a network. Where there is symmetry one expects that messages (requests for help, information, support) will be honoured (or dishonoured) equally by both actors, for they have invested equally in the relation. Where there is an asymmetric flow, one expects the person who has invested most in the relation to be more amenable to the requests of the other, rather than the reverse.

4. *Frequency and duration of interaction*

Frequency of interaction often leads to and is a result of the quality of the relation in the sense of multiplexity of shared roles and the nature of things exchanged; but this does not follow necessarily. For example, I see our milkman more often than I do my two brothers, who live on the other side of the Atlantic. Yet I exchange only money for milk with the milkman, as well as a non-committal greeting when I see him. In spite of not having seen them for five years, I have great affection for my brothers, and though I exchange little besides Christmas letters with them now, I would exchange much if called on to do so. Frequency of interaction, in short, may often be, but is not always, an index of the investment of the actors in the relation. The *duration* of the contact is perhaps a more telling index than frequency of interaction, as it is a measure of the amount of time (a limited resource) that people invest in each other.

Having discussed how the links in a person's network may be differentiated according to such interactional criteria as multiplexity, transactional content, directional flow and frequency and duration of interaction, it is now time to examine some of the structural or morphological characteristics of networks. In the next section we examine network links stripped of their interactional aspects. This approach can lead to a rather sterile over-simplification unless it is remembered that the links are *personal relations*, which can be extremely complex.

STRUCTURAL CRITERIA

The significant structural criteria of networks are size, density or connectedness, degree, centrality and clustering. These criteria are of more direct relevance to small, bounded (therefore partial) networks than to large, unbounded ones. Why this is so will become apparent in the next few sections.

1. *Size*

The most important structural criterion of a person's network, whether total or partial, is its size. This is because the other criteria are calculated as a proportion of the total possible or actual links in the network. Obviously where the partial network under observation is extremely large, the ratios derived from the total number of (possible) combinations will also be affected. This problem has been given little or no attention by sociologists analysing networks because most have been concerned with partial networks in circumscribed situations.[11] Most persons who have used the network concept have in fact examined what have been called 'action sets';[12] they have not been concerned with the latent links, i.e. those links not used in reference to a given situation.[13] Once the 'potential links' are also built into the analysis, as I believe they must be in sophisticated sociological models, the analytical problems become complex.

My Maltese informant Pietru Cardona in 1968 had a primary zone composed of some 1,750 persons. These were persons whom he had met and had dealings with in the recent or distant past. They formed the social universe of persons who could help him solve his problems. To calculate the degree to which these people interacted, via him or independently of him, thus a study of only his first order zone, required the construction of a 1,750 by 1,750 matrix. This is no mean feat, and if only a few variables are examined, the

DIAGRAM 2.5

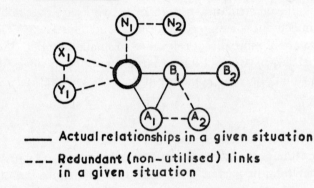

———— Actual relationships in a given situation

– – – Redundant (non-utilised) links
in a given situation

investigator has reached the memory limits of all but the largest computers. A study of the total first order zone is perhaps an extreme example. But even potential links in a partial network present problems. However, once actual and potential links are considered in relation to the second order zone—those persons known or unknown to Ego who can only be reached through members of his first order zone—the analytical problem becomes frightening. If, for example, each of the persons Pietru knows had a first order zone only of 500, they could place him in contact with no less than 875,000 other persons! Considering that Malta only has a population of 314,000, it is clear that Pietru can come into contact with certain people not known to him personally via several different first order links. Unless the redundant links are also built into the model one never really has a complete answer to the question illustrated in Diagram 2.5.[14] Why in a given situation were first order zone members A_1 and B_1 mobilized rather than X_1 and Y_1, and why second order zone member B_2 was also recruited though not A_2? In fact, unless the investigator also takes the redundant links into consideration, the questions cannot even be asked.

To sum up, latent links and second order zones are important, but they pose problems which have scarcely been considered by those attempting to use the concept of network for social analysis.

2. *Density*

The degree to which the members of a person's network are in touch with each other independently of him is also an important index. This index has been called the density of a network. That is, 'the extent to which links which could possibly exist among persons do in fact exist.'[15] It is hence an index of the *potential communication* between parts of the network and thus of the quantity and types of information (about Ego or others) than *can* be exchanged. When this information, judgements, gossip and so on is actually exchanged on a large scale, as often happens, for example, in a small village where every one knows each other, it tends to bring about a homogeneity of norms and values. It must be stressed, however, that network density is simply an index of the *potential* not of the *actual* flow of information. This is an important distinction, for one of the dangerous assumptions inherent in the network approach is that the measurement of density is a statement of actual transactions. This of course is a logical trap that must be avoided: a statement about form is not a statement about content. Nonetheless it is important, for it is a statement of the order *where A (form: high density), there a possibility of B (content: high volume of transactions).*

Formulated in this way an exploration of density can generate hypotheses which can be tested and we can thus gain insights into social behaviour.

Very often the persons studied make the same jump from form to content. They assume 'where contact, there communication'. Thus a person's perception of the density of parts of his network influences his behaviour. An example may make this point clearer. Cecil, another Maltese informant, had a long standing quarrel with his mother. Cecil was married and lived at some distance from his mother. His brother Charles, however, was unmarried and lived at home. Cecil got on very well with his brother until the quarrel with his mother. His brother would sometimes be obliged to take his mother's side in the dispute, for she is strong-minded and, after all, he lived with her at very close quarters. Cecil assumed (based partly on past experience) that all information he gave his brother was passed on to his mother. To avoid this, he began to take his brother less often into his confidence, and their relation deteriorated. Thus we can say that Cecil's perception of the strength of the link between his brother and his mother influenced his behaviour to the former: he began to communicate less with him.

I found myself also behaving in terms of the assumption 'where contact, there communication' in my own fieldwork situation. When I knew certain people to be in touch with others not present, I was very careful what I said about the others or about issues about which I knew they felt very strongly. I did not want to take the risk that my opinions would be passed along. Hence I was careful how I expressed them. I personally did not feel completely free to speak openly about my fieldwork in Malta (except to my wife) until I had left the island. Although the basic assumption 'where high density, there communication' must be demonstrated, most persons assume that it is true. That is, their perception of the density of their networks, irrespective of its accuracy, influences their behaviour. They are not prepared to take risks. These then are some of the reasons why density is an important measurement.

The density of a (partial) network may be calculated by means of a simple formula which expresses the ratio of the total possible links to the total actual links in (the portion of) the network under examination. This can be set out as follows:

$D = \dfrac{100\,Na}{\frac{1}{2}N\,(N-1)}$ % where Na refers to the total actual number

DIAGRAM 2.6

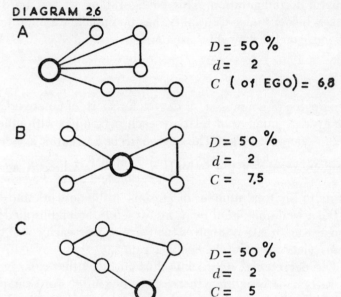

A

$D = 50\%$
$d = 2$
C (of EGO) = 6.8

B

$D = 50\%$
$d = 2$
$C = 7.5$

C

$D = 50\%$
$d = 2$
$C = 5$

of links (excluding those with Ego) if the network is ego-centric and N the total number of persons in the network (again excluding Ego).[16] If this formula is applied to Ego's first order zone set out in Diagram 2.1 it is seen to have a density of 66.6 per cent.

There are three persons in his primary zone ($N=3$) and two actual relations or links between them ($Na=2$), thus

$D = \dfrac{100(2)}{\frac{1}{2} \times 3(2)} = 66.6\%.$

There is obviously a relation between size and density, for where a network is large the members will have to contribute more relations to attain the same density as a smaller network. Hence one must be careful about comparing the density of different networks. Moreover, networks with the same density can have very different configurations. This is illustrated in Diagram 2.6. The three five-member networks sketched there have the same density but each has a different structural configuration. This configuration, as will be discussed below under Centrality, has potentially an important influence on the flow of information.

3. *Degree of connexion*

The degree of connexion, or *degree* for short, of a network, is the average number of relations each person has with others in the same network.[17] The degree (d) of a network is calculated by means of the formula $d = \dfrac{2 \times Na}{N}$, where N again refers to the total number of persons in the network and Na to the actual number of relations, which is then multiplied by two as each relation involves two persons who each count the same relation separately. See Diagram 2.6.

The degree of a network is thus an index that can give a correction or weighting to the density scores. For example, although the partial networks of Pietru and Cecil which exclude their fellow villagers have virtually the same density, when the degree of each of these partial networks is compared it is evident that the members of Pietru's network have more relations with each other than do the members of Cecil's network (see p. 122 below).

4. *Centrality*

Every person is naturally at the centre of his own personal network. But the objective position of a person in a given group or field of activity seen as a network of social relations, influences his chances of being able to manipulate people and information. The more central his position, the better able he is to bring about communication. Centrality is an index of the degree to which a person is accessible to the persons in a particular (non-egocentric) network.[18] Quantitatively the centrality of a person is usually calculated by adding the least number of steps (links) from each person in the network to every other one, and dividing this sum by the sum of the least number of steps from a given person to every other one.

DIAGRAM 2.7

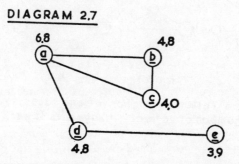

The centrality index (C) of Ego is thus calculated as follows:

$$C = \frac{\text{sum of shortest distances from every member to every other member}}{\text{sum of shortest distances from Ego to every other member}}$$

Centrality is a function not only of the size of a network but also of its structure or pattern, as can be seen from the differing centrality indices of the members of the network sketched in Diagram 2.7.[19]

Centrality is not only an index of a person's accessibility, but also of the number of communication paths which pass through him. This in turn is a function of the number of lateral links between the members of the network. Given unequal centrality, the more lateral links there are the less able the central figure is to exercise exclusive control over the flow of information. This is illustrated in Diagram 2.8, where the centrality of Ego is seen to vary inversely with the density of his network. In other words the power of a leader (or broker) is dependent upon the degree to which he monopolizes the flow of information, goods and services to and between his followers (or clients).

He thus has a vested interest in keeping his followers from establishing relations between each other through which such items could be exchanged independently of him.

DIAGRAM 2.8

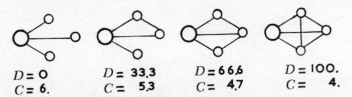

$D = 0$
$C = 6.$

$D = 33.3$
$C = 5.3$

$D = 66.6$
$C = 4.7$

$D = 100.$
$C = 4.$

Centrality is higher where density
(number of lateral linkages) is lower.

The strategic importance for information management and communication of a high relative score for centrality has been demonstrated in small group experiments, where it emerges as the most important variable.[20] Josephine Klein, in discussing the subject, has noted that 'in a differentiated network [where the centrality of the members differ] where only a limited number of transmissions are permitted, the most central person or sub-group will be the best informed and most influential.'[21] The most centrally located person in a communication network receives and directs the largest number of messages and because of this, has the most influence. All of which is quite logical. Centrality can only be quantified, however, in the case of relatively small, bounded networks. Nonetheless, the concept is a valuable one and can be applied, albeit on a more impressionistic basis, to a number of social situations.[22]

5. *Clusters*

Clusters are segments or compartments of networks which have a relatively high density.[23] The persons forming clusters are relatively speaking more closely linked to each other than they are with the rest of the network. Conversely, a cluster may be viewed as a compartment of a network which has a relatively low ratio of external relations as compared to

DIAGRAM 29

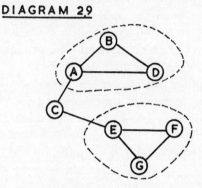

internal relations.[24] (See Diagram 2.9 which shows two clusters: cluster A, B, D and cluster E, F, G linked via C.) The existence of such clusters in his network if perceived by a person influences his behaviour for the reasons indicated in the discussion of density above. Pietru is aware that in his large primary zone there are clusters of persons who are highly interconnected. His behaviour to persons clustered in this way is affected by this knowledge. The clusters in Pietru's network are for the most part various categories of relatives, association members, neighbours, fellow teachers, and so on.

Clusters are thus often recruited out of different activity fields. The members of these different clusters can of course demand that a person play different parts. Sometimes such behaviour is inconsistent. A person may, for example, be linked at the same time to a crowd of hash smoking trendy dressers and a set of tweedy fox-hunting types. Although the parts he plays to the different sets of people are irreconcilable, he can continue to participate in both clusters as long as the interlinkage between the clusters is limited. An article in *Nova* recently provided an excellent example of a young London woman who was linked to seven different clusters, most of which required her to dress for and play special roles: (1) her immediate family, (2) her country cousins in Wales, (3) South Africans who knew her father, (4) a set of young mothers she met while taking her baby to the park, (5) some Army types whom she met through some of the young mothers and an ex-boyfriend, (6) a vaguely hippy lot of friends she met at art school and (7) a primmer set she is still in contact with from her girl's day school.[25]

If, on the other hand, a person cannot avoid cross-linkages and he wishes to remain a member of two different clusters, he must adjust his behaviour and his explanation of it in such a way that it is reconcilable to the members of both clusters. Valdo Pons discusses this point and notes of an informant in Stanleyville:

> In order to maintain his social relations he therefore had to be constantly exploring the consistencies and inconsistencies between several sets of views and norms. And any explanations and evaluations which he gave to members of one network had to be reconcilable with those given to members of any other network.[26]

Such a reconciliation of behaviour and explanation in terms of norms which are comprehensible and acceptable to members of different clusters leads to cultural and behavioral homogeneity. One can thus postulate that where there is a high rate of interlinkage between clusters, as there usually is if density is also high, there will be a greater degree of consistent behaviour than where such conditions do not prevail.

The degree of interlinkage between clusters is an index not only of the density of the network, but also of the multiplexity of the links. Where there is a high degree of interlinkage there is a great deal of overlap between activity fields. Interlinkage is merely another way of combining the concept of activity field and density.

Size, density, degree of connexion, centrality and clustering are all statements about the theoretical possibility of a person to transact. In the same way multiplexity, transactional content, directional flow, frequency and duration of interaction are indicators of the possible importance of various links. Together they help establish a statistical portrait of the form and content of a person's network. They help to build a model of his social universe which enables us to formulate hypotheses about the way he may behave, given the constraints of his cultural and physical environment. It is well to remember, however, that both the content and the form of networks of social relations are constantly shifting. Though the concepts discussed give greater precision to the study of social relations, they cannot be used to predict with certainty which course of alternative actions will be followed. But they increase the probability that we can predict more correctly by adding an extra dimension to our understanding of social behaviour.

CONTENT, STRUCTURE AND SENTIMENT

In dealing with the content of interaction and of the form it can take, I dealt with more or less objective criteria that can be quantified by observation or direct questioning. Of these, the most complex is the notion of multiplexity, for this was closely related to the notion of institutional activity fields. This is an abstraction from interactional reality of a different order than the others, and hence more difficult to use. (Is conversation exchanged between A and B because they are distant relatives, neighbours, fellow teachers, or all three?) Nonetheless I believe we must try to measure multiplexity, for this is one of the ways the interactional process is related to the institutional system. This I realize sounds here rather more like a declaration of faith than a scientific argument, but I hope that its relevance will become more apparent later.

Social relations, however, can also be examined in terms of subjective criteria. Now it is a difficult matter to determine just how far the social observer can build into his model the subjective sentiments of his informants. (His own subjective sentiments, albeit often unknowingly, have already been built into his analysis.) A thorough evaluation of these sentiments calls for the use of extremely complicated psychological and social psychological analytical instruments. This is one complication. Another is that by explicitly adding these subjective factors, the model becomes more complex and therefore more difficult to use.

Nonetheless this subjective evaluation must be added, for it works as a necessary correction to an over-reliance on the quantitative indices of content and structure. People often pretend that they like persons to whom they are bound by multiplex relations, and with whom they exchange a high volume of gifts and visits. If objective criteria alone are used these persons score high, and the researcher can easily be misled into assuming that this is an indication of the strength of the relation. Only by seeking a subjective evaluation from the informant will it be discovered that he intensely dislikes the high scorer. Thus the likes and dislikes of the informants and their view of the importance to them of the members of their network expressed in purely subjective terms add an important dimension that is all too easily overlooked.

Specifically, one can ask informants, as I did, to evaluate the various links in their network subjectively in terms of the emotional importance to them. By using these subjective criteria, which to an extent also correlate with the objective criteria discussed above, a model of a person's first order zone can be built. This will have, I suggest, a concentric form with at least five fairly well defined zones. These have been set out schematically in Diagram 2.10.

At the centre is Ego. Around him are clustered (I) a *personal cell*, usually composed of his closest relatives and possibly, a few of his most intimate friends. He invests a great deal of his material and emotional resources in these persons. Beyond his personal cell there is a range of people who are also emotionally important to him, his intimates. My Maltese informants distinguished a number of zones within this category of intimates. These could be broken down into two major ones, which, for want of a better term, I shall call

DIAGRAM 2.10

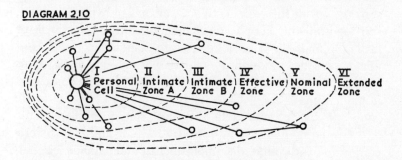

intimate zone A and intimate zone B. (II) *Intimate zone A* is composed of very close friends and relations with whom Ego maintains active, intimate relations. (III) *Intimate zone B* consists of both friends and relatives, with whom he maintains more passive relations but who nonetheless are emotionally important to him. Then there is a circle of persons who are important to him in a more pragmatic sense for economic and political purposes and the logistics of daily life. This may be termed his (IV) *effective zone*. A number of the people in this zone are there, rather than in zone V, because of their own networks. As these contain strategic persons who may be useful to Ego, he keeps his relations with them warm so he can gain access to the friends of his friends. Thus many in zone IV are instrumental friends rather than emotional friends.[27] Still farther from Ego in subjective terms is what could be called his (V) *nominal zone*, persons he knows but who mean little to him pragmatically and emotionally. He is acquainted with them, but that is about all; often he is uncertain of their names. They shade off into what might be called the ragged edge of his primary zone, the collection of people whose faces he recognizes, or those who remember that they have met him, though he no longer remembers them. These persons, and those beyond his first order zone, form the *extended zone* of his network.

Placement in these zones is continually shifting: just as the transactional and emotional balance in them is constantly shifting. From this perspective a person's network is a fluid, shifting concept. People, once met, remain forever in it, or rather, remain in it as long as Ego remembers them. But persons located today in the effective or nominal zones of his network, can in a matter of weeks or even days, become part of the intimate zone. Conversely, members of the intimate zone can be catapulted to the most remote corner of the effective zone, figuratively speaking. Minor and major shifts come about through disappointments and chance circumstances as well as through quarrels and such major events as marriage and death. Every transaction with a person is at the same time a reappraisal of the subjective placement of that person. This applies to the most intimate members as well as to those at the edge of the nominal zone. In chapter 5 I return to the relation between objective and subjective criteria in a more detailed examination of the personal networks of my two Maltese informants, Pietru and Cecil.

In the following section I try to use some of the concepts discussed above in an extended example which demonstrates the way in which an interactional analysis can furnish a better explanation of behaviour than classical structural-functional analysis.

3
Values and Interaction in a Conflict Situation

A person is often asked to decide between two parties each of whom seeks to persuade him that he is right by using arguments based upon equally important values. This places individuals in a dilemma: If both courses of action can be motivated by important values, what should he do? The situation in Vietnam with which many Americans were confronted is a case in point. 'Join the Army and fight the red menace in Vietnam which is threatening the American way of life and its trusted allies in South East Asia.' 'To defend your country in its hour of need, is the moral duty of every mother's son: united we stand, divided we fall.' Against these norms could be placed another equally telling set. 'The United States has become embroiled in a civil war in another part of the world through the ineptitude of its politicians and the manoeuvring of its military leaders'. 'Both are using the war for their own ends: the politicians to expand and consolidate the U.S. political hegemony in Asia; and the military as an arena in which new weapons can be tested, the flaccid peace-time armed services kept in fighting trim, and military reputations enhanced'. 'The war is being used to protect a corrupt, fascist regime from the defeat it would suffer from its socialist rivals in a free election'. 'The war is evil: it is therefore your moral duty not to join the Army'.

While many choose a particular course of action because

E

deep down inside, they believe that it is morally the right thing to do, many are not able to do so. They regard each set of norms advanced as equally telling. How then do they decide? Ultimately they do make a choice for which one of the normative arguments will be brought forward as motive. The question which concerns us is how they arrive at this choice. I shall argue that in most cases the choice as to which out of contradictory but equally telling normative arguments is chosen, depends largely upon the situation in which it is presented, the actors involved and the way in which they and others with whom they are in contact interact. My basic assumption is that *in a situation of conflict persons will attempt to define the situation and align themselves in such a way that the least possible damage is done to their basic values and to their important personal relations.*[1]

The extended example which follows is a summary of Kapferer's stimulating analysis of a dispute which occurred among fifteen African workers employed in the Cell Room of the Anglo-American Corporation's Electro-Zinc Plant in Broken Hill, Zambia.[2]

1. *Background*

Broken Hill is a town of some 46,000 located 86 miles by rail from Lusaka, in the heart of Zambia's Copperbelt. The main minerals mined at Broken Hill are lead and zinc. The cell room is located above ground and forms the last stage in the preparation of the mined zinc before it is exported. Briefly, the zinc, after being reduced to a solution elsewhere, is pumped into the cell room where through an electrolytic process purified zinc is deposited on the sides of aluminium cathodes housed in the cell boxes that give the room its name. The study focuses upon one of the three units which operate in the cell room.

The fifteen men involved in the dispute operate as a team and consist of eight strippers, four scale attendants, one dryer, one scrubber and the crew boss. (See Diagram 3.1.) The *strippers* (Abel and Donald, Damian and Soft, Abraham and Benson, Lotson and Maxwell) work in pairs at four stripping stands. Each pair lifts the cathodes out of the cell boxes on to the stand, strips the zinc sheets off the cathodes, cleans or renews these and replaces them in the cell box. The zinc sheets are placed on a block behind each stripping stand, from where they are picked up in small rail trucks and brought to the weigh office by the *scale attendants* (Joshua, Godfrey, Stephen and Noah), each of whom is assigned a certain number of stands in the cell room. Besides the work described, the strippers are also responsible for cleaning out the cell boxes and cleaning up around their stands. The working rate of the strippers is controlled by the crew boss on behalf of the management whose philosophy is: 'Haste makes waste.'

Dirty or eroded cathodes are placed by the strippers on special racks to be cleaned or, if too far gone, replaced by the *scrubber* (Andrew). Zinc sheets that are still wet with sulphuric acid are dried by the *dryer* (Henry), who also strips off zinc sheets that have so far defied the efforts of the strippers, and helps to hose down and clean up the unit's area. Finally, as noted, the *crew boss* (Jackson) tries to regulate the work tempo of the strippers and sees that the cathodes are properly replaced in the cell boxes. He is responsible to the European supervisors in the room for the work in his unit. From time to time he also helps the strippers and cleans around the stripping stands. The lay-out of the unit and the location of the personnel in this episode are indicated on Diagram 3.1.

The work begins at 7.00 a.m. with a break period from 9.15 a.m. to 10.00 a.m., and usually finishes at 11.00 a.m., or when the strippers have completed their daily quota of cathodes. All are paid on a piece work basis, with the crew boss receiving the highest rate, then the strippers, followed by the scale attendants and then finally by the scrubber and

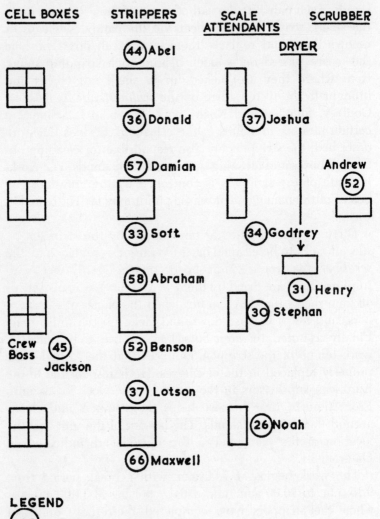

Diagram 3.1

THE CELL ROOM SETTING OF THE DIS-
PUTE BETWEEN ABRAHAM AND DONALD

CELL BOXES   STRIPPERS   SCALE ATTENDANTS   SCRUBBER

DRYER

(44) Abel

(36) Donald   (37) Joshua

(57) Damian   Andrew
                                (52)
(33) Soft   (34) Godfrey

(58) Abraham   (31) Henry
                     (30) Stephan
Crew   (45)
Boss   Jackson   (52) Benson

(37) Lotson
                 (26) Noah
(66) Maxwell

LEGEND
(100) = Person and age

Source: Based on Kapferer (1969 : 185)

dryer. It is clear that there is a certain functional connexion between the various tasks. They form a team, and co-operation is important. If this breaks down, quarrels result. To a certain extent the interaction of the personnel of the unit is dependent upon their task: the scale attendants, for example, and the scrubbers walk about, while the strippers work in pairs at a stand. But the interaction is not wholly dependent on the task: Noah, a scale attendant, walks about, but has little contact with the others, while Damian, a stripper, interacts with many. Other bases of interaction are tribal affiliation —(there are eleven tribes represented), age (these range from twenty-six to sixty-six), religion (seven) and authority in the work situation (Jackson is crew boss, and Lotson is shop steward). All influence to some extent the degree to which the fifteen men in the unit come into contact and interact with each other.

2. *The dispute*

Below is Kapferer's account of the dispute between two strippers, Abraham (stand II) who accuses Donald (stand IV) of working too fast.[3]

The normal clamour and hum of the Cell Room is suddenly broken by Abraham who shouts across to Donald at Stand IV, '*Buyantanshe* ("Progress"), slow down and wait for us.' A hush now settles on the Unit. For a while Donald takes no notice and Abraham calls '*Buyantanshe*' once more. This evokes a reaction and Donald retorts that he is not to be called by his nickname as he already has a proper name. Abraham replies that he only knows Donald by his nickname, '*Buyantanshe*'. His blood up, Donald shouts, 'We young men must be very careful about being bewitched.' Abraham assents, 'You are quite right, you will be bewitched if you don't respect your elders.' Donald is now almost beside himself with rage, and goes straight to lodge a formal protest with the Shop Steward, Lotson, against what he considers to be Abraham's threat of witchcraft. This done he then goes down the stripping stand reporting the matter to the Strippers and those Scale Attendants working nearby. He is just passing Stand III when he hears, as do others close at hand, Soft's very audible comment to Joshua that Donald must be drunk or else they . . . should not be seeing such behaviour. Donald storms across to Soft, and the latter, in an attempt to pacify him and to persuade him to return to his stand, says, 'I didn't mean *you* when I said that.' Jackson, the Crew Boss, who has hitherto been amusedly observing the dispute from the sidelines, now steps in and orders Donald to return to work, which the latter does, muttering angrily all the way back to his stand, 'I don't wish anyone to call me *"Buyantanshe"*, I have my own name, Donald.'

Work now returns more or less to normal. Occasionally small clusters of workers collect to discuss or enquire about the dispute; but the event is once more brought fully to the attention of the Unit workers when Soft comes to seat himself near Lotson at break time. Lotson asks him why he has quarrelled with Donald at work. 'It's my own business; Donald didn't hear me properly', mutters Soft. Others who are seated near Soft and Lotson now stop whatever they have been talking about and crane forward to listen. Damian and Jackson come from where they have been standing near Stand I and hover at the outskirts of the group surrounding Lotson and Soft. Soft now elaborates, 'Donald has taken too much beer and this is what has caused him to behave like this. Surely we all call him by his nickname!' Donald, who has been listening nearby, and prior to this had been discussing his version of the dispute with two of his friends, Godfrey and Stephen, impatiently breaks in, 'In my case please, I don't want anyone calling me *Buyantanshe* as I have my proper name, Donald. Drinking doesn't enter the case—the quarrel was caused by Abraham who insisted on calling me by my nickname and instead of answering properly to my protests, threatened to bewitch me.' At this Lotson bursts out with a disbelieving laugh and asks Donald for the real reasons behind his outburst: 'Was it because Soft called you a drunk? If so, this is not a real case.' Soft now intervenes and states that Donald has reacted in such a way because the comment came from a young man, 'Really', he declares, 'there is no excuse for Donald's behaviour.'

Abraham, who is seated near Stand I calls across to Donald to join him where he is sitting. (He addresses the latter as 'Donald'.) Everybody seated with Donald urges him to go, and after much prompting he does so. Lotson, Abel and Soft joke together that now Donald need not fear being bewitched any longer. Immediately on Donald's arrival at Abraham's seating place, Abraham asks him to go and sharpen his stripping hook. After having completed this service Donald returns the hook to its owner and then joins a group of Scale Attendants . . . who are seated near the Weigh Office.

For most workers in the Unit, including Abraham, the dispute seemed to be at an end. But that this was not so for Donald, was demonstrated a few days later. Donald again accused Abraham of witchcraft and used his suspicions of Abraham's malevolence as a pretext for applying for a transfer from the Cell Room to another section of the mine. His application was successful and he was transferred to underground work.

3. *Normative analysis*

A number of questions spring immediately into mind: Why did the accusation go from Abraham to Donald? Why were trivial issues such as Donald's supposed drunkenness and his offence at being called by his nickname emphasized instead of the major issues of rate-busting and witchcraft? Why did the majority support Abraham and not Donald? Norms relating to work tempo, witchcraft, respect of younger to older, soberness, the use of names were said to have been broken. It is obvious that the parties concerned brought forward various norms to support their positions.

Abraham's initial accusation was that Donald was rate-busting, and to understand the implications of this, it is necessary to see the work rate norm in context. As noted, the management via the crew boss seeks to hold the work tempo fairly constant. Management believes that regular, somewhat slower work is safer: it is possible to plan on this basis, and it avoids the damage and losses that would be caused if, for example, dirty cathodes were used in the heat of competition. But because the electrolytic process is a chemical one and takes exactly forty-eight hours, it cannot be hurried. Thus if the members of the unit finish their allotted work of stripping and replacing the sixteen cathodes ahead of time, they will be assigned other tasks for the rest of the normal eight hour working day, at no extra salary. Management hoped that this would occur, so that they would be able to bring the special four hour work day of the cell room workers into line with the eight hour day of the rest of the mine. On the other hand, if the task of stripping the quota of cathodes takes longer than the programmed four hours, the crew receive no extra money for their longer work. In these circumstances it is small wonder that an informal work tempo norm evolved.

Alongside the work tempo norm was another informal norm, keyed to the value of being strong and speedy. The work tempo was controlled until the break, but thereafter the stripping teams went flat out in an informal competition to see which could finish first, thus demonstrating superiority— and gaining a few extra minutes of free time at the end of the day. In the short period after the break no stripping team could get far enough ahead of the others to jeopardize the general work arrangement in the unit. What Donald and Abel had done was to disregard the 'go slow before the break' norm. Donald and Abel had been rate-busting in a very minor way, and thus to a certain extent jeopardizing the working arrangements of the whole unit. Yet if this was the reason for the dispute, why didn't the other workers bring this forward to explain their apparent alignment against him?

The answer to this last question lies partly in the cleavage between old and young in this work situation. The work in the cell room is heavy, and therefore more easily performed by the young. This in effect means that the younger men do proportionately more work than the older ones. There is thus a real fear among the older men that their flagging capacities will be noticed and that they will be sacked from their prestigeful and well paid jobs. There is thus pressure from the younger on the older men to work a bit faster and even to get rid of those who are lagging too far behind. Thus Abraham's accusation that Donald was rate-busting must also be construed as an attempt to protect the older men against the younger men.

Young and old strippers are usually paired, but, as can be seen on Diagram 3.1, there were two exceptions to this. Abraham and Benson, two older men, are paired at Stand II, and Abel and Donald, two younger men, are paired at Stand IV. Why the accusation went from Stand II to Stand IV may thus be explained in terms of the conflict between old and young: the stand with the oldest average age accuses the stand with the youngest average age. In fact, Abel and Donald, without working fast before the break had regularly been finishing first, and Abraham and Benson, with but few exceptions, always finished last. The slow tempo of these last two had on more than one occasion obliged at least one scrubber and several scale attendants to work overtime, for which they were not paid. Donald and Abel, unobtrusively but constantly had been demonstrating that younger men are better at their work than older men. In short, Donald by working rapidly expressed the superiority that many of the younger men felt, especially those, such as Lotson and Soft, saddled with older men.

The analysis so far has shown why the accusation went from Stand II to Stand IV; it has also, at least partly, explained why Abraham received no verbal support for his charge of rate-busting. It has not explained why the younger men who might have supported Donald abandoned him in favour of the older Abraham.

It might be possible to account for the failure of the younger men to support Donald by pointing to another norm which he apparently broke. In the ideology prevailing in the African township, and carried through in the cell room, the relations between older and younger are often expressed in kinship terms even though they are not related. In fact, in the sporadic contact that Abraham and Donald had, they addressed each other as 'father' and 'son'. When such reciprocal kinship terms are used between people, they are also expected to demonstrate the behaviour associated with the kinship roles: the son should be subordinate to the wishes of his father, and show the latter respect. Donald transgressed this norm in his snappish answer to Abraham's admonishment to slow down and in his subsequent behaviour. Donald's breach of this norm might explain why the other younger men—if they in fact regarded it as an important norm—threw their support to Abraham in spite of the extra work the older men caused them.

Unfortunately, against this possible normative basis for Abraham's support, can be placed Donald's voiced fear that Abraham might bewitch him. Abraham, it will be recalled, agreed out loud that this might in fact happen. In this cultural context it is believed that many older men have the power of witchcraft. This power is greatly feared, for it can bring about all manner of dire misfortunes to persons not in possession of it (hence especially to younger men). Thus the accusation and seeming admission of witchcraft should have mobilized support of the younger if not also of the older members of the unit for Donald. Yet in the face of this serious accusation Lotson merely laughed, and no one else referred to it. Was this because the members of the unit wanted to keep the older and younger workers from polarizing into two hostile factions and so paralysing the unit? Kapferer notes, however, that this fear of disunity was not strong enough to keep the group from splitting into such factions over similar disputes in the past.

Up to this point the normative analysis has explained why the rate-busting accusation took place and why it was directed from Stand II to Stand IV. It also explains why Donald accused Abraham of witchcraft. Finally, it also indicates why none of the other, younger men motivated their support for Abraham in terms of his rate-busting accusation. The normative analysis has not explained why Abraham and not Benson was the accuser, or why Donald and not Abel the accused. Nor has it explained why those drawn into the dispute should wish to keep the issues trivial, when in the case of similar disputes in the past they had not done so. Finally, the normative analysis does not explain why Donald was not able to muster support from the other young men, in spite of his excellent normative argument. In short in a situation of conflict many norms, values and attitudes are brought forward to account for behaviour, and it is rarely possible to explain the outcome only by referring to one or a combination of these. A normative analysis alone is insufficient. Echoing Kapferer, I shall argue 'that the amount of support a person achieves in a situation will be conditional on the structure and nature of his direct and indirect interpersonal relationships.'[4] That is, support is a function of network structure.

4. *Network analysis*

Kapferer began his network analysis by calculating the different types of exchange contents in the existing links between the actors in this drama. As will be recalled, he isolated five important ones: conversation, joking behaviour, job assistance, personal service and cash assistance. These he converted into an index of multiplexity by counting the number of different exchange contents for each link, considering a relation multiplex if it had two or more exchange contents. This way he arrived at an index of the multiplexity of the existing relations in the unit. The uniplex and multiplex relations of Abraham and Donald as well as the other members of the unit have been plotted in the form of a sociogram in Diagram 3.2.

Using the diagram as a basis, it is possible to calculate the relative strength of the networks of the disputants in terms of Density, Multiplexity, Degree and Centrality.[5]

	Density	Multiplexity: Star	Zone	Degree	Centrality
Abraham	72.2%	33.3%	53.8%	9	15.1
Donald	64.2%	12.5%	38.9%	8	11.1

This comparison indicates clearly that Abraham's network scores higher on all counts. He not only has more multiplex relations than Donald has, but the persons to whom he is linked share more multiplex relations than those to whom Donald is linked. This is expressed in the respective scores for star multiplexity and zone multiplexity. This last characteristic is especially important, for it enables Abraham to subvert persons not directly linked to him, as well as persons linked to both him and Donald by only uniplex relations. An example of the first is Stephen: Abraham by working through his multiplex tie with Andrew, who in turn has a multiplex tie with Stephen, can place more pressure on the latter than Donald, who only has a uniplex tie with him. A second example is Lotson with whom neither has a direct link. Abraham, however, can work through his multiplex ties with both Damian and Andrew who maintain multiplex ties with Lotson to gain the latter's support. Donald, on the other hand, can only approach Lotson through a single multiplex relation via Jackson.

DIAGRAM 3.2

RELATIONS BETWEEN THE ACTORS
IN THE CELL ROOM DISPUTE

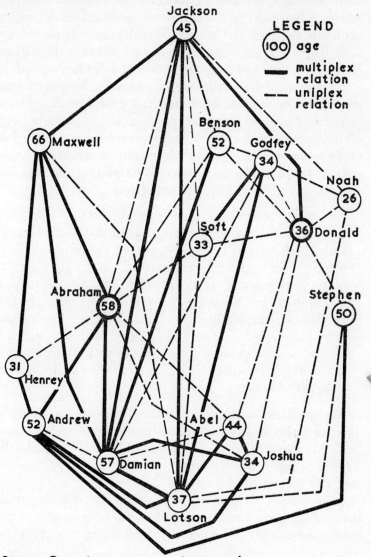

LEGEND

(100) age

—— multiplex relation

— — uniplex relation

Jackson (45)

Maxwell (66)

Benson (52)

Godfey (34)

Noah (26)

Soft (33)

Donald (36)

Stephen (50)

Abraham (58)

Henrey (31)

Andrew (52)

Abel (44)

Damian (57)

Joshua (34)

Lotson (37)

Source: Based on Kapferer (1969:231)

Significantly, Abraham also scores higher for centrality, which indicates that in comparison to Donald he occupies a more strategic position in the total network of multiplex relations that exist in the cell room. In fact, Donald, with a centrality index of 11.1, scores lower than anyone else except Soft, who scores only 10. Lotson, with 20.1, has the highest centrality index, and Damian, with 19.2, is a close second.

All but one of the persons who are linked to *both* disputants are linked by uniplex relations. The exception is Jackson, linked to Donald with a multiplex tie. Abraham can subvert all but Soft through paths of multiplex relations in either two or three steps. Donald disposes of no such multiplex paths outside Jackson. The case of Soft is interesting. He is in fact in a difficult position. Kapferer noted that

> His work position on Damian's stand placed him between two influential and committed men in the dispute, Damian and Abraham, and to have supported Donald could have infringed his work relationship with Damian. The difficulty of his work position could have contributed to his support of Abraham, but, what ever the reason, his suggestion that Donald was drunk brought Donald's wrath down upon him. This reaction influenced Godfrey, with whom Soft is tied by a close bond, to commiserate with him, an action which aligned Godfrey with Soft, and therefore, by association, with Abraham.

Though Jackson is indeed tied to Donald by a multiplex link, he is also tied by similar links to three persons who sided with Abraham: Maxwell, Damian and Lotson. The link with Lotson is especially important, for he is the shop steward, and the successful operation of Jackson's role as crew boss depends on his co-operation on the shop floor. By supporting Donald he might lose this, as well as the co-operation of that other influential person firmly committed to Abraham, Damian.

It should be stressed that the support of Abraham was

manifested almost immediately, before there was much opportunity for him to begin applying pressure to recruit followers. From this we must conclude that those who supported him did so because they perceived their relations in much the same way as has just been set out. In other words, all realized the difference in the configuration of linkages of the two protagonists and the fact that Abraham could exert more pressure through his network, the characteristics of which are expressed in their relative scores for density, multiplexity, degree and centrality. In short, they had more to lose by supporting Donald than by aligning with Abraham. This is why Abraham recruited more support than Donald. We are still left with the questions of accuser and accused, and why trivial issues were emphasized.

Why Donald was accused and not Abel can again be explained by reference to the relative strengths of their networks: Donald's is the weaker of the two. Abel has a particularly important multiplex link with Lotson, a powerful man, and with Joshua, both of whom are closely linked with Damian. In short, Abel was not as vulnerable as Donald. The accusation of rate-busting was directed at the person on Stand IV least likely to be able to retaliate effectively. That Benson did not initiate the accusation is perhaps explained in the first instance by the relation he shared with Donald, which would have been jeopardized. He could not reasonably accuse Abel, for his own network was considerably weaker than the latter's. He said nothing in the beginning, and later was mobilized to Abraham's side, not only by the fact that he worked with him, but also by virtue of his close relation—the only one he maintained—with the influential Damian. Being thus the more strongly linked of the two men on Stand II, Abraham issued the warning to Donald, the one with the weakest links on Stand IV.

Why rate-busting and witchcraft were not pursued as major issues can be explained largely by the attitudes adopted by Damian and Lotson, the two most powerful men in the unit. As shown on the diagram, Damian is linked to several younger men. If he had chosen to support the rate-busting issue or react strongly to the witchcraft one, he might very well have had difficulties with the numerous persons he maintained close relations with. He thus found it more strategic to appeal to a norm that was less controversial, and began to grumble about the lack of respect of younger persons to older persons. This was a very general issue and one not likely to arouse heated emotions. Lotson also supported Abraham. He maintained a number of strategic multiplex relations which were most important for his position as Shop Steward. In order not to jeopardize these he, too, chose to ignore the potentially divisive issues of rate-busting and witchcraft, and emphasize trivial issues, playing up the notion that Donald must have been drunk and misunderstood the situation. These trivial points could be stressed, because neither Abraham nor Donald were strong enough to define the dispute in terms of the divisive norms of rate-busting and witchcraft. On the contrary, it was in the interest of the two strong men, Damian and Lotson, to emphasize the trivial issues, thus protecting their many relations by preventing the faction fight between young and old that the two major issues put forward by the disputants would have caused.

The discussion up to this point has set out a number of the shortcomings of the structural-functional over-emphasis on normative systems. Behaviour cannot be explained solely in terms of norms and values: there are other forces at work besides normative constraints which must be taken into account. It was suggested that these 'other forces' lie in the area of interpersonal relations, which can be approached by viewing most interactions as transactions. In order to gain greater insight into the way in which interpersonal relations are structured, they may be viewed as a network. This makes it possible to measure systematically the diverse ways persons are linked to others and the reciprocal influence of interaction and network structure on each other. By means of a normative analysis the cause of the dispute, the arguments brought forward by the disputants and the direction of charge and counter-charge were explained. But the normative analysis could not demonstrate why more persons aligned themselves with one of the disputants, or why the conflict erupted between two particular individuals, or why the major issues were replaced by trivial ones. These problems were resolved by means of a meticulous examination of the networks and of the transactional balances of the disputants. The conflict and the eventual support of the disputants was explained by a combination of *both* normative (structural) and transactional analysis. While it is true that norms were used as window dressing for other motives in terms of which people acted, they also partly determined the arena and the issues.

Transactional analysis applied via the network approach must be used in conjunction with an analysis of norms. The one cannot be used without the other. The complementarity of the two approaches is set out and incorporated in the proposition which was verified by the data from the cell room: 'In a situation of conflict persons will attempt to define the situation and align themselves in such a way that the least possible damage is done to their basic values and to their important personal relations.'

Social behaviour cannot be explained by means of a single set of underlying values. One has to consider the total configuration of relations between people at a given moment in time. Social behaviour is the behaviour of people who are dependent upon others. Analyses that focus wholly on values, norms and symbolic systems excluding the relations between interdependent persons at a given moment, will always be distorted.

The configuration of relations, values and tensions is constantly in flux. It is dynamic. Thus any attempt to reduce them to a set of rules which can serve as a model for the society or group is impossible, just as it is impossible to predict accurately what will happen and how people will behave.

F

At best one can, through being aware of the many dimensions and factors involved, indicate the pattern and movement of relations. Moreover, by resisting the temptation to reduce complex variables to a static situation, by being aware of the inherent dynamism in such configurations, the observer may be able to indicate some of the processes operating and the direction of their movement. He thus gains insights and reduces the margin of error in his predictions, but he will never be infallible. The statistical portrait of the network of the members of the cell room indicated the balance of tensions at the moment of the dispute. The analysis was thus of a past event. Any attempt to predict on the basis of a table of statistics would be difficult, for the relations between the protagonists were in flux at the time their statistical snapshot was made.

Values and norms, transactions and network structure must thus all be taken into account. It has been demonstrated that there is a certain feedback between values and norms and the structure of transactional relations. To a certain extent, values may be confined analytically to the environment of the network, from where they place constraints upon the behaviour of transacting individuals. To this extent it can be said that values influence the structure of interaction, thus ultimately of the network in its morphological as well as transactional aspects. There are, however, other constraints besides norms and values which are part of the environment and which affect the structure—in the widest sense—of social networks. The nature of these constraints and the way in which they influence the structure of networks and thus interaction, as well as the reciprocal influence of behaviour on this social environment, form the subject of the next chapter.

4

Environment and Social Network

An anthropologist who has tried to relate environment, network structure and behaviour is Philip Mayer. Building on Elizabeth Bott's pioneering work, he linked differences in network structure to the rate at which Xhosa immigrants in South Africa were absorbed into urban institutions.[1] He showed how the small size, high density and multiplexity of the networks of certain categories of immigrants—the 'Red' Xhosa—encapsulated them and kept them tied to rural institutions and values, thus effectively blocking their absorption into the main stream of urban life.[2] Other immigrants from the same rural areas—the 'School' Xhosa—had large, less interconnected networks that contained a greater proportion of single-stranded relations which helped integrate them much more rapidly into the urban social scene.[3] They held an ideology which permitted and even encouraged them to expand areas of their networks linking them to urban institutions. Ideology, by affecting the network structure exerts an influence on behaviour. But in addition to ideology, biological, physical, social and personal influences also impinge on and affect the structure of networks, and thus behaviour.

BIOLOGICAL FACTORS

1. Sex

Such non-social factors as sex, age and genetic heritage affect a person's social relations. These cannot, of course, be seen as

completely disconnected from socio-cultural factors. Nonetheless, a person's sex influences the sort of relations he or she
maintains with others. In societies such as Malta, where there
is still a fairly marked cultural division between the social
worlds of men and women, a man has many more formal and
informal relationships with men than with women. But the
fact that a person is a man is a biological accident. (Though
modern surgery has made it possible for him to acquire certain female attributes.) Thus though Malta has many more
women than men—because of heavy emigration of men—
Pietru and Cecil, the two informants whose networks we shall
look at in greater detail shortly, have many more men than
women in their first order zones. The way in which a person
plays his or her ascribed sexual role can also influence the
relations he or she maintains with others. Where a woman
emphasizes her sex strongly she generates increased relations
with men, but by doing so she troubles her relations with
certain members of her own sex who are jealous of this
ability and her physical attributes, in part learned but also
inherited (though through plastic surgery and industry meagre
biological resources can now be inflated). On the other hand,
by being born without or by suppressing her female attributes
her attractiveness to men is limited, and thus the number of
men who try to establish (more intimate) contact with her is
reduced. Because of this she can probably maintain a larger
circle of intimate female friends. A woman with great biological sex appeal is often obliged to handle a greater volume
of relations with men than a plain Jane. Their natures may
also differ. Social relations with a sexually attractive woman
will often be single-stranded, transactional relations disguised
as multi-stranded moral relations. Unless she gets married
early and is well protected, such a woman will discover the
strong (sexual) transactional strand in the relationships that
men seek to establish with her. This, I suggest, can lead to a
certain suspicion or hardness of character. In short, because
of certain in-born physical attributes, a person develops a

network with particular structural characteristics. These in turn affect personality.

These observations can in fact be formulated as testable propositions. All other things being equal:

(1) sexually attractive women will have proportionately more males in their first order zones than unattractive women;

(2) the density of the male segment in the first order zones of sexually attractive women will be lower than that of unattractive women (it is in her interest to keep the men in her life separated), as will the multiplexity;

(3) and finally, the personality of sexually attractive women differs from that of unattractive women.

2. Age

It is also evident that the composition of a person's network is related to his age. The structural profile of his network changes during his life span. When he is young his first order zone is small and scores high for density and multiplexity. As he grows older, and his social horizons stretch beyond his home, his first order zone continues to expand, while its density and multiplexity decrease, though certain segments, such as immediate family and cliques of friends, continue to remain highly interconnected by means of multiplex links. This trend continues until late in life. But eventually there comes a point after which few new relations are made, and established relations begin to disappear as his acquaintances die. Owing to the increasing rate at which a person's circle of acquaintances is thinned out by death, he has at first more resources (emotional in-put, time, energy, though these too decrease with age) to invest in those remaining, thus initially converting more single-stranded relationships into many-stranded ones. On the other hand, because death removes without bias persons of his age and older from the various areas of society in which he was active, the interconnection between them also disappears and is not replaced. As his physical and mental powers fail, reducing his ability to get about and to communicate, his circle of acquaintances shrinks, and so does his interaction with all but a few. In structural terms, with old age a person's first order zone begins to decrease as does its density and multiplexity. This is in contrast to the first order zone of a child, which though small has high density and multiplexity. Quite obviously many factors affect this pattern, but in essence it is one that is biologically pre-determined and thus similar for everyone. Considering their intrinsic interest, the changes in the structure of the network over time, and the effects of this upon the behaviour and personality, especially of older persons, have so far received relatively little attention.[4]

3. *Personality*

As sex and physical appearance are elements in the genetic package that a person inherits, so are such basic personality traits as introversion/extroversion which have a marked effect on the size and structure of a person's network. Though I shall argue below that a person's social and cultural environment—including the size and structure of his social network—influence his personality in no small measure, the influence of genetic factors must not be forgotten. I mention this explicitly here, for I have rightly been reproached by a clinical psychiatrist for ignoring this element and trying to explain too much through social factors.[5] While I accept that genetic factors are important in determining a person's personality configuration, I must, because I am a layman in this highly specialized scientific field, simply state my belief in their possible relevance and then relegate them, unanalysed, to the biological environment and concentrate upon the social factors which influence behaviour and personality.[6]

PHYSICAL ENVIRONMENT

The physical surroundings in which the social network is embedded also exert considerable influence on its structural form. By physical surroundings I mean the immediate physical environment in which a person lives: whether desert, village or city, whether a hot or cold climate. People forced to move periodically in order to provide their livestock with water, such as the Bedouin and the Nuer, maintain a different network of relations than persons who live and work in small agrarian villages. These, in turn, have social networks which differ in certain respects from those of persons living in large urban centres.

1. *Place of residence*

The analysis of the difference between town and country, between life in a small-scale, bounded environment and one which is large-scale and open-ended, is one of the key problems in social anthropological analysis. All those who have written on networks have indicated that the concept of network can throw light on this problem. In some cases they have formulated hypotheses. These, however, have not been tested, for, as suggested above, to do so would bring the researcher face to face with one of the major unresolved problems in the use of networks: size. Social anthropologists as of yet lack the methodological sophistication needed to tackle this problem. Until this is achieved and a technique of network sampling is developed, they will probably remain untested. In spite of the limitations, however, it is useful to formulate propositions using the analytical variables set out in the previous chapter.

If the social networks of persons in a small-scale, relatively self-contained community are compared to those of persons in large urban centres we may expect the density of those in the former to be relatively high, as all persons know each other and effect certain exchanges. Because the activity fields in this small community overlap and the same actors play different roles to the same audience, we may also expect high multiplexity. Span and reachability will also be high. Variations in the structure of individual networks can of course be isolated by selecting certain elements exchanged, as Kapferer did in the bounded cell room. His study focused in effect on the variations in relationships between persons in one activity field. As soon as the number of activity fields involving the same people increases, as must occur in a bounded community in which people live, worship and work, the multiplexity and density ratios will also increase. In such communities we can also expect persons to have an excellent perception of the structure of the social networks of others. The high density and multiplexity leads to a rapid flow of information. Under these conditions, Bott and Mayer have suggested, the degree of consensus regarding norms is high, as consequently is the degree of social control. It must be stressed, however, that such isolated, bounded communities are largely ideal types, for they scarcely exist any longer, although they once formed almost the entire research menu of social anthropologists.

At the other extreme is the person who lives in a large city. The size of the universe from which he can recruit social relations is much larger, as is the range of institutions and activities in which he can participate. He has, potentially, a different public for every role he plays. Moreover, as each member of his city network is in a similar position, the speed with which people can reach each other, or circulate messages (their accessibility) is reduced. Neighbours often do not know each other, or if they do, exchange only nods. They most probably do not go to the same club, church or family feasts. Nor do they work together. In short, they tend to maintain single-stranded relationships with a large variety of persons.

The difference in the partial networks which the two Maltese teachers I worked with maintain at their respective schools, illustrates this last point. Pietru teaches in the primary school of the small village in which he lives. Cecil, born, bred and resident in town, teaches in a large secondary school. Although the latter has more than twenty male teaching colleagues, he in fact knows only one in another role. This is an older man, like himself an ex-Jesuit, whom he met while still a novice. He knows none of the pupils of the school in any but their roles as students. In contrast, Pietru has eight male fellow teachers. Of these, two live in the village. One is a priest, Dun Martin, with whom he has contact out of the school situation, for Pietru is active in various parish organizations. Moreover, as the standard-bearer of the Confraternity of the Blessed Sacrament, Pietru takes part with Dun Martin in the many parish processions. Though Pietru knows the other teacher well, he maintains a reserved distance, for they are in many respects rivals in the village status system. A third, older, teacher used to teach Pietru as a boy and he is very fond of him. Finally, he knows all the school's pupils in many different capacities. They are, as he is, members of the village. Some are his close neighbours, and others near or distant relatives. He also knows their parents. Certain boys help him in various parish activities. Some help their fathers to farm plots of land next to the many scattered fields which Pietru himself cultivates. With these he exchanges tools and held. Finally, he gives private lessons to many to prepare them for the stiff entrance examinations to the government secondary school system. In short, the partial segments formed by the occupational role sets of Pietru and Cecil differ strikingly: Pietru's has a much higher density and multiplexity than Cecil's.

The structural characteristics of urban networks, when compared to those found in small-scale, relatively isolated and stable communities, will score lower on density and multiplexity, especially on zone multiplexity (see chapter 3, note 5). In absolute numbers, the size of the first order zone is also smaller, for, owing to the greater number of single-stranded relations in a variety of activity fields, there are also fewer interactional situations and mnemonic aids. In my experience inhabitants of villages of up to about 3,000 know —in the sense of recognizing and knowing details about each other—all their fellow villagers. In larger villages not everyone knows each other. Thus each member of a tribe or village of around 3,000 can be said to have a first order zone of at least that size.[7] I suggest that few city dwellers have such large networks, for they do not have the same ascribed partial network of fellow villagers whom the village-resident constantly hears about and sees. He cannot forget them. The city dweller can and does exercise choice, and consequently has a smaller network. Because he does not see the same people constantly, he can forget people more easily.

Within cities, however, certain persons share highly interconnected networks with many multiplex links. Philip Mayer has described such networks for the 'Red' Xhosa immigrants, and Elizabeth Bott and Young and Willmott among working-class Londoners. These apparent exceptions to the type of urban network put forward above, can largely be explained by other factors which will be treated below. They form part of what might be called enclaves within the metropolis.

2. *Climate*

The idea that climate influences social behaviour is far from new. It is a factor with which most readers have had personal experience but find difficult to explain. Montesquieu argued in 1748 that climate influenced personality. Northerners were less sensitive, less passionate and more active than the Southern peoples. This influenced their political institutions. This became a classic theme and was taken up again by Madame de Staël (1766–1817) and by Taine (1828–93) to explain differences in art and literature. More recently Huntington (1924) and Markham (1947) sought to explain differences in economic and political development by differences in climate. They argued that a moderately cool, changeable climate induces people to greater mental and physical activity, hence industrial take-off first occurred in Northwest Europe and Japan. All these theories have been heavily criticized as over-simplifications: their proponents sought to explain complex processes in terms of one set of variables only. This was a serious, though tempting, error, for quite obviously many factors besides climate influence political institutions, literature, art and economic development. Nonetheless it is unfortunate that the effort to relate climate and social behaviour received such scathing criticism, for this blocked research (since academic researchers are very cautious people over-worried about their prestige) into a very promising field of inquiry. There is an important relation between climate and social behaviour.[8]

In warm climates much of the daily round of activities takes place in public. It is often too hot to remain indoors, hence cooking, washing, and even eating take place outside the house. In Malta, for example, as soon as the sun sets in the summer, the doorstep becomes the family living area in the villages. There, in the cool of the evening, the family congregates on chairs or on the ground to talk, eat, rest, and watch the television set located in the hot house. People come by on their way elsewhere and exchange greetings, for to ignore each other is impolite. Often they stop and chat, and for a brief moment join the circle. Moreover, in warm climates, food spoils quickly. This entails frequent expeditions to the shops. The average Maltese or Southern Italian woman makes several such shopping forays a day. On the way to and from the shops she meets people she knows, and often stops to exchange gossip. The men stroll along the streets in the evening, exchanging conversation with people they meet. These are relatively uncommitted contacts—in the sense that the exchange takes place in a public place and not in private—but they are frequent.

In a colder climate with more rain, the pattern of social relations is different. To begin with, much more activity takes place in the house. When it rains, as it does in all of north-west Europe for most of the year, one does not remain chatting for long in front of the grocer, or in the square: it is too wet and cold. Social contact takes place not casually, as it does in so many warm lands where people cannot help but meet each other, but by appointment. People meet each other in pub, club or home. The casual, non-committal contact typical of so many of the warm lands, disappears, or becomes at best less frequent. You visit each other rather than meet accidentally.

Now visiting usually involves being invited into someone's house. To do this you have to cross the threshold. Long ago Van Gennep perceptively noted the importance of thresholds and the many rituals that involve them. He observed that 'the door is the boundary between the foreign and domestic worlds . . . Therefore to cross the threshold is to unite oneself with a new world.'[9] Only people with whom a person has a special relation are invited or allowed to cross the threshold. People do not expect to be invited to visit by everyone they know. Hence if social exchanges are largely dependent upon this consideration, it is not surprising that they take place less frequently. In southern Europe people meet frequently by chance and talk, but they do so less often in the north. Who knocks on the door of an acquaintance by accident?

The inhabitant of Malta, or Italy or Greece meets many people by chance, and he is free to remain talking with them. Sometimes he cannot escape, for once you meet someone certain minimal exchanges have to take place if the relationship is to be maintained. For this reason it takes longer to walk between two equidistant points in a village or town in a warm country than it does in a cool one. A person keeps meeting people with whom he is obliged to talk. This and not lethargy, I suggest, accounts for much of the proverbial tardiness which has so annoyed Europeans in the tropics.

These climatic influences on social relations should be mirrored in the structure and transactional content of personal networks. All other things being equal, in a warm country, as compared to a cool one, the size of the first order zones will be larger, and as a result the density will be lower, as will the multiplexity. Though frequency of interaction is relatively high, many of the contacts are relatively superficial: they are non-committal, for one does not have to cross thresholds to interact. On the other hand, in a cold country, social networks will tend to be smaller, with the result that the relative density will tend to be higher, as will multiplexity. Since friends must cross the threshold and enter into the personal domain of the house, it follows that persons there will maintain fewer friendships, but that these are more intense than in warm climates.

Finally, consistent with this network structure and pattern of social interaction we would expect to find a difference in personality: the person living in a warm country being more open to casual conversation, thus more garrulous, more ready to strike up a chance, non-committal acquaintanceship than a person from a cool climate. The latter one would expect to be more reserved, less talkative, more inclined to enter into serious conversation if he talks and more open to entering into relationships involving a high rate of exchanges.

Is there empirical backing for these propositions? Having lived in the north of Europe, North America, Japan and England, as well as in Malta, Sicily, the Philippines and India, I should say that there is, but that the data has yet to be collected systematically. The contrast between the stiff, taciturn peasants and staid establishment figures in Sweden and their lively, garrulous counterparts in southern Europe, India and the Philippines, is striking.[10] But as with propositions concerning biological attributes and place of residence, climatic influences can rarely be considered completely in isolation, so that testing presents great problems.

IDEOLOGY

Above it was suggested that the differences in the rate of absorption of 'Red' and 'School' Xhosa into the urban way of life was related to differences in network structure, and that this was related to ideology. The Red Xhosa held an ideology which inhibited them from seeking out contact with people who were not like themselves. This ideology thus limited the expansion of their networks, encapsulating them in a tightly interconnected web of multiplex social relations with other Red Xhosa. This encapsulating network further served to isolate them from the main stream of the urban way of life. In contrast the School Xhosa held an ideology derived from their experience at the Mission school and their Christianity which encouraged the establishment of new contacts. Moreover through their new religion they were automatically connected with an open ended institutional network of the various Christian churches in the city.

This example provides a clear illustration of the way in which ideology influences behaviour through the way it affects the structure of social networks. But one does not have to go to an African town to observe this. In the Netherlands I notice very much the same thing between Catholic and Protestants, though I hasten to add that as of yet little systematic research has been done on this.

The thesis that religion influences behaviour is of course far from new. Max Weber in *The Protestant Ethic and the Spirit of Capitalism* argued that religion had an influence on economic behaviour. In brief, he pointed out that Calvinism with its doctrine of predestination and its concomitant ethic of hard work, thrift and ascetic renunciation of the pleasures of the world (to show that one belonged to those predestined to join God) created a climate favourable to the development of capitalism.[11] Hence modern capitalism 'took off', as it were, in the Protestant rather than in the Catholic countries of Europe where people did not hold such beliefs. This thesis has been criticized for failure to take sufficient account of other variables, such as differences in political development, economic resources, inventions, which in addition to the Calvinist ethic, created a socio-cultural environment favourable to the development of modern capitalism in northern Europe.[12] Again the argument was overstated by his followers and detractors (for Weber formulated it most carefully) in much the same way as was done by those who sought to demonstrate the influence of climate on political institutions, literature, art and economic development. Nonetheless, Weber's thesis is taken seriously. Quite obviously if the ethics or ideology advocated by a particular religion can be shown to influence economic behaviour, it can also influence social behaviour in other areas.

In the Netherlands, for example, there are differences in behaviour between orthodox Calvinists in the North and Catholics in the South.[13] The Catholics are described as more open, optimistic and vivacious, and the Calvinists as more sober, sombre and reserved. I have noticed that much more hospitality in the form of meals and entertainment is offered to visitors at the Catholic University at Nijmegen than at other Dutch Universities. The Catholic University budgets for this hospitality and the others do not, for it is considered less important. We and friends have noticed that Catholic doctors from the south of the Netherlands have a better 'bedside manner' than do their colleagues from the north, whether Catholic or Protestant; they seem to spend more time chatting with patients and getting to know them. In short, Catholics seem to be more interested in people, more conscious of cultivating and maintaining interpersonal relations. The reason for this can be explained partly by examining the respective ideological systems of the two religions.

Briefly, the Catholic needs to make use of other persons in order to obtain salvation. He is dependent upon the clergy for the performance of the many important rituals of his religion: baptism, confirmation, marriage and even the last rites on his death bed. Moreover, there are other rituals, such as confession, Mass, Communion, and the celebration of obligatory religious feasts, which he can perform only with the help of intermediaries. Not only does he require the assistance of others to practise his religion, he also approaches God through the saints who, because they are closer to God, and were once human, can be appeased and influenced to intercede on his behalf. There are striking similarities between the use of intermediaries in the religious field and the brokerage and patron-client relations which are particularly strong in Catholic countries. The importance of intermediaries, especially in the political field, is summed up neatly in the proverb often quoted by Sicilians and Maltese: 'You can't get to heaven without the help of saints', for political patrons in both cultures are referred to as saints. In Catholic countries the use of such intermediaries to reach valued ends is regarded as quite normal, and there is no moral stigma attached to doing so.[14]

Contact with other persons is not as important for the Protestant. He can obtain salvation by faith alone. This is taken one step further by the Calvinists in the doctrine of predestination: God has selected those who are to be united with him in heaven. Relations on earth with other persons have no influence over ultimate salvation. The emphasis in most Protestant churches is clearly on direct personal communication with God.[15] The niches in the facades of older Dutch Protestant churches that before the Reformation housed the statues of saints, now stare vacantly, like sightless eyes, at passers-by. The statues of the saints have been smashed; the religious intermediary between the mortal supplicant and the divine power who dispenses all good has been eliminated. A person does not need the help of others to obtain salvation.

Congruent with this is the ideology, very marked in the north of Holland, that to work through intermediaries to obtain a goal is morally wrong. This is especially pronounced among the middle and working classes. The upper class *regenten*, the Dutch establishment, are firm believers in the pragmatic importance of personal relations. People of course make use of other persons to pass on recommendations, solicit for jobs, obtain research funds and so on, but this is denied in public, for it is regarded morally wrong to do so. Many such relations, at least among the university-educated establishment, pass via *dispuut* (roughly the Dutch equivalent of the U.S. Greek letter fraternities and sororities) connexions. Since these are perpetual corporations, older members well placed in government circles and business can and do help younger members with jobs and recommendations among professional and social colleagues. Yet when I suggested that this is little more than a more formalized version of the patronage relations in southern Europe Dutch colleagues, surprisingly, were often shocked. In Holland there is an ethic that one should go it alone, and the concomitant—but often misguided—belief that a person's claim to a job will be judged on universalistic (i.e. rational) rather than particularistic (personal) criteria. That this does not always happen is most evident in the way in which personal relations played a role in the appointment of persons to posts as university lecturers (*wetenschappelijke medewerkers*). Until just a few years ago it was the practice for professors to appoint loyal clients to these posts, rather than to advertise for candidates as is done in Britain. This meant that a professor appointed his favourite bright and sometimes not too bright students (for the bright ones, especially if independently minded, could prove to be an embarrassment). The undesirable scientific consequences of this academic incest—which is certainly not limited to the Netherlands—have been sketched in the Introduction.

One other characteristic of social relations in a Calvinist society may be mentioned. This is the virtue attached to speaking one's mind bluntly. The bluntness of Dutch manners has struck foreign visitors over the ages.[16] This may be partly explained by the Calvinist stress on predestination: a person

G

is as he has been created; to disguise this, whether by means of fine clothing, make-up, or courtly manners, is hypocritical, therefore sinful. People who speak their minds in this way are regarded as virtuous; the flowery politeness of the Italian or Englishman is seen as hypocrisy. Social relations are thus often sacrificed to the ethic of honesty. The circumlocutions and extreme politeness used by people in many other cultures to protect their social relations, in the words of one of my (Protestant) students who had just received an effusive letter from a (Catholic) stranger to whom he had written for advice, are 'insipid nonsense' (*flauwe kul*). Not all social relations are strong enough to survive the often brutally frank onslaughts to which they are subjected by the Dutch.

I have argued that social relations are less important to the Protestant than to the Catholic. The latter is more sensitive to and therefore more considerate of the opinion of others. I suggest therefore that Catholics will have larger networks than Protestants and that these will contain more multiplex relations (though the score for multiplexity, since it is expressed as a proportion of the total number of relations, will not necessarily be higher). It will also take the Catholic longer to walk from point A to point B than the Protestant, for the former will spend more time on the way servicing his relations with members of his first order zone.

The above remarks also provide another view on the Weberian thesis of the relation between religion and economic behaviour. This was brought into perspective for me by a discussion I had with Cecil, my Maltese friend, on differences between Protestants and Catholics. He recounted a similar conversation he had with a Parsee businessman in Poona while in India as a Jesuit novice. The man had told him that he preferred Protestants to Catholics as employees. According to him they were more reliable: they were less often absent and usually came to work on time. The businessman also noted that the Protestant is brought up to make decisions for himself, and appears less influenced by the opinion of others. In line with the foregoing we may hypothesize that the Catholics were late because they stopped to talk to acquaintances met on the way to work, that they were absent more often because they attended religious feasts and family celebrations of relatives and friends, and that they were less prone to decide things for themselves because they were more closely tied to other persons and sensitive to the effects their decisions would have.

The above analysis serves to reinforce Weber's thesis. The maintenance of relations with others drains off time, energy and wealth. These are resources which, if invested in economic activity, bring about more rapid economic development.[17]

SOCIAL INFLUENCES

In addition to the influences from the partly ascribed biological, physical and cultural environment, there are influences from the social environment that affect the structure of social networks. I am thinking in particular of factors such as the kinship system, a person's occupation, his relative power and prestige, his education, and his rate of residential and social mobility.

1. *Kinship*

The kinship segment of a network is important, for in most societies the relations between certain categories of kinsmen tend to be morally sanctioned. These sanctions are particularly strong in societies in which persons are embedded in corporate kinship units such as lineages, clans, and other descent groups. Where a person is part of such a kinship system, he will have a number of ascribed relations with other members of the same group. These, depending upon the culture, influence to a lesser or greater extent the structure of his social network. If the kinship segment of his social network, even if not a formal group, coincides with the residential segment, he will have a social network with a high density and a high measure of multiplexity. Within social networks of this type there tends to be greater consensus regarding norms and values. As there are many links through which opinions can be made known and pressure applied, there will also be more pressure for conformity. There is thus less room to choose relations, and modes of behaviour. But though choice may be reduced when people are closely interconnected, it is not absent. As illustrated in the dispute between Donald and Abraham in the preceding chapter, in a face-to-face group persons can often choose between sets of norms concerning which there is a high degree of consensus.

2. Occupation

A person's occupation in no small way influences the content and composition of his network. As already indicated, his economic role set—the members of the partial network segment recruited in reference to his roles in the economic activity field—are an important part of his network. It is obvious that a teacher and a small farmer have very different economic role sets. The occupational relations of the teacher include fellow teachers, pupils and their parents, as well as the supervisory and administrative personnel of the department or educational system in which he works. The occupational relations of the farmer may include only a few fellow farmers with whom he exchanges tools and labour, a few agricultural experts from the department of Agriculture or the extension service, and the commercial contacts he must maintain with the persons from whom he buys his seed or live stock and those to whom he sells his produce. Thus a person's occupation influences the size of his network, the sort of exchange relations he maintains and the various categories of persons with whom he can if he wishes come in contact.

Where he plays several occupational roles, as does Pietru, for example, the number of relations quite obviously increases.

3. *Power*

Power is the ability of a person to influence the behaviour of others independently of their wishes. Power can be based on many factors. These include wealth and occupation or special relations which give access to strategic information, or resources such as jobs and licences that can be allocated by him. Wealth is generally an important power resource, and the wealthy are thus sought out by others who wish some share of the wealth. Unless they make a conscious effort to limit their relationships—and this is not automatic, for dependent clients form a resource which can be converted to obtain prestige and power in other spheres—their relations will tend to multiply. Thus a person with power will usually have a larger first order zone than persons with less power, though the multiplexity and density will probably be lower. Those who seek to establish relations with powerful persons will try to convert their initial single-stranded transactional relations into multi-stranded moral ones. By transforming the transactional link into a moral one, they hope to gain greater access to the resources he controls. The powerful have high social visibility, and may be included more often in the networks of the less powerful than the reverse. That is, a person may consider that he has a relationship with a powerful person, though the latter may not recognize this. One of the ways that people try to transform a single-stranded instrumental relationship with a powerful person into a multi-stranded moral one is by voluntarily performing many services to try and get the stronger party in a sort of debt relation. (This is called 'brown nosing' in United States Army slang, an allusion to a highly personal service.) Another way of transforming such relations in many Catholic societies, is to invite the powerful to become sponsors for religious ceremonies. That is, a powerful or influential man is invited to act as baptismal or confirmation godparent or wedding witness. I once asked one of the leading Maltese politicians how many godchildren he had. He laughed and said that he had no idea, but that it was well over a hundred. He had forgotten many of them, but he remarked that when the godfather or godchild wanted something they would call, often during his official office hours, and remind him of the relationship. Many more persons thus included this powerful man in their first order zones than the other way around.

4. Education

Education is an important resource, and thus is also a form of power. Education provides knowledge which not all people have. It is thus a resource which can be used to gain certain ends. Hence in most, if not all, societies, it gives prestige. In general one can say that the more education a person has, the greater the size of his network but the lower its density and multiplexity. It is well to remember that the density is relative to the size of the network. Scoring low on density does not mean that a person does not also have many multiplex relations. Educated persons know a wider range of people, for their social horizons are broader. Moreover in the process of acquiring their education they meet many people. By the time a person has obtained a higher university degree, for example, he has established many more social relations through his educational role as pupil/student than the person who has only completed an elementary education. This of course does not necessarily mean that the university graduate establishes more social relationships than the elementary school leaver in the ten to fifteen extra years he spends on his education. The range of new relationships made possible by education was touched on in the discussion of the difference in network structure of the School and the Red Xhosa. Education also serves to modify in a variety of subtle ways the ideological and moral precepts of a person. How these can influence the structure of a person's social network has already been discussed. Since the social network of a less well educated person will probably tend to be smaller, more interconnected and contain more multiplex links, we may expect that there will therefore be more channels through which social pressure can be placed on him to conform to the norms of behaviour and the values held by the members of his network. This consideration suggests that those with less education are less likely to accept new ideas or try out new techniques—to innovate—than those with more education. This is not only because their social horizons are more restricted—the usual assumption—but because the structure of their networks makes them more vulnerable to pressure exerted upon them to conform to the traditional way of doing things.

5. *Geographical and social mobility*

The degree to which a person remains stable, whether in geographic or social terms, also affects in very striking ways the structure of his network. A person who moves his place of residence places geographical distance between himself and a segment of his network. This means that he will have less opportunity to interact with those left behind, for to do so is often difficult if not physically impossible (though the availability of technological means—such as a telephone or a motor-car—modifies the impact of physical distance on the frequency of interaction). Moreover, by moving a person establishes new or re-establishes older social relations in his new place of residence. These new relations require servicing. Since his resources (time, energy, emotional input) are limited, he invests less in those left behind. A process summed up succinctly in the English saying 'Out of sight, out of mind.' But for a person nestled deeply in a highly interconnected network of multiplex links, moving is not easy. He is bound by it, tied to many others and vulnerable to the pressure which they exert upon him to remain, for his removal means a drastic reordering of social relations of the persons left behind.[18]

Thus once a person moves, the structure of his network changes. It becomes larger, the density decreases as does, usually, the multiplexity: he loses touch with old friends and neighbours in his former place of residence, and his new relations are at first usually not intimate. People in this situation find it increasingly easier to move than those who have highly interconnected networks of multiplex links. One of the characteristics of people in an industrial society is their increasing rate of residential mobility: most of the readers of this book will have moved several times in their lives. Each move is easier, in the sense that a person's network becomes less of an obstacle: the density and multiplexity is continually decreasing. As compared to those who have never moved, the networks of those who have done so several times often are larger but the density is lower, as is the multiplexity.[19] Such persons will probably have a smaller intimate circle of friends, for the removals prevent the multiplication of exchange relationships, a factor which leads to intimacy.

Much of what has been said about residential mobility applies to social mobility. People who are trying to get ahead in their careers, to climb higher on the ladder of social prestige, often move. As their income increases they move into houses and residential areas that are more comfortable and are evaluated in more prestigious terms. Thus quite apart from the creature comforts that can be gained by moving into a smart new house, the move also reflects (or often it suggests rather than reflects) a better job or a better income. In short the move may be seen as a claim to a higher prestige ranking than that associated with the house just vacated. Movement up the social ladder is also often possible only if a person is prepared to move to another city or country to take advantage of an opportunity which will advance his career.[20]

Often residential movement is brought about by a desire to get away from certain people, thus to lower the exchange content and multiplexity of certain social relationships. This may be because of quarrels; it may also be because neighbours are of a lower social status, or both. Although here the implications of moving up the social ladder have been discussed, people also move in the opposite direction. The financial and psychological costs of keeping up with the Joneses may be so high that a person may choose to move in order to cut his social costs.

Though social climbers very often move and so change the structure of their networks, they need not move to do so. By simply systematically exchanging less with certain persons, they cause much the same impact on particular social relationships as a residential move does. But to continue to live in the same place after 'turning your back' on old friends is not easy. The person who does so usually remains vulnerable to the resulting condemnation of his behaviour. The mutual links in his network that he shares with the old friends on whom he has turned his back carry him unpleasant messages and comments about his behaviour. It is usually easier to move away from people whom one wishes to see less often.

Social movement affects the structure of relations in the same way that physical mobility does. In fact social and physical mobility are often intimately related, as are various other social factors such as kinship, economic position, power and education. Certain occupations make possible or demand physical mobility—think of the academic, scientific and diplomatic professions. These in turn are related to the degree of education. These various factors often combine to produce power, not only in terms of wealth and high office, but also through the wide range of social relationships, which if carefully managed, form an important source of power.

PERSONALITY, CHOICE AND NETWORK STRUCTURE

In previous sections I pointed to the possible influence of inherited personality traits upon network structure. A person who inherits an introverted personality will make fewer intimate friends, and, in general, establish relations with fewer persons than a person who inherits a warm, outgoing personality. This indicates personality as the independent and network structure as the dependent variable. I think it more likely however that the arrows of causation point in both directions. That is, it seems plausible that the structure of a person's network, which as we have seen is influenced by a number of factors partly beyond his control—such as climate, ideology, kinship system and so on—also exerts an influence on his personality.

The chief problem of exploring this relation is the large number of variables involved for both network and personality structure. For example, extroverted and introverted personality types can themselves be broken down into a number of traits which in combination influence the way in which a person handles his interpersonal relations. The more important of these include the degree to which a person takes the initiative in social situations or is passive; accepts or rejects others; is sociable or unsociable; is friendly or unfriendly; is sympathetic or unsympathetic; and is at ease or is uncomfortable in company.[21] Similarly we have seen that a person's network structure also varies in terms of criteria such as multiplexity, size, density and degree.

I suggest there is a connexion between network structure and at least one of the personality traits associated with the extroversion/introversion opposition, namely sociability (in the sense of being 'willing to converse in a pleasant manner' —*O.E.D.*). All other things like culture, sex and so on being equal, a person who has a *dense* network (high score for multiplexity, density and degree) will be more sociable (to strangers) than a person with a *loose* network (low score for multiplexity, density and degree). A dense network is one which is typically found in an economically (and thus socially) undifferentiated village, town or urban quarter with a stable population, while a loose network is associated with an economically (and thus socially) differentiated village, town or city, with a mobile population.

The relation between dense network structure and a sociable personality is explained largely by what may be called conditioning and social control. A person encapsulated in a dense network is used to interacting in several different roles with most of the people with whom he comes in contact in the course of his normal pursuits. Moreover, the members of his network maintain similar relations among themselves. He is thus used to a fairly high volume of sociable relations, for conversation is a minimum exchange between people who are connected in many different ways. All or most of the relations he has with people in the course of his day are of this type. He has little experience with single-stranded relations and persons he does not know. He lacks the social experience to deal with them. Hence he tends to extend to the stranger the behavourial pattern with which he himself is most familiar, that of sociability.

In contrast, a person with a loose network is thus used to a relatively high volume of single-interest relations and, as in cities, contacts with people he may well never see again. He is, in contrast to the person with a dense network, accustomed to handling relations which are chiefly instrumental. He will hence be less sociable to strangers.

There is also another reason for a person with a dense network to be more sociable to strangers, especially to those he meets on his known territory. He may make an implicit assumption that the stranger is in some way connected to persons in his own network, and so be a friend-of-a-friend. The stranger may thus have a place in his second order zone. Hence he is sociable to him, he greets him, and often chats with him, exchanging small talk in the hope of finding out more about him so that he can 'place' him, and thus satisfy his curiosity. A person with a loose network, in contrast, has little reason to assume that strangers are friends-of-friends, for his own known social universe consists mostly of people whom he knows (or believes) are not in touch with each other. Hence there is no reason for him to be sociable for the sake of his friends, nor does he strive to 'place' the stranger, for he is constantly dealing with or encountering persons who are unknown. He has no particular curiosity about him. He passes the stranger without greeting, or if stopped by him, provides perfunctory answers without an attempt to engage him in conversation.

There are however at least two conditions which might tend to inhibit sociability even among people who have dense networks. The first is if a person has reason to mistrust or fear the stranger, as for instance peasants, who are ever fearful of tax collectors and other social predators. Sicilians of all classes are wary of outsiders. While the better placed Sicilian will try to engage the stranger in conversation to learn his business, the peasant ignores him in the hope that he will go away. This mistrust is often partly a consequence of relative social or cultural isolation.

The second condition which inhibits sociability is isolation in the geographical and social sense. A person, even if he has a dense network, will not be very sociable if he has an occupation which entails spending much time alone so that frequency of interaction is greatly reduced. I have in mind people isolated by nature, such as those who live in the north of Sweden, whose homes and farms are scattered over sparsely populated countryside. In fact, the taciturnity of those living in the northern districts of Scandinavia is proverbial. Banton mentions the case of an informant who when she married went to live with her husband, a customs official, on the barren Swedish-Finnish boundary in the north. She told him how at times 'an acquaintance of her husband would call on a social visit; he would come in and take a seat near the door; she would bring him a cup of coffee and after about twenty minutes he would leave, nobody said anything at all'.[22]

The implications of this discussion of the influence of network structure on personality, if true—and it can easily be tested—are rather frightening. As a continually increasing proportion of mankind is becoming industrialized and urbanized, there is also a concomitant increase in specialization, mobility and thus single-stranded economic and other social relations. Hence personal networks will increasingly assume the attributes of the loose network sketched above, with the related influence on personality. Thus not only is the world becoming filled with houses, smog, cars and noise, but people are becoming less sociable, more reserved and instrumental in their dealings with each other.

Finally, it is important to point to the problem of choice. Every person has a measure of choice as to just what the content of his relationships is going to be. Every time he interacts each person re-evaluates the exchange content of the various social relations he maintains. How often have each of us asked questions of the following order: Did we get a Christmas card from Tony and Em last year? How much should we spend on Maria's wedding present? What did she give us when we were married? Shall we invite Henry around for dinner? Dorothy was very cool last night! George might have given me a ride home! The quality of the relationship is thus constantly shifting. These changes can come about through events beyond a person's control, such as death or an obligatory move to a new post, but very often they are calculated. People can and do move to change the content or rid themselves of certain existing relationships, and give themselves the opportunity of establishing new ones.

The time, energy and emotional resources which a person can invest in personal relations are limited. He must choose how to invest these. I suggest that most persons can maintain intense exchange relations with only a limited number of people. In short, every person has what may be called a network management problem. Relations must be serviced periodically if the exchange content is to remain at the level desired. As a person's network is modified as he grows older, marries and rises in his profession, he must make choices as to which relations he will service and which he will ignore.

Marriage, for example, means that a man must drop some relationships from his own intimate zone to accommodate the influx of his wife's intimate relations. The many friendly relations a single person maintains are contingent upon his having enough time to service them and a place to meet them. Once married, a person has less opportunity to meet these persons: many places are restricted to unmarried persons. Moreover, he is no longer completely free to use his living quarters without making special arrangements: such as getting his spouse to approve of the visitor, or to remove herself to a back-room or to clean up (just what happens or does not happen rather depends upon the culture and the transactional balance between the couple). But besides these restrictions upon the place of the encounter, a married person has less time available. The need to work to support a growing family, the logistics of an expanding household, the establishment and the servicing of not only the relationships in his personal cell (wife and children) but also those brought into his intimate zone by his wife, all require considerable time. This shift in the allocation of time spent on certain relationships after marriage is foreseeable. Hence the last fling with the boys on the eve of the wedding that is such a part of west European culture. It marks not only a change of status, but it is in many respects a real farewell party.

The shift in relationships upon marriage, especially the loosening of the ties with one's own family and bachelor friends, is a gradual process. Nonetheless, over a span of a year or two, the changes are striking. Though these changes take place, as it were, in spite of a person's intentions, they are, in the final analysis, the result of limited choices.

A person may also consciously choose to restrict the size of certain zones. He imposes limits upon the type of exchanges he is prepared to enter into in a conscious effort to restrict the size of parts of his network. A serious and ambitious former colleague of mine provided a striking, if somewhat extreme, example of this. He had moved to a new university several years before we did, and for a period of three years he had canvassed and recruited new friends. Having left a considerable section of his intimate zone behind in his former place of work, he was searching for replacements. By the time we arrived he had found as many replacements as he could handle. He mentioned to us at a sherry party that he and his wife were no longer extending their range of friends as they 'could not afford the extra time' new intimate contacts would require. The net result of course was that his circle of intimates were all persons who had been at the university for several years. In this expanding university they constituted the 'old guard', the conservatives. He had few friends among the new-comers: to be able to include them in his circle of intimates he would have had to drop (or see less of) older friends. This was difficult owing to the investments in, and the on-going exchange relations he maintained with, them. Moreover, an old friend who has been dropped but still remains in the surroundings is much more difficult to cope with than a new-comer whom one scarcely knows. Thus for a number of reasons he considered the social costs of establishing friendly relations with new-comers too high.

I suggest this example is not an isolated case. In most organizations and communities with a turn-over of personnel a similar process takes place. Its results can be seen in the dichotomy noticed so often between the established old-timers who all know each other, and the new-comers, the outsiders. These though eager enough to meet the established, are rebuffed for many of the same reasons set out above. Thus quite understandably they look to other new-comers for support and friendship.[23] The established and the outsiders thus tend to form clusters or compartments. This affects not only the flow of information, but also the introduction and acceptance of new ideas. Since new ideas often come with the new people, these will find first acceptance with the outsiders. Because the established have their own relatively close communication and exchange circuits, they will come less in touch with and be less open to the new ideas. Hence they will be more conservative. This is one of the reasons why the establishment is often conservative and the outsiders or new-comers more progressive or open to new ideas. Any attempt to understand the acceptance and flow of new ideas must take into account the structure of the exchange circuits of the networks of the people concerned.

All this has taken us rather far afield from the influences affecting the structure of personal networks. But it is essential to be aware of the influences that choice has on the structure of, and transactions within, networks and the importance of these for various social configurations. We shall return to this in chapters 7 and 8 when dealing with various types of coalitions. The next chapter looks more closely at two personal networks in terms of some of the structural variables and influences that have been discussed up to this point.

5

An Exploration of Two Personal Networks

When I tried to apply some of the concepts set out in the earlier sections, particularly those dealing with structural and interactional characteristics of networks, and to test some of the hypotheses about the relation between environment, behaviour and personality, I could not find the published data I needed. Consequently I was obliged to attempt to gather this data myself.[1] I began with two informants in 1968, on a pilot study basis, planning to branch out and test findings more systematically on a wider sample. Collecting this data proved to be very difficult and very time-consuming, as did its analysis. Hence, for better or for worse, I have data on only two first-order zones.[2]

The following study is really little more than a first attempt to map and compare two first-order zones, and to relate the features of these to the observed differences in the environment, behaviour and personality of the two informants. I try to answer the obvious questions about the personal networks of Cecil and Pietru, my two informants: What is their cultural and social background? What are the objective structural and interactional characteristics of their respective networks? What are their subjective characteristics? Is there a relation between objective and subjective characteristics? What is the influence of the environment on the structure and content of the networks? What is the relation between network structure

H

and personality? Finally, I indicate some of the ways in which Cecil and Pietru use their networks to solve problems, and how these, the exercise of choice and other factors bring about changes in their composition and structure.

ENVIRONMENT: THE SOCIAL AND CULTURAL BACKGROUND

1. *Malta*

The Maltese archipelago covers 122 square miles. Malta, the largest and southernmost island, is 17 miles long and 9 miles wide, and covers an area of 95 square miles. There are just over 314,000 people on the Islands, making the Maltese archipelago, with a population density of just under 2,600 per square mile, one of the most thickly populated countries in the world. Slightly over half of the population lives in the urban area which centres on Valletta and the Grand Harbour; the rest live in clearly separated villages and towns which range in size from 900 to 17,000 inhabitants. No village, however, is more than an hour's bus ride from Valletta, and Gozo is only thirty minutes by ferry from its larger sister island.

Maltese see the family as the most important institution in their lives. The ideal household is composed of an elementary family living together in a separate house. Maltese have large families and reckon kin relationships equally through males and females. Each person is at the centre of a wide network of blood relatives, and relatives by marriage. Though the kinship structure is bilateral, there is a noticeable bias in favour of the mother's/wife's relatives. Maltese families are mother-centred and the contacts with relatives beyond the nuclear family are by and large articulated through women. Kinship obligations usually extend out to first cousins for men but as far as second cousins for women.

Malta may be said to have a service economy. Until recently

the Maltese lived off the income derived from providing services as civil servants, clerks, soldiers, skilled fitters, semi- and unskilled labourers to the British colonial and military establishments which governed the islands for years. Although Malta has been independent since 1964, she still largely lives off the services she provides, now to the ever-increasing number of tourists visiting the islands in search of the sun. Less than ten per cent of the islands' inhabitants are full-time agriculturists. Consequently most Maltese travel from their place of residence to their work-place, which is normally located somewhere in the expanding conurbation centred on Valletta, the capital.

As may be expected, there are considerable differences between town and country, and, especially, between the residents of the large, smart seaside suburb of Sliema and the inhabitants of small relatively isolated villages such as Farrug. The differences are not only a matter of dialect, but also of behaviour and interests. The Sliema residents regard the religious feasts, processions, and fireworks, so characteristic of village life, with abhorrence. The people in villages have a good deal of informal contact in streets and shops, but rarely visit non-kinsmen in their homes. Sliema inhabitants, on the other hand, arrange formal visits and frequent large receptions to which non-kinsmen are invited. Villagers deliver personally the invitations to attend their more modest baptismal, betrothal and wedding ceremonies; Sliema people post printed invitations, even to kinsmen who live close by. (Pietru wrote in 1971, however, that villagers now also post invitations.) The inhabitants of Sliema consciously as well as unconsciously imitate the behaviour and many of the attitudes of the English, who for so long ruled Malta's fortunes. Even the Maltese spoken in Sliema affects an English accent that contrasts sharply with the broad vowels and gutturals of the countryman. The latter, in turn, patterns his behaviour on the rural elite, the doctors, lawyers, and wealthy merchants, residing in the villages and rural towns.

Most Maltese are fervently practising Roman Catholics and there is traditionally a strong attachment to the Church. This has had an important influence on the moral code. It is especially noticeable in the field of kinship where the large families and strong bonds between members of the elementary family are supported by exhortations and sanctions of the Church. Nevertheless certain ideological divisions exist. These may be characterized as pro- and anti-establishment, for the Church and against the Church. In recent years this cleavage has become centred on political parties: respectively the Church-oriented Nationalist Party, which formed the Government until 1971, and the relatively anti-clerical socialist Malta Labour Party. Much the same cleavage has long been incorporated at the village level in rival factions which compete over the festivities in honour of their respective patron saints. The establishment faction is supported by the Church and includes most of the leading figures of the village and celebrates the official patron of the village. The anti-establishment faction, composed chiefly of the less influential members of the parish celebrates a local rival saint, often in contravention of the Church's interests. These ideological cleavages at the national level and at the village level actively engage most Maltese villagers. Such ideological commitments influence in no small way the relations between persons.

2. *Pietru*

Pietru lives in Hal-Farrug, a village of just over 1,200. Three out of four of the inhabitants work outside the village, chiefly as skilled and unskilled industrial labourers. In Farrug there are no striking differences in the standard of living, as there are in larger villages and towns. There is nonetheless a difference in the circle of acquaintances of a teacher and an unskilled labourer. The village is divided into two ritual factions which celebrate the feast of St. Martin, the parish's patron saint, and St. Joseph his local rival. These factions in turn focus on rival band clubs. The Labour Party is very strong in Hal-Farrug and is centred on the football club. Cleavage for and against St. Martin and for and against the Labour Party cuts through the village at all levels. It flares into intense rivalry at the time of the annual feasts of the two saints and at election time every five years.

Pietru was born in 1933, thus at the time of the first study he was about thirty-five years old. He had been married for three years and had one son. Pietru's father, a fairly well-off peasant cultivator, died when Pietru was four years old. His mother, though from the neighbouring village of Qrendi, remained in Hal-Farrug and supported her three daughters and son by continuing to farm the fields she had been left. It was a difficult life and she soon sent one of her daughters to live with her unmarried sisters in Qrendi, where she lives to this day. At the beginning of the war she became ill and, unable to get much help from her husband's brother and sister, both married and by village standards very well off, she and the children moved in with her own family in Qrendi. They returned to Hal-Farrug and her bombed-out house after the war.

Through a priest, a friend of the family, Pietru's mother was able to get him a place in a private school run by English monks. She paid what she could towards the cost of schooling from the meagre farming proceeds.

Pietru looks upon this period as one of hard work, for every day after school he had to work long hours in the fields helping his mother and sisters. In 1953 he tried the highly competitive entrance examination for the Teachers Training College. Apparently he was unsuccessful. I say 'apparently' because the Rector of his school telephoned the Department of Education in his presence and heard that he had passed the examination and was to be admitted. But when the list of successful candidates was published, Pietru's name was not included. Both he and the Rector assumed that he had been scratched in favour of some better-connected candidate from

Sliema. The Rector then helped him get a part-time teaching job at an institution run by the same religious order. Two years later he was admitted to the training college. He successfully completed the two year course of studies in 1957.

He was fortunate and immediately found a job in the Government Elementary School in Farrug. He continued to help his mother in the fields after school. He soon became engaged to a fellow teacher, a Valletta girl, who began to occupy his spare time away from teaching and farming. After a difficult year and a half, during which his fiancée persuaded him to abandon his attempts to win a Government scholarship to study agricultural science abroad, but was unsuccessful in getting him to adopt the customs and dress of the city, he broke the engagement.

Freed from his unhappy courtship, Pietru plunged into the social life of his village. He became an extremely active fund raiser for his band club, standard-bearer for the confraternity of the Blessed Sacrament, and the leader of the Catholic Action section for unmarried men. He also became the confidant of the new parish priest, supplying him with information about parish affairs and helping him with his numerous fund raising activities. During the political upheaval of 1961 and 1962, he became one of the Church's most vocal advocates in Farrug. At this time he also joined a national anti-Labour Party Church sponsored study group. His forceful advocacy of the Church's teachings alienated many of his former friends and acquaintances in this predominantly Labour village, where, in his words, 'you either agree 100 per cent or you are automatically an enemy'. I first met Pietru in 1960–61 when we lived in the village. He was then in his most active period in village affairs.

In 1962, Pietru, now twenty-eight, became engaged again, this time to a Sliema girl who had taught for many years in the village school. Having been rather badly bruised during his three year intensive participation in village politics, he withdrew almost entirely from the village arena. He devoted his free time for the next three years to getting to know his fiancée and to building a house.

Pietru has been married since 1965. He is still as active as ever, but he has little time to devote to village politics. Though he helps the new parish priest in his fund-raising activities and takes part in the village processions as the standard-bearer of the confraternity of the Blessed Sacrament, he no longer holds office in the band club and shows little interest in its activities. He still continues to help his mother in the fields and grows his own cash crops of potatoes, onions and tomatoes, which he works in the early morning before school begins and in the late afternoon. He also does most of the bookkeeping for the ever-expanding household bazaar run in his mother's house by an unmarried sister. During the last two years he has also been studying intensively to pass his 'A' level examinations in Economics, Social Geography and Maltese so that he may be qualified to teach in secondary schools and, possibly, to begin studying for a university degree. Four afternoons a week during the school year he and his wife run private classes in their home to prepare children from the village for the competitive Government secondary school entrance examination. And last but not least, he devotes a considerable amount of time to his growing family and helps his wife, who has none of her own relations in the village, with many of the household tasks. He also does much of the shopping for the family.

Owing to his retirement from the frontline of village politics, his continuing studies, and especially, his excellent results in getting his school and fee-paying charges through the secondary school examinations, he has regained some of the goodwill of the village which he lost during the heat of the 1962 political battle. His standing in the village is complemented by the quiet dignity of his Sliema born wife who, as we noted, taught in the village for many years before her marriage.

3. *Cecil*

Cecil, in contrast to Pietru, is Sliema born, though he now lives in Birkirkara, his wife's town. Sliema is a rapidly expanding residential suburb of some 21,000 persons. It is divided into three parishes and merges imperceptibly with other large suburban parishes to form the northern half of the conurbation centring on Valletta. For the past forty years it has been regarded as the best residential area of the island and many from the upwardly mobile government, military and business classes have moved there. It is predominantly a white-collar residential area. Many English and other foreign residents live there. Nevertheless there is a sizeable population of industrial labourers. It is thus an area characterized by sharp class divisions.

Birkirkara, where Cecil now lives, is a town of some 17,000. Though it gives the impression of being part of the urban sprawl, it is in fact a separate town and is one of the island's oldest parishes, with intense parochial patriotism. It is a stratified community composed of old established noble and professional families, shopkeepers, artisans and businessmen, industrial labourers both skilled and unskilled, and a fairly sizeable population of farmers. It has two active band clubs and an active political party club. It is the home base of the former Nationalist Prime Minister and his brother, the former Minister of Education. It also has a strongly organized labour faction which manages to return at least one member of parliament every election.

Cecil was born in 1940. He is the sixth child of a grocer, and has eight brothers and sisters. He recalls that he was very strictly brought up and was not allowed to play with the children on the street. He thus had little contact with his neighbours. Some of this parental vigilance was temporarily relaxed when his family moved in summer to a seaside house outside the town. Between the ages of six to twelve he was sent to a strict private elementary school. His father was very ambitious for his sons and obliged them to spend many hours closeted in their rooms studying. This regime was successful. One brother is a Franciscan priest, another a doctor and the third, who is also the only one besides Cecil to have married, is a university lecturer in England. His two older sisters have married; his two younger sisters are still unmarried.

At twelve he was sent to an exclusive, Jesuit-run secondary day-school. At seventeen he became a Jesuit novice and lived in the school as a boarder, and later transferred to the order's seminary. At twenty-one he was sent, at his own request, to the order's mission station in India. There he learned and taught Hindi as well as other subjects at primary and secondary level. He also obtained a degree in philosophy at the Jesuit university in Poona. From there he went to one of the order's secondary schools, where he ended up as vice-rector. In all Cecil spent five years in India before deciding to withdraw from the Jesuit order. At twenty-six he returned to Malta, where, after a period of searching, he found a teaching position in the government secondary school system.

When he came back to Malta he lived first with his family in Sliema and that summer moved to the family's new seaside house at St. Paul's Bay. There he met the neighbours and discovered that one of them was an ex-Jesuit of about his own age. He soon became engaged to the latter's sister. Next summer, in August 1967, he married and moved to his wife's town. He told me many times that he finds living in Birkirkara strange in comparison to life in Sliema. By his standards Birkirkara has much of a village about it. In the beginning he found it annoying that people from the neighbourhood into which he moved seemed to know a great deal about him. They also seemed to spend so much time talking!

In many respects Cecil is unsatisfied still. The considerable responsibility he held while a Jesuit, his education and the general background of his family leave him with unfulfilled aspirations. For the past few years he has been trying to get a scholarship to study social psychology in England. He seems gradually to be establishing roots in his place of residence, a process helped by the birth of two children. He sees his wife's relatives more often than his own.

4. *Comparative summary*

A number of factors relevant to the study of the structure of the networks of Pietru and Cecil emerge from this very brief description of their social environment. To begin with, there is the difference between town and country. Pietru's network is anchored in the rural area, that of Cecil in the urban. These differences are of considerable significance.

There is a striking difference in the range of activities in which the two engage. Pietru is not only a teacher who gives private lessons, he also farms, helps his sister run her shop, is a part-time student, takes an active part in the ritual life of his parish, and, finally, visits a wide range of relatives. Cecil's activities are largely restricted to his kinship and formal teaching roles. This difference in activity is of course partly a function of the difference between life in a small village and life in a large centre, that is, of their residential and social niches.

Cecil comes from an environment in which class differences are pronounced, whereas Pietru comes from what may be called a one-class milieu in which differences in styles of life do not seem to be permanent.

Pietru has climbed many rungs on the economic prestige ladder during his life, moving from farmer's son to teacher, and finally marrying a Sliema teacher and bringing her to live in the village. Moreover, he is well-off financially, with a large house, a good salary, and a fat bank account. Cecil's upward movement has been much less pronounced, though the move from shopkeeper to semi-professional status is not inconsiderable. On the other hand, he married the daughter of a skilled labourer and moved from Sliema to a rural town. Cecil is financially less well-off than Pietru.

There is also a difference in the geographical mobility of the two. Cecil has travelled widely, both within and outside Malta: between St. Paul's Bay in summer and Sliema in winter, and between Malta and several parts of India. Moreover, as already noted, he has now left his place of birth and moved to his wife's town. Pietru apart from the short period he lived in a neighbouring village as a boy and a three-week trip to Italy and Spain in 1961 with a group of teachers, has spent his life in Farrug.

These various factors have combined to make a difference in the personal prestige of Pietru and Cecil in relation to their immediate environment. Pietru is a relatively big fish in a very small pond, whereas Cecil is a smaller fish in a much larger pond. Pietru has high social visibility, whereas Cecil, partly because there are more teachers in his present environment, and also because he plays fewer social roles, has lower social visibility.

Pietru's immediate social environment is riven with ideological cleavages: the festa factions and political parties. These cleavages are not noticeable in Cecil's immediate surroundings. Various factors have combined to influence Pietru to take an unequivocal stand and play a part in these conflicts.

Finally, the differences in personality and character are also significant. Pietru has a hearty outgoing character. He is used to personalizing social relations—in the sense of exchanging small talk and information, in getting to know people—with bus conductors, shopkeepers and other strangers met in the course of his expeditions beyond the limits of his village and district. Cecil, though friendly, is more reserved in his dealings with people than Pietru. He is not as garrulous and does not appear to seek to personalize relations with strangers.

STRUCTURAL, INTERACTIONAL AND SUBJECTIVE
FEATURES

1. *Structural characteristics*

a. Size

The size of the two networks is easily compared. Pietru's
network includes 1,751 persons and Cecil's 638. These persons
are what we may call first order contacts: people with whom
Cecil and Pietru have or have had some contact. Both have
included a few people of whom they know but have not
actually met. These are persons who have married close
kinsmen abroad. They know that they will meet them as soon
as they visit Malta. In the meantime they know a great deal
about them through letters that are passed to them by family
members. Although each has done his best to recall, list and
discuss all the persons he knows, quite obviously many have
been left out, for the human memory is fallible. Persons under
fourteen have been excluded. In Pietru's case this involves at
least 450 village children whom he knows personally. Except
for the few unknown close affines mentioned, no second order
contacts were included.

b. Composition

Whom they know is more interesting. The networks can be
compared with regard to sex, age, education, occupation and
residence to indicate the relative spread of contacts throughout a number of important social categories. It is also important to ask in what capacity Pietru and Cecil know the
members of their networks. In other words, we must compare
the relative importance in each network of various activity
fields from which the members of the network have been
recruited.

Sex. Pietru's network displays a more even spread than
Cecil's 42 per cent of Pietru's network are women, while only
23 per cent of Cecil's are. This proportion roughly holds true
not only for the total network, but also for the many zones

and categories into which it can be divided. Of the total population of Malta 52 per cent are women.

Age. Pietru's network also shows a slightly more even age distribution than Cecil's. Pietru knows slightly more young persons—14–19-year-olds—than Cecil. He also knows slightly more older people—70 years and over—than Cecil. But except for the very old and very young, the age distribution in the two networks is similar.

Table 5.1 : Age

Age	Pietru	Cecil	Malta*
	%	%	%
14–19 yr.	9.4	4.5	14.7
20–29	20.7	24.3	21.3
30–39	28.3	31.5	16.9
40–49	15.7	16.6	15.3
50–59	11.0	13.0	12.5
60–67	7.4	8.3	11.9
70+	2.7	0.6	7.4
unknown	4.8	1.1	—
Total %	100	99.9	100
Number	1751	638	220,447

* Source : *Annual Abstract of Statistics, 1968*, Malta : Central Office of Statistics, 1969, p. 14, Table 4. The figures given for the first age category are 15–19 years rather than the 14–19 years I used.

Education. The educational composition of the two networks differs considerably. More than half of Pietru's network has had either no schooling or only primary schooling, as compared to only 14 per cent for Cecil. By contrast 65 per cent of Cecil's network has had secondary or higher education (seminary, teacher training, university), compared to only 32 per cent of Pietru's network.

Occupation. Considering that Cecil's network is on the whole better educated than Pietru's, it is no surprise that religious and white collar workers form just over half Cecil's network, but make up only one quarter of Pietru's. It is interesting to note, too, that though Cecil knows many more

Table 5.2 : Education

Education	Pietru	Cecil	Malta*
	%	%	%
Unknown	10.5	21.0	0.6
None	21.8	2.4	16.6
Primary	36.3	11.3	62.1
Secondary	16.4	32.3	18.6
Higher	15.1	33.1	2.1
Total %	100.1	100	100
Number	1749	637	215,316

* Based on unpublished material from the 1967 census kindly made available by the Central Office of Statistics.
The figures for Malta are for the population over 5 years not attending school, which is compulsory from 5 to 14 years. Those for Pietru and Cecil show only persons over 14 years, some of whom may still be at school.

priests than Pietru (145 as compared to 90), the latter knows more in Malta than the former (83 compared to 57). Both, however, know about the same proportion of skilled workers. Unskilled workers, on the other hand, are more important in Pietru's network than in that of Cecil. Not surprisingly, while four out of every hundred persons Pietru knows are farmers, Cecil knows virtually none.

Table 5.3 : Occupation

Occupation	Pietru	Cecil		Malta*
	%	%		%
Religious	5.1	22.7	}	31.6
Professional and white collar	19.2	29.6		
Skilled service (police, broker, shop etc.)	12.7	12.2	}	41.9
Unskilled service	28.2	21.5		
Skilled industrial	3.3	2.2	}	18.7
Unskilled industrial	9.6	0.5		
Agricultural	4.4	0.3		7.7
Other	3.3	1.4		—
Don't know	14.0	9.6		—
Total %	99.8	100		99.9
Number	1751	638		94,367

* Based on unpublished material from the 1967 census for the gainfully occupied population, kindly made available by the Central Office of Statistics.

Residence. Almost half of Pietru's network live around him in Hal-Farrug. In contrast, only one fifth of Cecil's network live in his place of residence, Birkirkara. Moreover, Pietru's network is clearly rural based, for 73 per cent of it is located in rural towns and villages, while only 10 per cent of Cecil's is. As can be seen from table 5.4, most of Cecil's network is located in various urban centres in Malta, while fully 25 per cent is situated abroad.

Table 5.4 : Place of Residence

Place of Residence	Pietru	Cecil	Malta*
	%	%	%
Farrug (Pietru) or	48.3	—	0.4
Birkirkara (Cecil)	—	20.2	5.5
Villages around Farrug	13.2	—	5.5
Sliema	5.6	21.5	9.0
Urban Malta	13.3	15.0	35.5
Rest of Malta	9.8	10.2	44.1
Abroad	7.3	24.5	—
Don't know	2.6	8.6	—
Total %	100.1	100	100
Number	1751	638	314,216

* The figures show the total population and are based on unpublished material from the 1967 census kindly made available to me by the Central Office of Statistics.

Although this last table shows that the geographical spread of Pietru's network in Malta is greater than that of Cecil, it is even more pronounced than is indicated: Pietru knows people in 40 of Malta's 44 parishes, while Cecil has acquaintances in only 27. Moreover, Pietru knows a number of persons in Gozo, while Cecil knows none.

c. Activity fields

It is now important to ask in what capacity Pietru and Cecil know the members of their networks. Fellow villagers make up the largest segment of Pietru's network. Cecil appears to know most persons in connexion with either their or his work. That is, they are part of each other's occupational role sets. Kinsmen, though forming the second largest activity field for both Pietru and Cecil, occupy a relatively larger place for Pietru, for 24 per cent of the members of his larger network are kinsmen. In contrast, only 17 per cent of Cecil's network are kinsmen.

Table 5.5 : Activity Field

Shared Activity	Pietru	Cecil
	%	%
Occupation Economic	19.9	41.4
School/College	0.5	11.6
Kinship	23.9	16.6
Association and similar interests	6.1	4.1
Village	40.6	0.4
Neighbour	4.8	11.0
Miscellaneous	1.5	14.5
None	2.6	—
Total %	99.9	99.6
Number	2020*	821*

* These totals exceed the number of persons in each network since some relations derive from more than one activity field.

d. Density

The density of Pietru's network is 23.7 per cent and that of Cecil's 5.2 per cent. Briefly then, more members of Pietru's primary zone are linked to each other independently of him than is the case with the members of Cecil's primary zone. At least this is the way each perceives the density of his personal network, for it is important to remember that only Pietru and Cecil, and not the members of their primary zones, were asked to indicate which persons knew each other. Thus this density index is their subjective perception of how communication/exchange could potentially take place.

We must not lose sight of the fact that conclusions so far have merely been numerical statements about the composition of the networks. Table 5.5 indicates only that a relation exists between Cecil or Pietru and a member of his network which may be expressed in terms of a particular activity field.

This tells us nothing about the quality of that relation or its relative importance. Phrased differently, how well do Pietru and Cecil know the members of their networks? Is there a relation between the size of a given activity field and the importance of the persons in it to Pietru and Cecil? I attempted to answer these questions by examining the content of their relations in terms of what is exchanged.

2. *Transactional content*

The type of exchange relations which Pietru and Cecil maintain with members of their network is set out in table 5.6. From this it appears that Pietru maintains more personal relations with more members of his network than Cecil, though he also ignores a greater portion of his network. He also seems more personal, that is, he exchanges more conversation, visits and gifts than Cecil. He seems less noncommittal: while 57 per cent of Cecil's network are persons with whom he exchanges only greetings or civilities, these categories include only 28 per cent of Pietru's network. In contrast, Pietru exchanges conversation, information and visits with 40 per cent of his network, while Cecil maintains these types of exchange relations with only 20 per cent of his much smaller network.

Table 5.6 : Exchange Relations

Type Exchange	Number		%	
	Pietru	Cecil	Pietru	Cecil
Ignore	537	138	30.7	21.7
Greet only	288	191	16.4	29.7
Civilities only	204	174	11.7	27.3
Conversation/ information	560	69	32.0	10.3
Visits and gifts	140	60	8.0	9.3
Don't know	22	6	1.3	0.9
Total	1751	638	100.1%	99.4%

I

Table 5.7: Exchange Relations and Activity Field

Type Exchange	Occupation		Kinship		Village	
	Pietru	Cecil	Pietru	Cecil	Pietru	Cecil
	%	%	%	%	%	
Ignore	3.2	20.3	21.3	8.8	41.2	—
Greet only	6.5	29.1	15.7	24.3	23.0	—
Civilities only	21.4	30.1	8.1	36.8	10.8	—
Conversation/information	63.8	14.4	26.9	6.6	21.9	—
Visits and gifts	4.7	5.3	24.8	21.3	2.9	—
Don't know	0.2	0.6	2.9	2.2	0.2	—
Total %	99.8	99.8	99.7	100	100	—
Number	401	340	483	136	846	3

In table 5.7 exchange relations are compared to certain activity fields. It is clear that the activity fields which numerically seemed so important to Pietru (village) and to Cecil (occupational role sets) are considerably less important in terms of exchange relations. While the village is proportionally important for Pietru in terms of his total network, he exchanges conversation and visits with only one out of every four fellow villagers. Thus with three out of four persons in his village he maintains only nominal relations. Pietru also appears to maintain closer relations than Cecil with the persons with whom he shares occupational role relations. Although this category is numerically the most important in terms of Cecil's total network, he maintains only nominal relations with or ignores (does not greet) 80 per cent of the persons within it. Pietru, in contrast, maintains nominal relations with or ignores only one third of the persons with whom he shares occupational role relations and exchanges conversation and visits with two thirds of them.

It is also obvious in table 5.7 that Pietru maintains much more intimate exchange relations with his kinsmen than Cecil. In fact, he exchanges conversation and visits with 51 per cent of his 483 kinsmen, while Cecil does so with only 28 per cent of his 136 kinsmen.

Finally, from table 5.8 it is evident that most of the people whom Pietru ignores (i.e. does not greet when they meet) are fellow villagers, while most of those Cecil ignores are people whom he knows because they are members of each other's occupational role sets. While Pietru and Cecil visit more often with kinsmen than with persons from other activity fields, fully three quarters of the people Pietru visits are kinsmen, while considerably less than half of Cecil's visits are with kinsmen.

Table 5.8: Activity Field and Exchange Relations

Shared Activity	Ignore		Greeting		Conversation		Visits	
	Pietru	Cecil	Pietru	Cecil	Pietru	Cecil	Pietru	Cecil
	%	%	%	%	%	%	%	%
Occupation	2.2	41.0	8.0	44.0	36.2	45.8	12.0	22.5
School/College	0.4	9.0	—	5.8	0.1	20.6	0.7	10.0
Kinship	17.9	7.2	23.3	14.7	18.4	8.4	77.3	35.0
Association/ similar interests	4.2	4.2	1.8	2.7	9.8	7.5	2.0	6.3
Village	67.0	—	58.6	—	25.3	—	1.3	—
Neighbour	2.5	16.9	5.5	12.0	5.4	14.0	6.0	6.3
Miscellaneous	0.2	21.7	1.5	20.9	2.5	3.7	0.7	20.0
None	5.6	—	1.2	—	1.4	—	—	—
Total %	100	100	99.9	100.1	99.1	100	100	100.1
Number	552	166	326	225	707	107	150	80

3. *Intimacy zones*

Each informant was asked to separate from his total network those persons who in some way meant something special to him. This decision was made on a purely subjective/emotional basis. It is interesting to note that Cecil and Pietru, quite independently, each selected 132 persons from his total personal network. Moreover, each classified 10 persons in a first, the most intimate, category. These include spouse, parents and most siblings. Beyond this *personal cell* (zone I, see p. 47), there is a second zone of approximately 20 persons with whom they maintain especially close relations (zone II). While zone I for both consists mostly of relatives, zone II, though composed chiefly of relatives for Pietru, is made up largely of non-relatives for Cecil. Finally, the third zone consists of approximately 100 friends and relatives with whom Pietru and Cecil maintain more passive contact but who are subjectively very important to them (zone III). I did not ask them to classify other members of their networks, those in what I have called zones IV and V (p. 47).

Who are the 132 people in each of the zones of intimacy? They reflect closely the relative importance of the various activity fields and, interestingly enough, exchange relations set out in tables 5.5 and 5.6. Kinsmen form the largest category for Pietru (45 per cent compared to 21 per cent for Cecil), whereas persons with whom he shares an occupational role are more important for Cecil. Pietru is also more personal with the members of his intimate network than Cecil: he exchanges visits with 52 per cent of them, while Cecil visits only 29 per cent.

4. *Comparison*

The salient differences between the two networks which emerge from this very cursory comparison include the following. Pietru's network is larger than Cecil's and appears to have a more even distribution of the sexes, age groups, educational and occupational categories as well as a more even geographical spread in Malta. Kinsmen appear to occupy a more important place in Pietru's network than in that of Cecil, and the density of the former's network is higher than that of the latter. Finally, Pietru has a tendency to personalize a greater proportion of his social relations in the intimate as well as the non-intimate zones of his network than Cecil.

The striking difference in size of the two networks may be explained partly by the fact that Pietru is seven years older than Cecil and thus has had time to meet and maintain contacts with a large number of persons. But it does not account for the fact that Pietru knows almost three times as many persons as Cecil. A second explanation might be that Pietru plays more occupational roles than Cecil. He is after all schoolteacher, farmer, tutor, informal assistant of the parish priest, member of a religious confraternity and band club as well as father, son, husband and kinsman. It is apparent, however, that many of these roles derive from his niche in a small village. He is a patron, a big fish in a little pond. Furthermore, because he is socially prominent, people seek contact with him, and do not let him forget them. Moreover, by simply being a native of the village, his network is larger than Cecil's by some 846 persons—his fellow villagers. Cecil, as a city dweller, has no comparable ascribed segment in his network. Without this ascribed segment their networks are more nearly comparable: 805 to 638.

Another important factor in explaining the difference in size is Pietru's tendency to personalize his relations to a greater extent than Cecil. He therefore has more guide-lines to aid his memory. The details he learns through conversation help to fix persons in his memory. Moreover, by personalizing relations, he creates multiplex ties. Through these he more easily meets new persons. Expressed in another way: people seem to be more important to Pietru than to Cecil, therefore he knows more.

Finally, it is important to note that Cecil's training as a Jesuit entailed a high measure of isolation, a systematic effort to eliminate or curtail contacts with non-Jesuits—especially family and former friends—and a rapid rate of geographical mobility. These all served to limit the number of persons with whom Cecil could maintain contact and remember.

The more even spread of Pietru's network in terms of sex, age, education, occupation and residence can be explained by the fact that he is a villager. This even spread must be seen as an ascribed attribute of his network. There is an even distribution of sexes in the village, as well as of ages. Pietru is well educated, most of the villagers are not, though an ever larger proportion of village teenagers are going to secondary school. Besides this, villages like Farrug are reservoirs of skilled and unskilled labour. Pietru grew up with these persons and still lives at close quarters with them. Cecil has no such bloc of non white-collar workers in his network. Similarly Pietru knows more people in other villages than Cecil, because he is a villager himself: village teachers form blocs in opposition to town teachers in the training college and associations of which Pietru is or was a member (and also in the secondary school where Cecil teaches). Furthermore, his own large kin network is anchored in the villages and through the many kinship ceremonies he meets people from other villages. Moreover, the custom of celebrating the patron saints of villages attracts people from other 'rival' villages who come to enjoy the spectacle and compare notes. Festas are occasions on which old acquaintances are 'serviced' and, through them, new contacts are made. This is perhaps a cultural explanation, but an important one nonetheless, for Pietru attends ten to fifteen festas a year. Cecil only attends one, that of his wife's parish, and that only since he has been married. Sophisticated inhabitants of Sliema, especially of his generation, regard it as provincial to show great interest in these festas.

How can one explain the greater number of kinsmen in

Pietru's network? To begin with, there could be a demographic reason. In his genealogy he listed the descendants of eight married uncles and aunts of his parents. They produced no less than 182 living second cousins. Cecil in contrast could name only two married siblings of his grandparents, and they have produced only three living second cousins. This sound demographic reason for the greater number of kinsmen in Pietru's network would perhaps be sufficient if it were not for two additional factors. First, I strongly suspect that Cecil's grandparents had more married siblings than he in fact knew and therefore listed, for he noted three persons of whose exact relationship he was unsure but whom he guessed were probably second cousins. Secondly, Pietru consistently listed more relatives in every genealogical category than Cecil. For example, Pietru knows 88 of his wife's relatives, whereas Cecil knows only 31 relatives of his wife. Even though Pietru has been married eighteen months longer and could have met more affines, and he unquestionably cultivates many of his wife's relatives because they are better situated socially than he, it does tend to support my contention that kinsmen are more important to Pietru than they are to Cecil and therefore he knows more. This is also supported by the higher rate of exchange relations that Pietru maintains with his kinsmen (see table 5.8) and the more important place they occupy in the intimate portion of Pietru's network (45 per cent opposed to 21 per cent for Cecil).

The question we must answer therefore is why are kinsmen more important—in the sense of receiving a higher social investment—to Pietru than they are to Cecil? Can this be explained by Pietru's more gregarious nature? It could be argued that because people in general seem to be more important to Pietru than to Cecil, and that kinsmen are a special category of people, that they therefore receive proportionately greater attention from Pietru.

Have we reached the point where the essential differences between these two networks have been reduced to a difference in personality between Cecil and Pietru? I think not. In fact, I see personality here as the dependent rather than independent variable. As the differences in sex, age, education, occupation and residence were explained in terms of Pietru's village niche and Cecil's town niche, so the difference between village and town environment also explains why kinsmen are more important to Pietru and why his network scores higher on density.

Why are relatives more important to a villager than to a townsman? To answer by saying that kinship is more important in village subculture is to beg the question. To plead culture, I think, is an admission of defeat. It is merely an excuse for stopping analysis. To some extent culture is the normative rationalization of patterns of behaviour. Though there is feedback, of course, the rationalization is of less interest than the underlying sociological explanation of those behavioural patterns. Kinship is important in villages because they are moral communities of which membership (in the case of those born there) is ascribed. As a kin network is built up of relations which normatively are morally sanctioned (by church as well as public opinion)—this is also true in the city —the kin network is a moral, ascribed segment of the total network. This moral network segment in turn is partly embedded in a moral community. This in combination with the many-stranded relations which exist between inhabitants of a small village indicates some of the reasons why the enforcement of kinship norms is much more efficient in a village than in a town. Although the kinship segment of Cecil's network is also a moral network, it is not embedded in a moral community of which he is a member. Thus, if he does not honour his kinship obligations, and as I could demonstrate he is indeed very cavalier about these, his offended kinsmen cannot appeal for justice to non-kinsmen who can exert influence on him in several other roles because they are members of the same moral community. In contrast, Pietru lives at relatively close quarters with many of his kinsmen. If he offends them they can appeal their case to persons who form part of the moral community of which he and they are members.

Moreover, a failure to discharge obligations to kinsmen could well jeopardize relations with other villagers, who might assume that he would also betray the relations he shares with them.[3]

These various reasons combine to ensure that Pietru meets his kin obligations more punctually than does Cecil and that his own kinsmen do likewise. Thus, the fact that Pietru lives at close quarters in a village with a large number of his relatives, ensures that he knows more relatives and sees them more often and that they meet their obligations to each other more faithfully than is the case with Cecil. Given the same norm, there is more pressure to conform to that norm in a network that scores higher on multiplexity, density and degree.

Pietru's network scores higher on density than that of Cecil primarily because it includes a compartment (or partial network) of no less than 846 persons that has a density of 100 per cent, namely his fellow villagers, all of whom know each other. If these villagers, and those persons for whom no data was available, are removed from the two networks, it is interesting to note that their respective density scores become almost the same: 5.4 per cent for Pietru's, and 5.3 per cent for that of Cecil. But in spite of the similar density scores, each member of Pietru's corrected primary zone (excluding villagers) is linked with an average of 42.8 other persons in the primary zone (this is the degree, see p. 40), while the corresponding figure for Cecil is only 31.7 persons. The discrepancy between these two measures of the amount of interrelation between the members of the two primary zones is explained by their different sizes, for size is of crucial importance in evaluating the significance of density scores.

The greater degree of interconnection between the (non-village) members of Pietru's network may be attributed principally to the presence in his first-order zone of large, densely interconnected segments or compartments. These include a bloc of 170 primary school teachers, 54 policemen, 60 members of the clergy, and nearly 500 relatives.

In short, the greater density of Pietru's network is due principally to the place that fellow villagers occupy in it, as well as to the important place assumed by kinsmen. For if almost half of his primary zone is composed of fellow villagers, almost one quarter consists of relatives, which in turn form segments (his mother's, his father's and his wife's relatives) which have high internal density.

Why then does Pietru personalize his social relations to a greater extent than Cecil? Is it because their basic personalities differ? I think that their personalities do differ. The reason for this is less genetic than social. I have already suggested that sociability is found more often in villages than in towns, and conversely, that a more reserved personality is more common in a large town with a mobile population than in a nucleated village with a stable population. Why do villagers personalize their relations? This is chiefly because most villages are highly interconnected communities. In a village any person with whom one has dealings knows all the other persons in the village (beyond 3,000–4,000 this is no longer true). They are therefore used to associating with people who have similar backgrounds and know the same people. They thus can exchange information about shared experiences, problems and acquaintances. They do not do so all the time or with all villagers, but it does mean that there are no anonymous persons in the village: everyone knows everyone else.

City people are used to persons with whom they have only single-stranded service relations. In a city there is a category which can be called the anonymous service fringe. These are the people with whom one has relatively frequent dealings, such as bus conductors, shopkeepers, neighbours, etc., but about whom nothing is known. It is significant, I think, that Cecil did not know the name of fifty non-relatives with whom he had regular dealings while Pietru listed only one such case. Pietru begins talking easily to strangers such as bus conductors and shopkeepers, Cecil does not. I am suggesting that because Pietru is not used to single-stranded anonymous relations, he cannot handle them. Consequently, he takes steps to ensure that relations do not remain single-stranded: he begins conversation and searches for common ground. Cecil, on the other hand, used to travelling and life in a relatively impersonal urban centre, is accustomed to such impersonal relations. They form a familiar category. He can handle them. He therefore does not seek to personalize single-stranded relations.

The difference in sociability between Cecil and Pietru is similar to the difference between the latter and his city-bred wife. Pietru's wife does not have the sociable nature of her husband. On her shopping expeditions through the village she does not talk a great deal, although she is not taciturn. Her reserved relations with the shopkeepers and neighbours are regarded as rather unusual by the people of Farrug, while they see nothing unusual about Pietru's talkativeness. In contrast, Pietru's long conversations with strangers are looked on as exceptional behaviour in Sliema, while his wife's reserve is not. I have already pointed to this same contrast in sociability between Cecil and his village-bred wife. Cecil is somewhat reserved, and his wife, according to his standards, is very talkative. I know the cases discussed are few. Nonetheless I suggest there is evidence to associate a sociable personality with a person who is brought up and lives in a highly connected moral community of no more than 3,000 to 4,000, and a reserved personality with a person who has been brought up in an (urban) area with a relatively low density.

STRATEGIC LINKS AND PROTECTORS

Both Pietru and Cecil use their networks to cope with the manifest problems of daily living and to solve the more complicated problems which they, like all of us, face from time to time. This means that each must keep two different sets of contacts serviced: those for the minor problems and those for the major problems. Pietru for example, consciously maintains a friendly exchange of conversation with his neighbour, Salvu Abela, the village street sweeper, who is also an experienced, hard-working builder and stone mason. He receives advice on building matters from Salvu, including on the delicate matter of how best to get a building permit, and can borrow a wheelbarrow, ladder and other tools from him when he needs them. In return Pietru gives him cabbages and other plants. Pietru noted that if he didn't treat Salvu in the friendly way he does, he wouldn't get this help. He went on to observe that by not being 'proud' and being friendly with a range of people, he saves himself a great deal of money every year. He maintains the same sort of exchange relations that he has with Salvu with a host of other villagers. He is thus able to borrow tools for clearing his sewage pipes (often blocked in Malta), other building tools, parsley and celery, onion seeds and tomato and cabbage plants, to mention but a few of the items he listed for me. Cecil who plays fewer roles and is more conscious of his status as a school teacher than Pietru, does less manual work, and consequently does not need to maintain the range and number of friendly relations that Pietru does with his neighbours.

Both Pietru and Cecil also consciously maintain relations with persons who might one day be useful in helping them resolve the many major problems which are inherent in any complex, industrial society: hospitalization, a brush with the law or one of the many government departments, income tax, disputes at work, and advice about, or even better, a price-reduction on, the purchase of major household appliances. As already noted, the Maltese call contacts who can help solve more complicated problems 'saints'.

1. *Pietru*

When I asked Pietru to note down useful contacts he replied first of all that 'Those people I can rely on as helpful are those I have already listed on my family tree, especially those who are related to my wife.' He then went on to list fourteen saints. Of these, four are well-placed, all-purpose patrons each of whom has a wide range of contacts leading into all major activity fields. Two of these are favourite uncles of his wife; one is a highly-placed business executive and the other a senior civil servant (Table 5.9, Nos. 1 and 2 respectively). Pietru remarked approvingly of the latter that 'He knows where the Devil sleeps' (i.e. that there is not much that he does not know), and knows 'everybody from the Prime Minister to the simplest messenger at the Law Courts.' These are his most important protectors. The two other all-purpose patrons are monsignori, former parish priests of Hal-Farrug who have moved on to bigger parishes. Each of these has an extremely wide range of influential contacts throughout Maltese society, but especially in the Archbishop's Curia and in government departments and ministries.

Besides these four important patrons, Pietru maintains relations with persons strategically located in various activity fields. These include a nurse at the government hospital, a clerk at the Medical and Health Department, two clerks at the Department of Agriculture, a senior official of the Malta Union of Teachers, an executive officer at the Inland Revenue Department, an executive officer at the Public Works Department, another monsignor at the Curia land office and an executive at the broadcasting company (for Pietru is interested in journalism).

Moreover, through helping his sister with the business end of her little shop, he knows thirty-three businessmen from whom he can obtain a large variety of household articles and appliances at wholesale prices. Finally, because his mother's house is situated opposite the village police station, and his brother-in-law is a policeman in the village, he is on good terms with no less than fifty-four policemen stationed all over the island. Besides being generally useful contacts, these policemen enable him to make telephone calls 'without too much shyness', for few people in the villages have telephones. In short, Pietru feels himself to be relatively well covered in the event of illness, disputes at work, problems with the government departments, the Church or the police. In table 5.9 below I have summarized some of the data I collected on the fourteen saints Pietru listed.

2. *Cecil*

Cecil listed nineteen influential relations, five of whom are abroad. His most important saints and the ones he knows best are his two older brothers. One is a priest with a very wide range of contacts, and the other is a doctor, who besides knowing important people also has specialized contacts with the hospital. These, together with a friend, a clerk with a private firm who also knows very many people, constitute his all-purpose patrons: persons with whom he maintains a high rate of exchange and who know many people throughout Maltese society. Besides these, he has relations with people in several specialized fields: those who can help him in his present job, those who may be able to help him further his plans to do post-graduate work at a British university, and those who can help him maintain or establish contact with India, Australia and England. These last are important in view of his uncertain plans for the future, for many Maltese emigrate to Australia and England. Finally, he also listed a person who can help him obtain photographic equipment at reduced costs, for his hobby is photography. I have summarized data on these persons in table 5.10.

Table 5.9: Pietru's Saints

Con-tact No.	Occu-pation	Type of help and field of influence	Inti-macy zone	If re-la-ted	Exchange Relation Visit	Conversation	How long ago	Last meeting Du-ra-tion	If plan-ned	How long known
1	Finance	All kinds via influential friends	II	x		x	15 days	30 min	x	6 yrs
2	Executive Officer	ditto	II	x		x	1 mo	30 min	0	6 yrs
3	Business Executive	Cheap spirits and drink	IV-V	x		x	2 mo	30 min	0	6 yrs
4	Nurse	Hospital	IV-V	x		x	–	2 hrs	0	3 yrs
5	Clerical Officer	Med. Dept. and Health	III	0		x	1 mo	30 min	x	6 yrs
6	Monsignor	All kinds via influencial friends	IV-V	0		x	2 mo	15 min	0	22 yrs

Oversight or miscalculation can lead to movement away from the centre, just as unexpected success can bring about movement in the other direction.

Pietru described how little oversights can have serious consequences. If for example, you failed to greet someone, either because you didn't hear or see him, he would usually respond in the same way next time you met him. Before you knew it the affair escalated and you were no longer on speaking terms. He indicated that this was the cause of the strained relations between himself and a number of the inhabitants of Hal-Farrug. He then went on to describe how one oversight on his part had cost him a close friend who became the only hostile person in his network. This was a certain Miss Farrugia who had been a very good friend of his family. She became hostile because he did not invite her to see his new house before he moved into it, though he had invited a number of close relatives including all his first cousins, with whom his relations are reservedly competitive. Though Miss Farrugia was not related, she obviously considered herself so close to Pietru's family that she should have been invited. Pietru had simply forgotten her and she has never forgiven him. Though invited to his wedding, she did not come, nor did she send a present. When she sees him in the street now she turns the other way. She has broken completely with him and he is chagrined at this. He reciprocates her behaviour, though he does so rather reluctantly.

We have already seen how a miscalculation, or rather the more mercenary calculation, of the electrician mentioned above was responsible for his swift removal from Pietru's circle of intimates. But as an unsuccessful attempt to mobilize someone can sour their relation, so the success of an operation may strengthen it. Pietru was pleasantly surprised at the help he received from the school teacher and the policeman (table 5.11, nos. 6 and 7) in his quest for books, and after the transaction he promoted them to his intimate zone. Cecil reacted similarly to the assistance he received from his uncle

L

who helped him obtain his job, and the friend of his brother who bought him a camera.

In short, circumstances over which an individual has little or no control and his own transactions ensure that the relative weighting that he gives to his relations is constantly shifting. In this and in the preceding chapters I have attempted to indicate some of the interactional and structural characteristics of social networks and their interrelation as well as the way they are affected by the environment and, through these, behaviour and personality. The emphasis has been rather heavily upon the way in which environment, network structure and the manipulations of others impinge upon an individual. Although this bias has been present, I have also repeatedly pointed to the way in which individuals themselves are in large measure responsible for the contents and structure of this social field. It provides a recruitment field for the action sets and communication paths which they must build to solve certain problems. In the remaining chapters we shall be considering egocentric social systems, such as cliques and factions, which have more organizational characteristics than the social networks examined up to this point. These social forms may of course also be viewed as social networks or clusters in a larger network of relations. These are brought into being for the most part by the specialists in network relations to whom we now turn.

6

Social Manipulators: Brokers as Entrepreneurs

As villages, towns and cities develop at points where communication channels—roads, rivers and railroads—meet, so various social forms develop at points where important networks intersect. These points of intersection are persons. Every individual provides a point at which networks intersect. But not everyone displays the same interest in and talent for cultivating relationships with strategic persons and manipulating these for profit. Moreover, to operate this network of strategic links—his enterprise—profitably, such a person must also stay ahead of competitors. This he can best do by using techniques or resources which have not been tried before in the same social situation, or arena. In short, he innovates. This means that he is also prepared to take certain risks, for the outcome of an innovation is usually not certain. A person who builds and manages an enterprise for the pursuit of profit in the course of which he innovates and takes risks may be called an entrepreneur.[1] Now the resources an entrepreneur manipulates are of two distinct types, although they are very often found in combination. The first are resources, such as land, jobs, scholarship funds, specialized knowledge, which he controls directly. The second are strategic contacts with other people who control such resources directly or who have access to such persons. The former may be called *first order resources*, the latter *second order resources.* Persons who dispense first order resources may be called *patrons*. Those who dispense second order resources are *brokers*.[2] A broker is thus a special type of entrepreneur: one who controls second order resources and manipulates these for his own profit. Brokers are thus highly expert network specialists. We may explore how brokers operate their roles by trying to answer four questions: What do brokers do? Who becomes a broker? How do brokers make a profit? and, How do brokers build a career?

WHAT DO BROKERS DO?

The short answer to this question is that a social broker places people in touch with each other either directly or indirectly for profit. He bridges gaps in communication between persons, groups, structures and even cultures. Such persons range from 'connecting relatives' who direct the communication between kinsmen and whose profit motive is more latent than manifest, through political middle-men whose medium of exchange is services, information, and votes, to such specialists as marriage and real estate brokers whose relations approach the commercial as their tariff is largely paid in cash. The anthropological literature abounds with examples of brokers, for the manipulation of others is a fascinating subject.[3] Think also of the popularity of spy stories—a spymaster is an excellent example of a broker who carefully builds up a specialized information gathering network—and accounts of criminal brokers, such as Mario Puzo's recent bestselling novel about an American *mafioso, The Godfather*.[4] But perhaps the simplest example of a communication broker is the telegrapher who sends a message for a client. Many companies have waxed fat on man's need to communicate with man. And so have social brokers.

A broker is a professional manipulator of people and information who brings about communication for profit. He thus occupies a strategic place in a network of social relations viewed as a communication network. It is therefore quite legitimate to look to communication theory to see if it provides analytical tools which can help sociologists ask relevant questions about the operations of brokers.

Communication theorists have reduced a communication system to five fundamental elements:

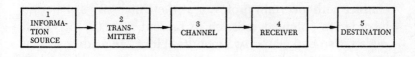

The information source selects the message to be sent. The transmitter changes this into a signal that is sent via a communication channel to the receiver and thence delivered to destination. According to communication specialists, the important questions to ask about a communication system have to do with the amount of information, the capacity of the channel, the coding process used to change a message into a signal, and the effects of noise (interference).[5] To these I think anthropologists must add one more: the tariff charged for transmission, for this is where the profit lies.

The simplest illustration of this model is given by isolating the steps involved in sending a telegram. (1) You formulate a message and pass it on to (2) an employee of the telegraph company. He checks it and calculates the tariff according to the number of words, the destination and the channel to be used. If your credit is good you can pay later, if not you pay cash. He then passes the message on to another, who codes it and transmits it via (3) radio waves. It is then (4) received, decoded and delivered to (5) the destination. If the noise has been minimal—and this is a function partly of the channel used, the message and the coding techniques, all of which are also dependent upon the tariff—the message arrives as given by the information source.

Most of the communication transactions an anthropologist encounters are considerably more complicated than this example, but the processes involved are similar enough so that the model and the related questions apply. Take the case of my Sicilian friend Salvatore.

Salvatore, a student from Syracuse who had worked in the west Sicilian town of Leone, wished to come into personal contact with a certain professor at the University of Palermo in order to obtain permission to present a thesis, for which registration had closed two months before. He made a special trip from Syracuse to Leone to discuss this problem with *Avvocato* Leonardo, the Secretary of the Christian Democratic Party in the town. Six months before, while he was still in Leone, Salvatore had helped Leonardo prepare a draft of an important memorandum on the town which had been requested by the party's provincial leaders. Salvatore explained his trip by saying, '*Leonardo mi doveva questa*', Leonardo owed me this (favour). Salvatore knew the lawyer was in touch with many people in Palermo and felt sure that through him he could come into personal contact with his professor.

Leonardo was willing to help and gave Salvatore a card to his cousin, the personal secretary of a Palermitan official, asking him to help. He also offered to let Salvatore copy his thesis, which he pointed out would save a great deal of bother since it was a good thesis and had been presented to a different professor a few years before. Salvatore thanked him but replied that he wanted to do his own thesis, 'for the experience'.

Armed with Leonardo's *raccomandazione*, introducing him as his *carissimo amico*, his dearest friend, Salvatore set out for Palermo. The following day he met Leonardo's cousin and explained what he wanted. The cousin suggested that he see his brother, who knew many people in the University, and in his turn gave him a card. That evening Salvatore met the brother who said that he knew the professor's assistant, and gave him a card introducing him as his *carissimo amico*. The next day Salvatore called on the assistant with his *raccomandazione* and explained his case in full, asking what he should do. The assistant replied that he could arrange matters with the *Professore* but only on condition that Salvatore make electoral propaganda in Leone and the surrounding area for the *Professore*, who was standing for the Chamber of Deputies in the election the following month. Salvatore understood and pretended he lived in Leone, and not in Syracuse, which was outside the electoral district in which the *Professore* was standing, a fact which made him quite useless. The assistant then telephoned the *Professore* and made an appointment for Salvatore.

Salvatore went to see the *Professore* and explained his wish to present his thesis that June. The *Professore* looked rather doubtful, until Salvatore mentioned that he was impressed with his public spirit, and had already spoken about his candidature to several of his friends in Leone. The *Professore* loosened up at once. He indicated that the thesis should not present a problem. He then wrote a letter for Salvatore to take back to a former student of his in Leone, whom he also asked to help in his campaign.

Salvatore returned to Syracuse, via Leone, where he delivered the letter, and at once began to work on his thesis. Eventually his thesis, which was very good, was accepted and today Salvatore has his degree. The *Professore*, however, was not elected.[6]

Using the formal model of a communication system, the example of Leonardo may be analysed in the following manner. Salvatore, the information source, had to get a message to his professor. His own direct channels to Palermo were not suitable. He thus selected a powerful transmitter whom he knew controlled a variety of channels into Palermo. Leonardo, the broker, is of course the transmitter. The channels he controls are role relations embedded in his personal network.

In a simple model, the transmitter (broker), is in direct contact with the destination. The communication system is thus reduced to but two role relations *source-broker* and *broker-destination*. The broker then functions as coder, transmitter, channel, decoder, receiver, delivering the message personally to the destination.

Our Sicilian case, like many things Sicilian, is a good deal more complex. Leonardo selected a strategic channel capable of carrying this searching type message along a communication path the links of which were not known beyond the first one. Of the many channels he could use, he selected his first cousin, a kinsman placed strategically in the Palermo political scene. The relation he shared with his cousin was a channel of high capacity and low tariff. Moreover, his credit with his cousin was extremely high, owing to the variety of role relations he shared with him. For the same reason this channel was multipurpose—capable of carrying messages of various types. Some of the channels Leonardo controlled, notably through the formal Christian Democratic Party apparatus, were used almost exclusively for high tariff political messages. It would thus have been uneconomical to use these channels for this message. Moreover, because of the low political content of Salvatore's message, it might have been seriously affected by noise had he selected a purely political channel.

After selecting the channel, Leonardo coded the message by scribbling an introduction on the back of his visiting card. The code used of course depends upon the channel, the message, and last but not least, the tariff and the credit rating of the transmitter. Leonardo transmitted the message by sending Salvatore, with his introduction, to see his cousin. The latter acted as a relay, receiving, decoding, selecting a new channel, recoding and transmitting to the next link in the path, who acted similarly. The willingness of a broker to act swiftly as a relay for a message sent by another broker is a reflection of the high credit rating of the initial transmitter and of the anticipated tariff. The credit relations between the various kinsmen in the communication path were excellent; and the professor's assistant hoped to book a profit much later, when his professor was elected. Until then, like a good, loyal university teaching assistant, he tried to help his patron in every way conceivable.

Obviously there are several important differences between this case and the sending of a telegram. To begin with, the channels are personal relations, and not radio waves. These are not constant and messages sent are subject to much noise. Personal relations are very much affected by the number of messages sent and received and their tariff. One person, Leonardo, performed a complex series of operations which in the case of sending a telegram took several persons to do (selecting and providing the channel, coding, transmitting). Moreover, he furnished access to a series of relays which ultimately guided the message to its destination. This complete service is what gives a good broker his power. Another difference is that the tariff in all transactions was not cash but past or future services. Salvatore had in fact paid in advance. A final and obvious difference is that the information source—himself—moved along the channels, thus reducing noise. This is not possible in a telegraphic communication system (though the sung congratulatory telegram adds a dimension in this direction!).

There are, however, a number of important similarities. To my mind the most striking is that the tariff varies according to the message, destination and channels used. Secondly, the ability to send effectively (with little noise) depends upon having access to select channels. Finally, the ability to send messages rapidly as well as the number and capacity of the channels, varies directly with the credit rating of the broker.

WHO BECOMES A BROKER?

Who becomes a broker depends on two sets of criteria: the structure and content of his social network, and his willingness to use this for personal gain. Where a person has a large network with a high score for multiplexity and exchange content he can operate as a broker. But he must be willing to manipulate his social relations for profit. Not everyone is prepared to do this. Pietru, for example, has a network of strategic relations that he could place at the service of less influential fellow villagers, if he were inclined to do so. But he is not interested in cultivating and exploiting relations as a broker: he finds the idea repugnant. Similarly, a secondary school teacher I know in Sicily told me that he refused to run a second time for the office of municipal councillor because to be successful he would have had to make use of *mafiosi* to recruit votes. Considering the sort of pressure that they would have applied to gather his votes, and the type of messages they would have expected him to transmit once elected, he declined to use them. He said to have done so would have been immoral. Without their support he knew he could not be elected. This might have been a rationalization of his inability to muster enough personal votes to be elected, but I don't think so. Thus in discussing brokers we must accept as a given quality a willingness to manipulate other persons, although in some cases—and here I am thinking of certain academic colleagues among others—the brokers concerned are not fully aware of the degree to which they in fact manipulate others.

As noted in an earlier chapter, the structure of a person's network and the use to which it can be put are influenced by many factors from his social environment. Although it would seem to follow from the discussion on ideology above (pp. 78–83) that there should be more Catholic than Protestant brokers, I have no evidence that this is so. There is, however, certain evidence that centrality, the time available to manage his social relations, and power over first order resources are of particular importance in assisting a person to become a successful broker.

1. *Centrality*

The objective centrality of a person or group may be determined by a variety of factors. Bailey has shown how the Konds of Orissa used a particular untouchable caste as a buffer to avoid having to come into direct (and hence polluting) contact with the surrounding Oriya 'outsiders': they used the untouchables as their messengers. Since the Konds spoke a separate language a number of the untouchables learned Oriya. When the British and their Oriya-speaking interpreters came and sought contact with the Konds, they quite naturally worked through the bilingual untouchables. Since the latter arranged their contacts with the Konds, the British assumed them to be tribal officials, and attributed high status to them. As the frequency of contact between the Konds and the outside world intensified, the untouchables exploited their central position between the two rival cultures for their material and political profit.[7]

Similarly, other persons because of occupation, education, age or any number of fortuitous circumstances may come to occupy positions within, and thus also between, two cultures, or organizations, thus providing a bridge between them. This central position is used to carry and to transmit messages. But it must not be thought that the role of broker is found only in the less developed countries, where the cultural gap between bureaucrat and uneducated peasant is usually immense. Brokers are also found in complex industrialized societies where the multiplicity of powerful, interlocking government departments form a maze almost as impenetrable to the educated businessman as to the peasant. While in many complex societies specialized agencies, such as citizens' advisory bureaux, trade-unions and other groups, have taken over from individual brokers, there is still ample scope for the private entrepreneur. Washington's Bobby Baker after all was not a character in an Asian drama, but the leading figure in a well-publicized farce set in one of the world's most industrialized societies.

In a dynamic social field in which there is considerable movement a fixed position can become a central point. Urban beerhall owners form important links in the networks of immigrants to African cities, for they provide fixed points in a series of fleeting relationships.[8] Much the same is true of the shops and work-places of village specialists. Though in villages there is not the same flux of transient immigrants as in African cities, there is constant movement along the streets and between houses. Shopkeepers, café owners, cobblers, barbers, tailors and other craftsmen who work in the village can talk with a variety of persons while they work. Because they are always there many people stop to talk, pass on information and ask them to pass on messages. They thus become key links in the information network of a village. During fieldwork in Sicily, Malta and Montreal I made constant use of shopkeepers and artisans: not only because I found them always at home, in contrast to other informants, but also because I learned that they were usually well-informed. For the same reason many villagers meet in these shops, cafés and work places to catch up on the news of the day. These places often develop into regular meeting places for cliques of friends. Pietru, for example, laughingly referred to his unmarried sister's bazaar as the 'Central Office of Information'. It was a place where he could go to find out rapidly the latest news in the village, either from his sister or from one of the other women invariably present in the shop talking to his sister. If by chance they did not know the answer to a question (and I often got him to ask questions for me as well) he would leave it with his sister, who would elicit responses from other clients and pass them on to him later in the day. Pietru's sister, and through her Pietru, were remarkably well-informed about what went on in the village. Shopkeepers and craftsmen occupy central positions in village or neighbourhood communication networks. This gives them a strategic advantage should information management be required as, for example, during electoral campaigns. This is a position they can often exploit for profit if they choose to do so.

2. *Time*

A person who has more time to devote to the management of his social relations is more likely to have more multiplex social relations and to be better informed than others. These are assets for a broker. To make a profit from his relations, he has to be able to devote time to servicing them. This is essential for the success of his enterprise. A person whose occupation allows him to invest time in servicing relations while he works, such as the shopkeepers, café-owners and craftsmen discussed above, is thus in a particularly fortunate position. Others may also be able to find the necessary time because they control economic resources which do not require much time to manage, such as a wealthy landowner whose adult sons work under his nominal direction. Yet others, with occupations which do not permit much free time or enable them to service relations while at work, will have to do so in their free time after work. If they have families of their own this time will have to be taken from the time they would otherwise invest in playing the role of husband and father. If they do so they may be in for trouble at home. In this respect a bachelor, a widower or a man with grown children is in a more advantageous position than a young father, who will have to invest more time in his family roles, though this varies with the culture. The number of bachelors who have been successful in politics—and Britain's Edward Heath is currently the most prominent—is striking.

3. *Power*

Power, in the sense of control over first order resources, is another attribute which enhances a person's ability to operate as a broker. Obviously the ability to influence the behaviour of others independently of their wishes is helpful if a person wants to send certain messages, or activate a communication path. The more powerful a signal, the less chance that it will be disturbed by noise. Moreover, powerful signals can be transmitted over considerable distance, for they activate relays—other persons who are prepared to receive, recode and transmit the message along a path selected from their own network. The power of the signal can derive from the multiplex quality of the relationship that is used, as was the case of the relationship between Leonardo and his cousin. It can also stem from the power that backs up a request to transmit a message, thus forcing the next link to use his own most favourable onward link under fear of reprisal. This is what happens when *mafiosi* 'assist' persons to transmit messages.

Willingness to manipulate relations, a central or strategic location, ample time to service relations and power are all attributes which help a person become a broker. But besides these attributes, a person must also have the ability to turn his social relations into a profitable enterprise. This requires a good measure of skill and cunning.

HOW DO BROKERS MAKE A PROFIT?

Brokerage is a business. A broker's *capital* consists of his personal network of relations with people; in brief, his communication channels. As noted, these are role relations. All role relations are governed by the notion of reciprocity or *transaction* (see p. 25). Interaction must thus be seen as a strategic game with each party trying to gain value or at least break even. This value I call tariff. Whether a person makes a profit very much depends on the tariff charged by the other parties in the transaction, as well as other social costs, and, ultimately, on the interest he is able to exact. The tariff is rarely specified and normally paid later.

Tariff is the value which the broker derives from the transaction. This can consist of services, information, status, good will, even psychological satisfaction. Only rarely does it consist of money, for reasons which will become clearer below. The fee for Leonardo's services as broker was Salvatore's help with the development report. Salvatore's expertise in this field must of course be viewed as a first order resource (capital) which he controlled. Salvatore's fee for his service was the message Leonardo sent. This tariff, of course, had not been specified when the transaction was begun. Both felt that they had made a profit.

Tariff, however, is rarely paid at the moment of transaction. Rather, a social transaction is not usually a simultaneous exchange of services. More usually there is a considerable time lag between exchanges: 'Communicate now and pay later' or 'Pay now and communicate later' are the slogans that govern the transactions of brokers. They are statements about credit.

If a broker's capital consists of the actual communication channels he controls, his *credit* consists of what others *think* his capital to be. They are thus dealing in expectations—future possible services—rather than dead certainties. Social brokers of the type discussed here operate almost exclusively with credit. The tariff is rarely specified; it is left as an understanding that something will be exchanged at a later date. If it were specified and promptly paid in full, as is so easy to do with a monetary transaction, the account would be closed and there would be no special (debt) relations between the transactors. It is in the interest of both parties to keep the channel open, either by underpaying or overpaying at a later date. The strategy is to avoid specifying the tariff.

This strategy was evident in the episode described at the beginning of the book. *Professore* Volpe was able to get his son admitted to the university and to exact an apology from his angry colleague because he and his brother enjoyed high credit, at least with certain *mafiosi*. Their credit was partly due to the reputation and activities of their father, who had been able to provide valuable protection in the past. This credit together with their own astuteness ensured that they were still a force to be reckoned with, for, as the example clearly demonstrated, they could make themselves respected. Thus the apology extraction mission which the *mafioso* voluntarily organized is partly a reflection of the credit of the Volpe brothers, and partly a continuation of an exchange of services between persons who find each other useful. It was also clearly a means by which the *mafioso* could demonstrate that he was able to deliver the goods, thus was a person able to make himself respected: in short, a person with credit. The tariff for the service was naturally left vague, for it was in the interest of both parties to keep the relation between them open, thereby maintaining their interdependence. Both *Professore* Volpe and the *mafioso* assumed they would need each other's help again.

Debt is of course a function of credit, for it is its reciprocal. It is also a statement of credit, for it is proof that the creditor has faith in the ability of the debtor to provide services. Thus to be in debt is a demonstration of credit—as any one accustomed to paying in cash discovers when he tries to establish a credit rating to get a loan. (In Canada I discovered that because I had no debts I had no credit rating, and without a credit rating I found it difficult to obtain goods on credit when I needed to!) It is often said 'Tell me who your friends are that I may tell you who you are.' Equally one can say 'Tell me who your creditors are that I may judge your credit.'

Because one is never quite sure of the extent of a broker's capital (who and how good his contacts are), it is easier for him to increase his credit than for someone whose capital consists exclusively of first order resources. These latter are more easily observed and, moreover, are finite, whereas the network of a broker is open ended, thus potentially infinite. The credit of a patron is thus more limited than that of the broker. That is, the extent of his sources is known. The broker, in contrast, works behind a screen of ignorance and no one quite knows how far he can reach. He deals in speculation and hope. A political leader, for example, usually can recruit a greater following by playing the role of broker rather than that of patron. By being a broker he deals in *promises* to consult others who control the first order resources his followers desire. As patron he must *dispense* first order resources, and these of course are not unlimited.[9]

The broker thus provides communication services and tries to land people in debt, thereby increasing his own credit, for each debt is an open communication channel or return service. There is of course a risk that people will not reciprocate as expected, that they will default. After a broker's credit is well established, people offer him their services, thus establishing credit with him. This is an investment in the future. Salvatore willingly provided services to Leonardo because he knew Leonardo had a range of excellent contacts that, one day, might be useful. Thus by controlling second order resources, Leonardo was able to gain access to first order resources which he used for his own benefit (to increase his use to his party, thereby increasing his credit with strategic political brokers). The ability to bring about communication rapidly is largely determined by credit, and credit is naturally dependent upon ability to bring about communication. It is a cumulative process.

The profit a broker derives from his activities stems from two sources. The first is interest: the second his capacity to convert his capital and credit (his network and the faith people have in his ability to use it for or against them) into other resources. These must offset the costs, both social and material, he invests in the transaction.

As *interest* I regard, not the return service, which I see as the fee, but the possibility of deciding *just when and just what* will be offered as a return service. It is this flexibility which gives the broker his high credit: people can be led *to think* all sorts of things about the nature of his network and

M

his ability to manipulate it. With the patron they can come *to know* its limits much more quickly.

Second order resources can very often be converted into first order resources: property, political office, better employment.[10] Conversion thus broadens the power base of the broker: it enables him to dispense first order resources to clients. But conversion is tricky, for by becoming also a patron, the broker becomes unequivocally tied to his promises to make his first order resources available. Unless he is able to dispense these to his clients, his credit diminishes rapidly, for he is now no longer able to deal in futures and probabilities, which are the stock in trade of the broker. Once his credit as a patron is placed in jeopardy, his credit as a broker is affected. As escalation of credit is cumulative, so is de-escalation.

Leonardo, an admirable broker with high credit, sought to convert his credit as a broker into political capital. His credit within the local section of the Christian Democratic Party, bolstered by promises to strategic figures, gave him enough support to become mayor of his town.[11] But his resources as mayor were limited, and he owed and promised much to many. He was not able to dispense the first order resources (jobs and contracts) that his clients expected. He began to lose credit. Within a year he was unseated as mayor, and shortly after that, his credit in ever more rapid decline, was ousted from his strategic post as secretary of the party. This loss closed down a whole network of strategic communication channels. But although his credit was declining rapidly, he was still able to retire from the local arena to an excellent teaching post he had finally secured in Naples, after much intrigue, before his credit collapsed entirely. Though bankrupt as a broker, by astute conversion of his second order resources into first order economic resources, he was able in the end to achieve his goal, the security of a good government job.

The moral to this little Sicilian episode seems to be that if a broker does decide to convert his assets (capital and credit), he should think twice about converting them to political resources. Slow conversion to economic resources would seem safer, though the profit may not be as great or as rapid.[12]

BROKERAGE AS A CAREER

1. *The career model*

Given the desire to manipulate people as resources in order to move ahead, a person who starts from a niche which gives him a high measure of centrality, a certain amount of power and prestige and the time to service his relations can become a broker.[13] His first problem is how to get people to make use of him. He must sometimes even cultivate a need for his services. Given this need, he must not only be able to pass messages, but must also be in touch with other brokers, patrons and clients who can ensure that the messages are acted on. If his prime capital consists of one powerful patron —and a broker beginning his career cannot be expected to know a range of patrons—it means that his influence is limited to the resources that patron controls. If, however, his capital consists of or includes a powerful broker, then the types of message he can transmit are more varied, and thus he can build up a clientele of debtors more rapidly. Though the debt relation for a favour obtained via another broker is not quite as binding as it is when obtained from a person who dispenses first order resources directly.

A broker must build up credit by producing the goods. Though a broker merely passes a request along, and thus the blame for failure in theory falls on the decision maker or the more powerful broker to whom it was passed, ultimately he is also affected. This is because failure reflects upon his standing with the decision maker, upon his ability to select a correct channel along which to route the request, or upon the (low) priority rating he assigned to the message. Clients know that a broker receives many requests which must be routed along the same channels and that it lies in his power to code and transmit them in such a way that they receive priority. Thus ultimately the ability of a broker to expand his credit depends on his success in obtaining favourable replies for his clients.

As his credit expands, so does the volume of messages he handles, and hence the number of persons in his debt— providing always, of course, that he has followed the dictum of the successful Gozitan village politician (whose nickname, incidentally, was 'The Saint') I once asked for the key to his success: 'Do much for people but ask little in return.' A broker with a clientele of persons in his debt is in a strategic position in most political systems. He can produce votes for persons seeking elected office. If he agrees to provide votes for a candidate and the latter is elected, he gains an important new channel in his expanding communication network. Most politicians, whether European or non-European, are powerful brokers, who have as clients important civil servants who, in fact, make the decisions their voters seek to influence.

This is because many civil servants in Europe, the United States and in the so-called developing countries owe their positions to the intervention of a politician or some other influential person. They are thus in debt and vulnerable to influence. But even in those cases where this is not so, a civil servant is often prepared to help a politician obtain a favour for a voter because by helping him this way he gains a hold over a person who may later be useful. Most civil servants somewhere during their career need help to gain promotion, protect a particular policy or in general to block the manoeuvring of a rival.

The ultimate aim of the local broker must always be to develop his own range of contacts who control first order resources so that he does not have to work through other brokers, for as long as he does so he is dependent upon them.

Assuming he has been successful in his operations, that he

has developed a network of strategic channels to key decision makers so that he needn't work through other brokers, that he has eliminated rivals and that his credit is high and his debtors numerous, he is then in a position to convert his second order resources into some valued end such as a good job with the administration or political office. If his educational qualifications permit, he may well choose the first course and enter the civil service where he becomes a loyal administrative client/broker of the politician who helped to place him. The municipal, provincial and regional administrations of Sicily, for example, are filled with persons who worked for years at the local level as brokers for various politicians. Their positions are secure in the sense that they have tenure of office and a pension.

If, however, their educational background is such that they cannot qualify for a good, pensionable post, they often have no alternative but to try to convert their brokerage role to political office. This however is hazardous. Though they can call in their debts and so obtain votes, these will normally be insufficient to elect them. Moreover, they will in all likelihood be opposed by the politicians for whom they acted as local agents, since these stand to lose their monopoly position and thus that portion of the local support that the brokers gain. Politics is a zero sum game. Moreover, if elected, a politician has to fight continually to maintain his position, for every four or five years his clients express his credit rating in the votes they give him. Thus to protect his credit he must also establish his enterprise as a monopoly: rival communication channels must be destroyed. This generally means a certain amount of manipulation and rather ruthless calculation.

This is in short a model of how a broker may operate his role to gain power and office. It has been illustrated in part by the career of Leonardo. Because he had the educational qualifications, he could convert his brokerage role into a sound pensionable post with the government when his credit collapsed. Data gathered by Mart Bax, on the other hand, provides a fascinating illustration of the career of Tadgh O'Sullivan, an Irish broker without these educational qualifications, who sought to convert his resources into political office.[14]

2. An Irish broker

To be able to follow the career of Tadgh O'Sullivan it is necessary to know something about some of the rules of the political field in which he operates.

The parliament of Eire consists of two chambers, the upper chamber, or *Seanad*, and the lower chamber, the *Dáil*. Only the latter is elected directly by the voters. The Dáil is the most important political arena and there is much competition to become a *Teachta Dála*, Member of Parliament, or T.D. for short. There is also local government at the county level, and the elected Members of County Council, M.C.C.'s for short, have a good bit to say about the allocation of resources of direct relevance to the voters, for their tasks deal with roads, public health and sanitary services, housing, public assistance and so on. The dominant party in Eire at the national and often at the county level is the Fianna Fáil, which has been in power since 1932 for all but six years. The party rests on its parish clubs, each of which sends three delegates, including the local secretary, to the regional organization. The regional organization selects candidates for local government office and also sends delegates to the constituency organizations which selects candidates for the Dáil. The parish clubs also send candidates to this constituency convention. Because of the close contact the M.C.C. has with the electorate, it is of considerable strategic importance for the T.D. to be an M.C.C. at the same time, and Bax notes that nearly three-fourths of the T.D.'s are in fact also M.C.C.'s. But to cover areas in their constituency where they do not have direct personal access, and they cannot be everywhere at once, they must recruit local brokers who can act as their link with the voters. This brings us to Tadgh O'Sullivan, broker extraordinary.

Tadgh O'Sullivan occupies an admirable niche to start operations as a political broker. To begin with he is a bachelor of 45 who lives with his mother in a town of about 900. He thus has a good deal of free time to devote to his many activities. Secondly he has several strategic occupations: he is the town's shoemaker and the electricity meter reader, tasks which place him in touch with a wide range of people whenever he chooses (for he can read the meter whenever he needs an excuse to drop in on someone). He is also secretary of the local Fianna Fáil party club of which his father, who died when Tadgh was at secondary school (thus obliging him to leave school and seek work) was one of the founders. As secretary he routes messages from the local party members to politicians and government departments for action. Because of his strategic position he was approached by an M.C.C. from the district with a request to funnel many of the requests through him. In return he arranged to get Tadgh a job as local reporter for a regional newspaper. As secretary of the political club he also attends regional and constituency party meetings.

Tadgh moreover holds important local and regional offices in the Gaelic Athletic Association which place him in contact with another circle of influential people. These positions also enable him to dispense favours to certain towns. He is instrumental in deciding which town will be the venue for important football and hurling matches between teams whose home facilities are insufficient to accommodate the teams or the crowds anticipated. The local merchants and publicans who benefit from these matches make it possible for him to get extra financial credit and to buy goods at reduced prices. Moreover he gains important goodwill from the clubs owning the facilities used, for they receive a percentage of the gate.

With his range of contacts, interests, central location and jobs that permit him to talk to people in private to hear their 'confessions' (their requests for assistance) he was ideally suited to play an important brokerage role for pub owner Sean Dwane, a young T.D. and M.C.C., in a tight race for re-election. In order to get Tadgh sufficiently in his debt, on the hook, as it were, Dwane arranged for him to be promoted to regional reporter of the newspaper for which he had been a local stringer. This is a steady and pensionable job. Moreover, it meant that Tadgh could travel around the whole constituency on his own and Dwane's business at the newspaper's expense!

Dwane proved to be an excellent contact, and was able to deliver the goods, both for individual requests that Tadgh funneled into him as well as for the village. His credit rose, as did that of his local broker, Tadgh, to whom people began coming in increasing numbers with their problems. But though Tadgh developed power through his ability to route messages to Dwane, this power was based almost exclusively upon the single relationship he had to the influential Dwane.

Nonetheless, increasingly confident, Tadgh sought nomination as candidate for membership in the County Council. This worried Dwane, for it will be remembered he was also an M.C.C., and he feared the loss of the votes that Tadgh would be able to draw from him. Thus by manipulating his network—buying a drink here, making a promise there, giving some favours and so on—he was able to block Tadgh's nomination and so preserve his monopoly position as the sole link with the bureaucracy at the County Council level. This manoeuvre strained the relationship between the two, but as they both needed each other politically, they patched up a working arrangement.

Having learned that you can only get so far on credit, Tadgh now began to concentrate on building up his own contacts with persons who controlled first order resources. He began to subvert a number of Dwane's influential friends beyond his local area. He also scored an important political triumph by obtaining sewage connexions for a row of local houses completely without Dwane's intervention. This increased his local credit enormously. He also began to agitate against a number of Dwane's policies at regional meetings.

At this point he developed a new and extremely important link in his network. He became one of the liaison officers between the party's national executive in Dublin, and the constituency. This entailed fortnightly visits to Dublin to report on the functioning of constituency clubs, county councillors and T.D.'s. He now had direct access (without Dwane's help) to some of the top men in the party and the government. This increased his credit throughout the constituency, for he was now a broker with channels able to carry extremely weighty messages directly, swiftly and with little interference. He demonstrated this, for example, by telephoning a minister and, in a matter of hours, securing the release for a district businessman of an important consignment blocked in Customs. The grateful businessman assured Tadgh that he would help him any way he could at election time.

At this point Bax ends his account of the rising fortunes of Tadgh O'Sullivan, poised as it were in mid-attempt to convert his many debt relations with people into political office. If he succeeds in building a coalition of persons (such as club secretaries) who can help him solve the management problem of funneling 'confessions' and votes to him, I have little doubt that he will be elected M.C.C., and perhaps eventually move on to T.D.

It is persons such as Leonardo, Tadgh O'Sullivan and Séan Dwane who, through manipulating strategic relations in their networks in their drive to attain their goals, construct the coalitions which form the subject of the next chapter.

7
Coalitions

The coalitions which people form in their drive to attain their goals are temporary alliances. Although their internal structure and organization vary enormously, all coalitions are built by individuals who are dependent, in different ways, on each other. Because the very existence of a coalition depends not only upon the specific and varied goals and resources of the individuals who compose it, but also on the relations between them, they are unstable. In time, goals alter, resources shift and relations between people change. Moreover, the *ad hoc* nature of coalitions makes them ideally suited instruments to exploit new resources in changing situations. Coalitions may thus reflect changing circumstances, they may bring about change, and, by their very nature, are constantly subject to change. They may disappear as certain goals are achieved, or they may evolve into social forms of a different structural order, such as more permanent associations, often transforming their social and cultural environment in the process.

Coalitions, though present in all societies, play a more important part in organizing activities in some than in others where formal associations rather than coalitions organize the same activities. Why this should be so is an intriguing question and seems to be related to the degree to which a nation-state or community of interests has developed in a society. But before discussing this problem it is perhaps advisable to examine some of the characteristics of coalitions and the variety of combinations which they can assume.

VARIETIES OF COALITIONS

In spite of suggestions to narrow the meaning of coalition to 'the joint use of resources to determine the outcome of a decision', thus giving it a specifically political connotation, I find it more convenient to use it in the ordinary, broader English sense.[1] By *coalition*, therefore, I mean '*a temporary alliance of distinct parties for a limited purpose*'.[2] Of course, defining a concept does not make it a social reality. Concepts only mean what they are defined to mean and are not realities except for those societies in whose languages the concept exists. There is in fact an impressive range of such concepts in virtually every society studied. The definition of coalition is general enough to cover this range of organizational forms, some of which will be discussed shortly. On the other hand, the definition is also restricted enough to set coalitions off from corporate groups. When the term corporate group is used by social anthropologists, it usually means 'a corporate body with a permanent existence; a collection of people recruited on recognized principles, with common interests and rules (*norms*) fixing rights and duties of the members in relation to one another and to these interests. The common interests can be called property interests if property is very broadly defined.'[3]

In contrast to the concept of corporate group, that of coalition implies temporariness: a coalition is entered into explicitly in order to achieve a limited purpose. But as time goes on it may accumulate more tasks. The duration of the coalition will obviously vary with the length of time it takes to realize that purpose. Some coalitions prove to be viable units and longevity results. Alliance implies the joint use of resources: one is committing resources to achieve a goal. But these resources, though used jointly, remain linked to the person who brought them into the coalition and who may remove them at any moment. The nature of the commitment as well as the resources can thus vary from member to member. Obviously a certain amount of co-ordination must take place, and this gives the coalition a measure of organization. That is, there is present a certain co-ordination of social action in terms of the given ends of the coalition.[4] The parties in coalition usually remain distinct, their individual identity within the alliance is not replaced by a group identity, nor is their individual commitment replaced by an ideological commitment to a uniform set of rights and obligations, which is characteristic of corporate groups. This does not mean, however, that behavioural norms, shared rights and duties and long life may not develop. In short, it is quite possible for a coalition to acquire some of these features, and for it to develop into a corporate group.

As the commitment and the resources invested may vary from member to member, so can their individual motives and interests. A landlord forms a coalition to fight an election. His limited aim is to become mayor. The aim of the second member of the coalition may be simply to gain sufficient political leverage to obtain a job for his dim-witted son. To achieve this he commits his resources—the votes of his own labourers, for he is also a landlord—to the coalition. The labourers agree to support the coalition by giving their votes to protect their relations with their landlord/employer, and so on. It is obvious that the aims and interests involved are relative, for the pragmatic goals of individual members may differ widely from the coalition's normative aim (assuming it has one). There may thus be many different limited interests which can be realized through commitment to a particular coalition. As noted, the instability of coalitions derives partly from this, for as soon as one member attains his limited aims or sees a more expeditious means of achieving them, he will be ready to drop out and, consequently, to remove his resources.

The suggested definition makes no statement about the means of recruitment to the coalition, or about its size. Agreement to join may be obtained by coercion as much as by altruism and self-interest. Coalitions can vary in size from a few friends who meet regularly with the sole purpose of sharing common interests, to tens if not hundreds of persons who enter into an alliance in order to mobilize support for a particular politician or cause. It also seems worthwhile to note that coalitions may comprise individuals, other coalitions, and even corporate groups; and most show a concentric form of organization, with core and peripheral members.

Some of the coalitions for which terms exist in the ethnographic literature are cliques, gangs, action-sets and factions. In examining these it may be helpful to note the way in which certain features interact. The features concerned can include: (1) a centrality of focus in the form of a single central ego (a leader or core); (2) a clearly defined goal apart from mutual affection or interest; (3) internal specialization apart from the possession of a leader; (4) clear recruitment principles; (5) density and interactional content; (6) behavioural norms *vis à vis* other members (thus a common identity); and (7) the presence of rival or competing units in the environment.[5] My object in examining these features is certainly not to attempt to classify coalitions. It is simply to explore to what extent attention to these features can provide insights into coalitions in general. The four forms of coalition have been selected rather arbitrarily. Terms, such as salon, coterie, entourage, machine, social circle, team, clientele, following, and so on, designate many other types of coalition. In fact, if only these seven features are combined in terms of their presence or absence, no less than 256 possible combinations can be generated. It is senseless to try to attach terms to them all. Not the term but the interplay of features is important to the social analyst.

CLIQUES

A clique is a coalition whose members associate regularly with each other on the basis of affection and common interest and possess a marked sense of common identity.[6] This consciousness of kind sets the clique off from the sociometric or objective clique defined as a cluster of persons all of whom are adjacent to all others.[7] A clique is a relatively constant collection of persons who see each other frequently for both emotional (or expressive) as well as pragmatic (or instrumental) reasons. It has an objective existence, in the sense that it forms a cluster of persons all of whom are linked to each other. It also has a subjective existence, for members as well as non-members are conscious of its common identity.

Most people have been and still are members of one or more cliques. I personally have been a member of quite a number. In common with many, I suppose, the most important and longest enduring clique was the one of which I was a member during secondary school. I still occasionally contact some of its members, although we now have little besides that once shared membership in common. I also belonged to several cliques in the different units in which I was stationed during my period of service with U.S. Army, and I was a member of various dormitory cliques at college. Since my college days, however, friends have been recruited on an individual basis. Thus, although some of my current friends do know each other, we do not all meet regularly and cannot be considered a clique.

The most important clique I belonged to during my period in the army in many respects provides a typical example. It came into being in February 1947, shortly after we were posted to an isolated village about thirty miles outside Trieste, on the border with Yugoslavia. All of the members of the clique planned to go to university, in general felt themselves to be slightly better educated than the other members of the platoon, and were interested in something besides sex and getting drunk.

I joined the outpost at the same time as *Rossi*, whom I had met briefly before and knew to be interested in going to university. At the outpost I met *Harry*, with whom I became quite friendly. Although Harry had been to an exclusive military preparatory school, he was unquestionably the messiest soldier in the platoon. At school he had learned almost everything there was to know about the fine art of gold bricking, or getting by with minimal work. He could always give advice about matters military and, especially, how to do little but seem busy. He could also be relied upon for an intelligent conversation. Through Harry I met *Herman*. Herman was the only member of the clique who had been to university, where he had spent one year studying engineering. At the university he had been a member of the Reserve Officers Training Corps and had played football on the first year squad. Moreover, he had been singled out by the Army as leadership material and had just completed a two months' course at the Non-Commissioned Officers training centre at the Lido in Venice. Herman was in all ways a well-scrubbed, beautifully-pressed and gleaming example of what a soldier could look like. Indeed, he later became corporal. Herman, however, had a satellite, *Joe*, a boy from a rather poor Tennessee family. Joe had met Herman at the Lido N.C.O. training course and had been devoted to him ever since. Under Herman's influence he ceased the carousing and wenching that he had engaged in before going to the Lido.

It is probable that Herman, because of his superior education and his soldierly bearing, was the *primus inter pares* in terms of the values and problems we dealt with. The five of us spent much of our free time together and constituted a clearly discernable group of friends in the hut in which our platoon was quartered. A sixth man, *Mervyn*, sometimes joined us. He was a friend of Rossi and vaguely planned to go to university. The five of us, Herman, Joe, Harry, Rossi and

myself, regarded ourselves as 'buddies'. We were also regarded as such by other members of the platoon (see Diagram
7.1).

DIAGRAM 7.1

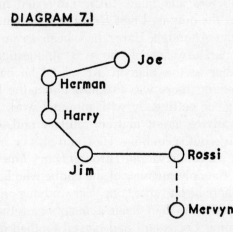

We all spent a good deal, if not most, of our free time with
each other, but the pattern of interaction between us was by
no means symmetrical. Joe spent most of his time with Herman, and the two bunked next to each other. I saw a good
deal of Herman, as did Rossi, but Herman spent more time
with Harry than with us. Harry divided his time, I should
say, equally between Herman and myself. I saw about as
much of Rossi as I did of Harry. Rossi, on the other hand,
although he spent most of his time with the four other members of the clique, and especially with me, spent a good deal
of time with Mervyn, who sometimes joined us.

Our activities were rather simple minded. We considered
ourselves moving on a higher plane than the rest of our
platoon, most of whom spent their free time getting blind
drunk—one combat veteran and his friend would get so
drunk on *grappa* that they would take bites out of glasses in
a local café (until the proprietor took to serving them in water
tumblers)—and conducting sexual extravagances with Trieste
whores. In contrast, when we got an evening pass to Trieste

we devoted our time to the pursuit of what we regarded as higher activities. We went to the cinema and generally dined in a good restaurant, where we could rub shoulders with officers and the white collar soldiers from the various headquarter companies stationed in Trieste. What we did not do was to indulge in *grappa* and girls. Our free time at the outpost, and later when we returned to the cantonment just outside Trieste, was usually spent talking or reading.

The clique began to dissolve when we moved into the cantonment, for we were all stationed in different barracks, and Herman became corporal. This gave him responsibilities and a status which placed him clearly apart from the rest of us. About three months after we returned to Trieste we began to be shipped back at different times to the United States and the clique finally broke up.

This clique is typical in many respects of the cliques which have been described in the literature.[8] While it is true that some of the cliques described have leaders, it does not follow that all cliques do. The literature as well as my own experience provide cases to the contrary.[9] In our army clique Herman, because he had actually been to the university for a year, symbolized for us most clearly the aspirations of further education and the more sophisticated way of life this implied. Therefore although we regarded ourselves as equals, Herman, seen objectively rather than subjectively, was the focal point. The clique had been built up around him.

A clique usually has no clear common goal other than the exchange of confidences, conversation and other emotional experiences between its members. Members come together to be in each other's company. Cliques may, however, become specifically goal-oriented, and, conversely, certain members of a goal-oriented action-set may form a clique. My army clique as well as those described in the literature had no specific goals.

Cliques normally show little or no internal specialization, unless it be in terms of roles assumed by certain members

N

such as clown, Don Juan, story-teller and so forth. Certain capabilities of the members may, if the occasion demands, be placed at the service of the clique. But because the clique is not a goal-oriented coalition, these special capabilities have little functional importance for the coalition. In our army clique the only degree of specialization present was the role of messenger and odd job man which Joe occasionally assumed for Herman and only for him. He and Rossi often played the clown, he as a Hill Billy and Rossi, who was a second or third generation Italian-American from Jersey City, as an immigrant Italian tough man. Herman was a clean-cut model American soldier, with no sense of humour. We together possessed a pool of talents which served us well. Herman had contacts with Non-Commissioned Officers and through them obtained useful information. He could also sometimes protect clique members from extra guard duty. Harry could provide expert advice on how to get away with as little work as possible. Joe shared the idiom and southern background with most of the other members of the platoon, and could thus lay contact with them. As I recall it, my only use was that I knew several good restaurants in Trieste and, what was more important for the clique, knew how to behave in them, for my father on a business trip to Europe had visited me in Trieste and taken me out to eat several times. Rossi was an amusing conversationalist, and a most sympathetic listener to those with problems. Perhaps it is in fact the combination of these particular capacities which enabled the clique to survive for as long as we were together.

A clique has no clear-cut principles of recruitment. Shared characteristics and (this grows later) mutual affection seem to be the primary recruitment criteria which emerge from the literature. Any given body of persons who are in touch with each other and share characteristics tend to gravitate towards each other: they have a common fund of experiences which provide an initial point of contact. Members of a clique thus very often have similar interests and aspirations, are roughly the same age, are of the same sex, come from the same social class and do similar work. This was certainly the case with our army clique, for we all had an interest in further education and an aversion to what we regarded as the debaucheries of the rest of the platoon. We were all on eighteen-month enlistments with the Army, except Joe, who had enlisted for three years. We were all between eighteen and nineteen years old. Moreover, all of us, with the exception of Joe, were, generally speaking, middle class. As mentioned he came from a working-class family in Tennessee. These generally shared but amorphous characteristics were what we had in common.

All members of a clique interact with each other. Nonetheless, all cliques seem to exhibit a certain degree of structuring which corresponds to the frequency and content of the interaction. It is useful to speak of *core members* of a clique, who participate all the time, *primary members*, who meet sometimes with the core and rarely alone, and *secondary members*, who are on the fringe, as it were, and participate infrequently.[10] This structuring is obviously partly a function of the size of the clique, for it becomes more pronounced the larger it is. Its principles could be discerned in our army clique. Although all of us met each other together and separately almost daily, Herman, Harry and Joe formed the core. Rossi and I could be regarded as primary members. Mervyn, who sometimes spent his free time in the barracks with us, and came along occasionally to Trieste, was clearly a secondary member. This distinction between core and peripheral members is characteristic of all coalitions.

Cliques have clear-cut norms of behaviour and a sense of common identity. These two characteristics are intimately linked. Norms can only develop among a collectivity which has a consciousness of kind. Besides specific norms that are unique to certain cliques, there seems to be a general one of loyalty to the members and a conscious preservation of the confidences shared between members when dealing with outsiders. The overriding norms in our army clique were chastity and moderation in alcohol. Towards the end of our period in Trieste Rossi succumbed to the influences of another clique to which Mervyn belonged. One evening, after he had been very thoroughly steeped in alcohol, he was introduced to one of the favourite whores of the other clique. She promptly seduced him on the pavement behind some bushes in a park. He was most sheepish when members of the other clique teased us with the episode, for we had a reputation as clean living young men.

Cliques are not necessarily rivals of or in competition with other cliques. As they come into being to fulfil the desire of the members for companionship, they do not compete for prizes or scarce resources. It is obvious, however, that if a clique adopts a clear-cut goal to attain a prize which is sought by others, rivalry can develop. Our army clique was in no sense a rival of or in conflict with the many other cliques in our platoon and company.

I have analysed cliques rather extensively because they are, apart from coalitions of intimate kinsmen, the most important type of coalition in terms of emotional investment.[11] A clique serves as a vehicle for an effective element which counterbalances the formal demands of the organization in which it is embedded, and makes life more meaningful. As Eric Wolf perceptively noted, a clique 'may reduce the feeling of the individual that he is dominated by forces beyond himself, and serve to confirm the existence of his ego in the interplay of small group chit-chat'. And more instrumentally, cliques may render '. . . an unpredictable situation more predictable'. . . and provide 'mutual support against surprise upsets from within or without'.[12]

In spite of the importance of cliques, they have received relatively little analytical attention, for they have defied classification.[13] Though cliques have received attention at the descriptive level, in common with the other social forms dealt with in this book, they have not been taken seriously into account by theorists. These, whether structural-functionalist or marxist, have generally tended to view societies as being composed of formal, neatly bounded groups of institutional complexes. Hence cliques are regarded as ancillary, secondary or interstitial, although their existence, composition and operation is critical to the understanding of the formal organizations and groups on which sociologists normally concentrate.

GANGS

Sociologists have made very little progress in formulating an operational definition of gang which distinguishes it from other kinds of social grouping.[14] By gang therefore I mean a leader-centred coalition whose members associate regularly on the basis of affection and common interest and possess a marked sense of common identity. In short, a gang is a large clique with a single leader who is both the symbol and central focus of the coalition. Alongside this single central focus, it shares with the clique the other characteristics set out above. In contrast to the clique, however, the activities of the members of a gang more often take place out of doors, and tend to be more varied. As used in common English speech, gang has a pejorative connotation, and is used to refer to bands of boys or young men bent on mischief, or to an enduring coalition of delinquents under a single leader. If the term is stripped of its pejorative connotation, however, it refers to a leader with a band of followers between all of whom there is a high rate of interaction, common interest and, perhaps to a lesser degree, affection. There is an abundant literature on juvenile gangs but considerably less has been written about leader-follower teams.[15]

Perhaps the best known gang is 'The Nortons', described by William Foote Whyte in his classic *Street Corner Society*.[16] The young men who gathered around Doc received their name from the Norton Street corner on which they assembled. They came into being as a coalition in the early spring of

1937. *Doc*, 29, was the gangs pivot. (See Diagram 7.2.) Doc had been the leader of a kids' gang in secondary school. He had had to beat up the former leader of the gang, Nutsy, to achieve this position. Doc had been able to beat up all the other boys, and they accepted his leadership. He told them what to do and protected the gang, plotting strategy against other boys' gangs. The old gang broke up when they left secondary school. The only member of his old gang that Doc continued to see was his very good friend *Danny*, 27. Doc and Danny stayed together. Danny eventually developed a partnership in a dice game with *Mike*, 29. Mike had been the leader of another kids' gang during his secondary school period. After that he ran a bar which had been closed by the police, and later a restaurant. Doc and Danny spent a good deal of their time in the restaurant. Danny and Mike eventually set up their dice game and befriended *Long John*, 24. As his brother had received a life prison sentence for murder, Long John was most anxious to leave the influence of the delinquent gang of which he had been a member. Mike and Danny helped him break away and he worked for them as look-out. *Nutsy*, 29, was the only member of Doc's former gang who had continued to spend his free time on Norton Street. He had become the rallying point of a group of younger men. His special friend was *Frank*, 23. *Joe*, 24, was a good friend of both these men. *Carl*, 21, and *Tommy*, 20, had formerly been members of another gang but they now accepted Nutsy's leadership. *Alec*, 21, had been a school friend of Joe's younger brother. He used to hang around Norton Street to be near Joe, whom he admired. *Fred*, 25, was a personal friend of Doc who had protected him from Danny and some other boys who, as a practical joke, had tried to extort *Mafia*-type protection money from him while he worked at his uncle's store. Doc explained the joke to him and since then he had regarded Doc as his benefactor. Doc had met *Lou*, 24, when he worked for the Norton Street Settlement House and had been friends with him for several years. *Angelo*, 25, was also a special friend to whom Doc had given a certain amount of protection and encouragement to overcome his shyness when he first arrived as an immigrant.

Doc returned to Norton Street early in the spring of 1937. Nutsy, and his own followers Frank, Joe, Alec, Carl, and Tommy, respected him and accepted his leadership. They gathered around him. Doc's personal friends, Angelo, Fred and Lou followed, as did Danny and Mike, whose gambling game was located nearby. Long John followed them. Diagram 7.2 sets out the relationship which existed at the moment the gang came into being.[17]

DIAGRAM 7.2

DOC'S BOYS: "THE NORTONS"

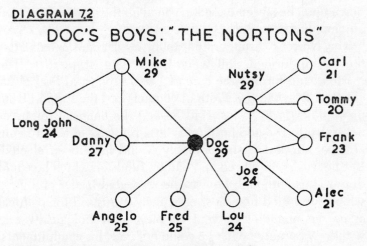

Source: Based on Whyte (1955: 3-51)

Doc, Danny and Mike may be viewed as forming the inner core of the gang, with Long John as a satellite. Whyte calls them leaders. They together had a wide range of contacts, and accompanied the younger men whenever they had dealings or business with persons outside the district. Doc, in contrast to the others, was, at the time the Nortons came into being, unemployed and could spend more time hanging around the street corner than they could. Thus he had the time which the others lacked to invest in servicing relationships. Moreover, he had been the leader of the boys' gang on the same street. He was clearly the leader: 'The Nortons' had been built by him and around him.

The activities of the Nortons, besides general conversation on the street corner and in the cafés, was centred primarily on bowling and, occasionally, on girls. But the members were supposed to spend their time on their fellow members. When a rivalry began to develop over the girls, they stopped their association with a girls' club. Generally speaking the members of the Nortons did not indulge in heavy drinking, extravagant wenching and gambling. Long John was looked down upon because he used to spend all the money he earned on gambling.

The Nortons disintegrated about a year and a half after they were formed, following Doc's fling at politics. The Norton gang formed the core of Doc's support in his bid for election. Doc had the width of contacts and the support from many other local gangs. Had he had the financial resources necessary to provide hospitality and presents to his growing army of supporters, he probably would have been elected. But he was unemployed and had no funds on which he could draw. Thus, although he was the respected leader of a gang which supported him most effectively in his bid for political office, he nonetheless went to pieces psychologically and withdrew because he felt he could not meet his commitments. His failure in the political arena affected his standing among the Nortons, for he had betrayed their trust. Mike, who had been particularly active in organizing Doc's campaign, ceased to look upon him as a leader, though he remained his good friend. Doc in fact stopped trying to hold the Nortons together, and the gang began to disintegrate. The Nortons had been built by and grew up around Doc; when he withdrew under the pressure of events, the gang began to fall apart.

A gang, as exemplified by the Nortons, clearly has a central focus in the leader. But it cannot be said to have a clear common goal other than the amusement of its members. The gang exists for the benefit of its members. In fact it is interesting that when the Nortons did develop a clear common goal, namely to promote the candidacy of Doc, the internal roles were so radically redefined that the members destroyed the gang. It is also not possible to speak of clear internal specialization within the gang. Although Whyte describes Mike and Danny as Doc's lieutenants, they can scarcely be regarded as his delegates, as others did not accept orders from them in his absence. At most they can be considered as something of a buffer between Doc and the others as far as the flow of communication is concerned. Nutsy, on the other hand, whom Whyte does not regard as a lieutenant, appears to have had more authority over Frank, Joe, Alec, Carl and Tommy, than Mike or Danny had. They clearly formed a clique within the Nortons. Other than that there appears to be no internal specialization, although this was clearly present when the gang became a goal-oriented political action group. The gang appears to have had no recruitment principles other than the general congeniality of its members and their acceptance of Doc as their leader. Nonetheless, there was a clear sense of unity and an awareness of a common identity. They were as conscious of this as non-members were. Doc, together with Mike and Danny, with Long John as a satellite, formed the central core of the gang, with perhaps Long John, Angelo, Fred, Lou and Nutsy as its primary members. The rest can be regarded as secondary members. It is also significant that these peripheral members, as can be seen from Diagram 7.2, are somewhat younger than the other Nortons. The Nortons possessed certain norms of behaviour, foremost among which was the loyalty and help they were expected to display to other members.

Finally, it may be noted that gangs like the Nortons are not primarily conflict groups. That is they are not in competition with other like units for honour or valued prizes. This of course does not mean that they do not, upon occasion, compete with others as a unity, as the Nortons did during certain bowling matches. Many gangs, however, especially those composed of somewhat younger men, and boys' gangs, do compete avidly with rival gangs for honour and control of territory, women and even petty criminal enterprises. Usually the structural characteristics of these fighting gangs are similar to those of the Nortons, although the number of peripheral members is considerably larger, especially when they clash, for many join the fray. Such gangs not only have clear goals, but also provide physical protection for members against the depredations and assaults of rival gangs in areas where the State is unable to do so. This is increasingly the situation in larger metropolitan areas, where the understaffed police force has to cope with underprivileged, exploited and increasingly rebellious ethnic and minority groups and the generally escalating level of violence. Much of the literature dealing with gangs refers to coalitions of this type.[18] Such gangs combine the characteristics of coalitions such as the Nortons with those of the more task- and prize-oriented action groups to be discussed in the next section.

ACTION-SETS

By action-set I mean a set of persons who have co-ordinated their actions to achieve a particular goal. This definition is somewhat general, but it does not imply only a purposeful mobilization of members by a single leader or clique to achieve a particular goal.[19] While not questioning that an element of leadership is eventually necessary for the successful co-ordination of activities to achieve a goal, we should not rule out the possibility of a more spontaneous merger of people who think alike and gradually discover that they do. There leadership emerges as or after they join forces.[20] The definition is thus broad enough to include the wide variety of work parties and action groups which abound in the ethnographic (and sociological) literature. Examples of some of these are the agricultural teams and boat-crews described by Blehr in the Faroe-Islands; the Ilokano *daklis* fishing groups recorded by Scheams; the beer drinking sets in Burundi described by Trouwborst; the economic *combinazioni* observed by the Schneiders in Sicily; and, closer to home, the murder teams described by Valachi.[21] Besides these, every reader will be familiar with action-sets he has mobilized to wallpaper a room, to celebrate his wife's birthday or perhaps to block the destruction of a piece of nature by a new motor-way or water reservoir. Others perhaps will be more familiar with the economic coalitions built by entrepreneurs in the business world to replace key figures on a board of directors, to develop and market a new product, or perhaps to take over a firm.

Chapter 6 provided an example of the least complex kind of action-set: the attempt by one person to obtain the help of another to achieve a goal. Salvatore mobilized Leonardo, who launched him along links in his network with whom Salvatore constituted a series of two person action-sets of very short duration until he attained his goal of a personal introduction to his professor. Raymond Firth has provided details of a more complicated action-set which remained in being for six days to repair a canoe on the little Pacific island of Tikopia.[22]

The first day Chief Ariki Kafika and some others chopped down the tree destined for the repair of the canoe. The next day the chief and his son assembled about twenty kinsmen, relatives by marriage and neighbours to carry the timber to the coast. No one was in command of the party and opinions were given freely by all. Although the chief himself did not help, his son and the son of an other chief did. Next day, after a ceremony, the repair of the canoe began under the direction of an expert, who was the brother of the deceased builder of the canoe. Firth notes that sixteen men were present. On the fourth day there were twelve men present. Some helped only at the ovens for the cooking, others alternated between the boat and the ovens. The expert apparently took no part in the cooking. The following day there was a big feed where there were twenty-six persons present. Some came only for the feast and slipped away after eating. They apparently did no work. On the sixth day the chief's son distributed food and various valuable objects as a reward for the help. The expert and non-kin received slightly more than kinsmen. Although the actual work on the canoe was carried out by men, women were present all the time bringing food and various items.

Anton Blok recently analysed a series of more complex action-sets which remained in being for years and co-ordinated a diversity of activities and personnel.[23] He describes how the coalition of Domenico and his two nephews Nicola and Michele, which had held a lease to about a thousand hectares of land on the Baronessa estate near the Sicilian town of Genuardo between 1902 and 1914 was attacked and defeated by a rival coalition. Domenico and his two nephews formed the core of the action-set. They did not work the land themselves. They were assisted by a number of *campieri*, local strong men in their service who policed the estates ensuring that livestock was not rustled, crops were not pilfered and that the various categories of workers made no extravagant claims. These *campieri*, in the absence of effective State control over this hinterland, formed the private police force of Domenico and his nephews. In addition to contracts with their *campieri*, they also had to recruit to their coalition on a contractual basis, herdsmen to look after their large flocks of sheep and sharecroppers and landless labourers to farm their extensive lease-holding. Besides these, they had to maintain good relations with persons who could transport their produce to processing centres, with millers who converted their wheat into flour and with local and regional politicians who could provide protection. The most important of these was the landowner of the estate, who lived in

Palermo. In short, it was a highly complex coalition co-ordinated by a clique headed by Domenico.

In September 1914 Domenico's enterprise was challenged by a rival coalition headed by Edoardo. Edoardo moved to wrest the Baronessa landholding from Domenico. To do this he built up a coalition of ten men who lived, as he did, in the neighbouring town of Adornò. All were *campieri*, of whom five, including Edoardo, worked on the Baronessa estates leased by Domenico. The other five performed similar functions on neighbouring estates. They were thus all strong men, men who could make themselves respected; in short, *mafiosi*. Edoardo made his move as the six-year lease on the Baronessa complex was about to expire. The coalition of *campieri* recruited the support of a noted outlaw, Grisafi, and his band who, in return for protection, information and possibly some other remuneration which Blok does not mention, undertook to place Domenico's enterprise under severe pressure. Well supplied with detailed information by the Adornò coalition partners who were employed by Domenico, Grisafi made his move early September 1914. Grisafi first tried to blackmail Domenico, and then tried to kill him and one of his retainers in a raid on his land. Although Grisafi did not succeed in making off with any of Domenico's cattle, he did kill fifteen oxen and injured several others that were ploughing in the fields that day. Domenico, because he and his nephews lacked sufficient protection and male kinsmen willing to enter into coalition with them to defend their interests, capitulated to Edoardo's pressure. He did not try to renew the lease. Edoardo and his *campieri* henchmen thus took over the lease of the estates formerly held by their employer. They entrenched themselves firmly and built up a vast enterprise. In the next few years they became involved in a number of clashes with rival estate owners as well as the forces of the law.

It is worth noting here that the coalition of Domenico had a long life. It was co-ordinated by a clique but had a shifting composition. In fact, it included a number of short-term coalitions recruited for ploughing, harvesting and transportation. These were all very short-term task-specific coalitions. Edoardo's coalition also called into being short-term action-sets to carry out specific objectives. The most striking of these was the coalition constructed between the five *campieri* working on the Baronessa estates and Grisafi and his band. Edoardo's coalition was also internally specialized. Some members provided central planning, others gathered information and, finally, Grisafi and his entourage carried out the physical violence.

All action-sets appear to have a central figure or a clique whom we may call the leader. As we have noted, although co-ordination comes from this leadership element, it may not have been instrumental in building up the action-set. The leader or the leadership clique in many cases acts as co-ordinator of recruitment once the action-set has come into being, and supervises and co-ordinates the tasks of the various members. Though in the case of the *daklis* fishing set and the Tikopian canoe repair party, these responsibilities were delegated. In all action-sets there is a measure of internal specialization, with certain persons being assigned or assuming specific tasks. The membership of the action-set is fairly clearly defined in the case of smaller coalitions, such as the dyadic sets recruited by Salvatore, the murder teams in which Valachi participated and the Faroe Islands boat crews. This limitation of members is demanded by the situation. But the membership, or the degree of exclusiveness, of larger action-sets is relative. It is often difficult to establish the exact composition of such coalitions, for people at the fringes drift in and out of the action. The Tikopian canoe-repair party lasted six days and the number of those co-operating ranged from two to twenty-six, excluding female helpers. Firth noted explicitly that some persons appeared only to eat, and then slipped away after the meal. Similarly, it is virtually impossible to set out in detail the membership of the series of related coalitions which Domenico and Edoardo co-ordinated in pursuit of their goals. At most we can make a distinction between a core clique and primary and secondary members. Again, the pattern emerges of a core and periphery.

Shared social relationships between all members prior to recruitment (outside the action situation) is not a necessary condition. In other words, in network terminology, all members are not necessarily adjacent. In all cases, however, some members shared prior social relations with some others, usually with the leader or members of the central co-ordinating clique. Obviously, if the action-set is small, all members will have some contact with others in the action situation. But in a large set this need not be so. Unquestionably all members of Domenico's enterprise did not share relations with each other nor even with the core, for many had been recruited via intermediaries who were members of the primary zone of the coalition.

Working together does not necessarily generate norms of behaviour which carry over outside the work situation: people may simply continue to act towards each other in terms of other shared roles. This also implies that there is not necessarily a sense of common identity. Moreover, within the work or action situation certain norms of behaviour do develop among some of the members, especially with regard to the specialists. This is also a variable dependent on the size and duration. Finally, it is worth noting that action-sets do not necessarily compete with other units for prizes or power. This, however, depends very much on the particular goal of the coalition. There were no rival action-sets competing with the Tikopian canoe-repair party for the timber or for members or even for honour. On the other hand, competition for such scarce resources is the raison d'être for the structure and action of the Sicilian coalitions.

FACTIONS

Factions have attracted more attention from anthropologists than any other form of coalition. But it is only really since the 1950s that they have become the subject of serious study.[24] The reasons for this have been touched on in the first chapter: until recently social scientists, at least social anthropologists and sociologists, were concerned primarily with the analysis of enduring relations, corporate groups. Coalitions and factions in particular, patently do not fit into this concept of the subject matter of the social sciences. Factions have in fact been described in all parts of the world, although the most numerous and detailed descriptions have come from India.[25] They are in fact forms of social organization that are basic to any political process. The structural characteristics of these coalitions and the problems of their leaders form the subject of this section. First, however, it is important to be clear about just what factions are.[26]

By faction I mean a coalition of persons (followers) recruited personally according to structurally diverse principles by or on behalf of a person in conflict with another person or persons, with whom they were formerly united, over honour and/or control over resources. The central focus of the faction is the person who has recruited it, who may also be described as the leader. The ties by which the leader recruits a following are diverse. They may range from kinship to neighbourhood; from economic partnership to the old school tie. They are usually personal links, though sometimes some followers in their turn will also mobilize the support of members of their own networks. The links with the leader may thus range from single-stranded transactional relations, to many-stranded moral relations.[27] This is clearly indicated in the following example of Maltese factions.

The story of the origin and development of the festa factions in Hal-Farrug is in many respects similar to the accounts of the rise of factions elsewhere. The conflict between the partisans of St. Joseph and St. Martin originated almost a hundred years ago. Before 1878 there were no factions in the village; everyone co-operated in the celebration of the feast of St. Martin, the patron of the parish. By all accounts the annual festa was a humble one, and lasted only one day. This period is described as an idyllic time, a sort of mythical period during which the village was happy and united. Much of the organization of parish affairs, including the celebration of the patron, appears to have been in the hands of a clique of influential persons. This often happens if the parish priest is weak. But in 1878 a new parish priest arrived and the scene began to change. Dun Guzepp, the new priest, was young and strong-minded. He was determined to wrest control over local affairs from the establishment clique. He began to create a rival force. Moreover, as he was from a village where there was a strong devotion to St. Joseph, he first established a confraternity dedicated to his namesake. He thus began to enrol followers in a formal moral association under his direct leadership. This gave him a considerable hold over his followers. The first feast in honour of St. Joseph was celebrated in October 1878 to mark the formal establishment of the new confraternity. Although the new secondary feast was at first a simple affair, it and the titular feast grew rapidly during the next few years. In 1880 the new confraternity dedicated an altar in the church to its patron. By 1886 some persons were beginning to grumble about having to pay for another feast. There was a feeling of 'you collect for your feast, and we'll collect for ours'.

In 1888 an incident occurred which changed the course of the rivalry between the supporters of the two saints, which until then appears to have been rather mild, as most people celebrated both saints. Dun Guzepp, who was the financial administrator of the parish church, tried to increase the rent on some of the local property it owned. There was an outcry. Some persons went to the bishop to complain. Not only had Dun Guzepp been diverting parish funds collected for other

o

purposes to buy new street decorations for the feast of St. Joseph, they protested, but he was now raising rents on church property to continue this work! The complaints resulted in an investigation, following which the administration of the parish church was taken from Dun Guzepp and given to a prominent member of the village who favoured St. Martin. This was an important loss of power and, in this poor living, a serious loss of revenue, for the administrator receives a commission on all fiscal transactions. The parish priest had lost the round to the local establishment which traditionally organized the celebration of St. Martin. This defeat, not surprisingly, infuriated Dun Guzepp. From that day onward, according to the accounts I heard, he threw his full support openly behind the feast of St. Joseph, and in so doing divided the village openly into opposing factions, forcing all persons to choose sides. He eventually built up the feast of St. Joseph to a scale that rivalled and eventually surpassed the celebration of St. Martin, which continued to be organized by the village establishment. He recruited his following—or rather the followers of St. Joseph!—not surprisingly from the anti-establishment elements in the village: the uninfluential, the poorer families and, so several informants indicated, many young men. Though he is reported to have pressured some into joining, most came willingly. Through the new cult they could gain offices and perform functions which hitherto had been monopolized by the circle of the village elite who had surrounded the former parish priest. Today the supporters of St. Joseph still occupy the lower rungs of the local prestige ladder.

This somewhat brief account of the establishment of the festa partiti in Farrug will be expanded in chapter 8. Nonetheless it is clear that rivalry is basic to the existence of a faction, for a faction supports a person engaged in a hostile competition for honour or resources. The conflict is thus political. The prizes for which they compete may also include access to the 'truth' (a form of power) and hence be ideological, as in a religious group or church which is then converted into a political arena.[28] Moreover, factions compete with other coalitions for the same prizes. Though the conflicting units are thus functionally equivalent in the sense that they compete for the same prizes, they may be unequal in terms of organization and size and have access to different resources, and thus employ different strategies. This will be made clearer in the following chapter when 'establishment' and 'opposition' conflict groups are discussed. Finally, factions are conflicting units formed within a larger encapsulating social entity such as a village, association or even another coalition, which had previously been united.

The structural characteristics of factions differ. There may be variations in the multiplexity and density of the network of relations within the factions. The area around the leader may be more closely connected. He may be tied to a number of persons—his brothers, for example—by multiplex ties. These persons with him form the core of the faction. The core/follower ratio is an important structural variable.[29] Where there is a strong core, the faction often acquires a number of corporate trappings. Among the most important is the permanence of the group, for if the relation between the members of the core is many-stranded and based on moral (ideological) factors as well as transactional ones, they may stay together longer. The longer the faction remains united, the more corporate characteristics it acquires. These may include a common ideology, property, and bureaucratic organization. These in turn lead to and follow from persistence in time. The relative strength of the leader is another important variable. This varies according to the importance of his own resources relative to those of his followers. Where he is strong he can direct the conflict of the group more accurately.

There are several factors which have a bearing upon the structure, evolution, number and strategy of factions. I have called these the problems of management and new resources.

The first is an internal problem and the second derives from the environment in which the factions operate.

A faction leader desires to win. To do this he must be able to manoeuvre his available resources more effectively than his rivals. One of his most important resources is the size of his following and his control over their actions. These provide him with a management problem.[30] He must build up as large a following as possible with the minimum expenditure of his limited resources. Moreover, the number of followers he can recruit on a purely transactional basis is limited. As he maintains personal links with each of his followers and these are structurally diverse, he is forced to spend much of his time and energy (finite resources) on servicing these links in order to keep his followers tied to him. There is thus an upper limit to the number of followers he can keep tied to him given his available resources. The longer the conflict remains unresolved, the longer the faction remains in being and the more resources the leader must expend, thus the poorer in resources he becomes and the more difficult he finds it to satisfy his followers. Moreover, the longer his followers remain mobilized (that is, linked actively to him) the greater is the likelihood that they will establish contact with each other independently of him. Once they start comparing their benefits from the leader, they may discover these to be unequal. The leader must then spend more time acting as a judge in conflicts between followers competing for his limited resources. If he is not successful in this role of judge, discontent may begin to form. Discontented members may switch allegiance to a rival faction leader, or unite in a coalition to challenge their own leader. Discontent thus weakens the hold a leader has on his followers.

There are at least two ways in which any leader can expand the size of his following beyond the limit imposed by his finite resources. The first is by introducing an ideology; the second by establishing what we may call a bureaucracy.[31] Dun Guzepp did both. Ideology can, of course, be the cause of conflict. There is often faction forming along ideological lines in churches, sects and political parties. But ideology can also be manipulated. By introducing an ideological or moral content to the relationship that he has with a follower, a leader establishes an extra hold over him. He can do this by giving his following a collective symbol and a sense of purpose by using causes, such as defending democracy and motherhood, helping the poor, or, as we saw in Malta, honouring a saint and performing a ritual. These are known and thus safe. Only if these fail will he attempt the riskier task of innovation. (Riskier, for if he fails he loses more credit than he would have had he tried a known—safe—symbol or technique.) By virtue of this ideological tie each follower is now linked to him by a many-stranded moral tie. He follows not only because he is going to get something from the leader (land, protection, brokerage, presents, a job) but because he and his leader are making the world safe for democracy, protecting mothers, or the poor, or honouring St. Joseph. They have a common cause. This not only gives the leader an extra hold over his follower; it also permits him to divide his resources over more followers. It introduces a sense of purpose to the following. They can now express their allegiance to the leader (or defend it against critics) in moral terms. When this happens, the following has a consciousness of kind, a moral purpose.

The second way for a leader to increase his following is by introducing forms of bureaucracy. He can, for example, attract as a follower a person who has his own following, and Dun Guzepp attracted at least one such big man. This increases the size of his following, but at the cost of less power over his followers. The first allegiance of these new recruits is usually to their own immediate leader. The leader's authority over the sub-leader is also limited, for the latter controls resources in his own right. These give him power. Finally, such sub-leaders are potential rivals for the leadership, as they are points of potential fission. As they gain power, the leadership is no longer exclusively in the hands of one person, but in those of a clique of persons, one of whom is *primus inter pares*, a first among equals.

A leader can also delegate various time-consuming tasks (recruitment, allocation of resources, judgement, mediation, brokerage, combat, ritual celebrations, etc.) to specialists in the manner of a corporation president who is assisted by vice-presidents in charge of sales, production, promotion, and so on. The leader is the co-ordinator. Dun Guzepp, for example, later delegated a number of his tasks in the parish to prominent followers. Ideally, co-ordination is a specialized task which only he is capable of performing. In practice these specialists learn each other's tasks and become rivals of the leader, even as vice-presidents rise to topple a weakening corporation president.

The most efficient solution to the management problem is to introduce an ideology and a specialized bureaucracy. This is one way political parties come into being. But with this solution, however, there is always the danger of the means becoming the end. That is, the group rather than the leader makes the first claim upon the loyalty of its members. Rivals then challenge the leader and defend their right to do so by claiming it is for the good of the group.

In a relatively stable situation (i.e. where the environment of the factions remains constant) if the factional conflict persists, the coalitions will become increasingly structured. The factions may thus, with time, become permanent competing structural units which are not leader centred, but group centred. This in fact happened to the festa factions discussed above. Their transformation will be discussed in greater detail in the following chapter.

The availability of new resources in the environment may also seriously affect the intensity of conflict, the structure, the permanence and even the number of factions. I have in mind resources of two sorts. The first are new techniques for fighting or attacking a rival or recruiting followers, such as a

new ideology, source of employment, funds. The second are
new prizes for which persons (the leaders) compete, such as
political or administrative office, a job which confers honour
and power. They are of course not unrelated, for the new
means that a leader uses to bind his followers, become the
prizes for which the latter compete. Many writers dealing
with factions have attempted—though not very systematically
—to relate increases in factional conflict to social change.[32]
In situations of social change, however, there is an increase
of factionalism because there is an increase of new resources.

First of all, new resources create conditions of uncertainty:
Neither the first party to use a new technique or strategy nor
its rival are fully aware of how to use it or how to combat it.
This very often leads to overcommitment of other resources
and a rapid elimination of the rival or, if the technique back-
fires, the user. By elimination here I mean dissolution of the
faction or its transformation into a group of another structural order that is no longer a faction. The evolutionary cycle
of the coalition is thus accelerated. Secondly, the introduction
of new political and religious ideologies and systems not only
provide new moral symbols for antagonists to use; they often
also provide new spoils. Thirdly, new spoils, such as elected
office, very often cannot be exploited successfully by existing
corporate groups (such as lineages) which are not flexible
enough. Members can be subverted by factional leaders and
so destroy the political capacity of a corporate group such as
a lineage that because of rigid membership rules, cannot
expand rapidly enough to compete for the new prizes.[33]
Finally, the very introduction of new resources divides
people into two camps: those who see them as desirable and
useful, and those who regard them as a threat to their traditional moral order and/or their political or economic positions. Hence so many authors have pointed to the presence
of 'conservative' and 'progressive' (or modern) factions.[34]

A faction thus has a single leader and a clear common goal.
It does not necessarily have an internal specialization,

although it may acquire it. There are no clear-cut recruitment rules, for as has been suggested, the means by which persons are bound to a faction leader differ considerably. As with other coalitions, it is often difficult to speak of clearly demarcated boundaries. In the periphery there are a number of members about whom the leader cannot be sure. While they proclaim allegiance to him, they may do the same to his rival. While all faction supporters are linked directly to the leader or to one of the clique (core) around him, they are not necessarily in touch with each other. The level of density or adjacency is low or absent. Finally, faction members do not usually share behavioural norms with all other members of the faction, either acting in factional context or outside it, although in the case of the 'moral' Maltese festa factions, they may.

DISCUSSION

The features of coalitions touched on in the introduction have proven useful analytical guidelines. All the coalitions examined except the clique had a centrality of focus in the form of a central co-ordinator or leader. Although in objective terms Herman, the leader of my Army clique, can conceivably be considered as the central figure, there are examples in the literature of cliques without a clear central focus consisting of a single person. On the other hand all coalitions display a distinction between a core of persons who meet more often and peripheral members. Coalitions thus display a concentric pattern. The relations between the core and the supporters is probably of some importance. Coalitions grow in vulnerability as the number of peripheral members increases in relation to the number of core members.

A clearly defined common goal apart from mutual affection or interest was present only in the action-set and the faction. The action-set is clearly goal-oriented and is defined in terms of the goal which the central figures in the action-set are pursuing, even though the motives of other members may reflect other goals. The goal of the faction is clearly to acquire scarce resources for which others are competing. This sometimes involves prestige and so may involve the destruction of resources commanded by a rival in order to reduce his prestige and honour.

Internal specialization is always present only in action-sets, where a certain division of labour and talents among the members appears to be necessary to achieve the goals. Specialization, however, can develop in any of the coalitions. As indicated in the discussion on factions, it may be a function of the size of the coalition: where the number of members grows beyond the ability of the leader to manage his relations with members personally, he may have to split up his tasks and introduce the help of specialists. Even in Doc's gang there was an indication that Mike and Danny assisted him to carry out some of his duties as leader. They accompanied younger members when they sought contact with government institutions and important persons outside the gang's territory.

None of the coalitions examined had clear-cut rules of recruitment which made it possible to indicate objectively all members. In all the coalitions, except perhaps the chain of dyadic coalitions built by Salvatore, there were one or more peripheral figures about whom it was rather difficult to decide objectively. Subjectively, however, each member has a very clear idea who is and who is not a member, although all the other members would probably not agree.

Only in the clique and the gang do all members appear to interact with all other members. That is, in the two cases examined, there appeared to be a hundred per cent density. All members are adjacent to all others. On the other hand, gangs can grow very speedily if they become fighting gangs. Some who join do not even know which gang they are joining: they are merely target-oriented. But clearly, even though all members of a clique, and at least the core group of a gang, maintain relations with each other, the transactional content, directional flow and frequency of interaction varies considerably between members. There seems to be a more even flow between the members of a clique than between the members of a faction, where the relations are more asymmetrical and the configuration can assume the pattern of a star with the leader at the centre.

The high density of cliques and gangs correlates with the development of behavioural norms *vis-à-vis* other members and a sense of common identity. These are the result of the intense interaction of the members. This in turn appears related to the length of time the coalition remains in being and its size: the longer it endures and the smaller it is, the greater the likelihood that the members will get to know each other and develop behavioural norms, and thus a sense of common identity.

Rival or competing units are always present in the environment of the faction. This was clearly a coalition in competition with other persons or coalitions. Aside from the central role the faction leader plays in building the coalition and recruiting members, leadership appears to be essential in bringing about the high degree of co-ordination a coalition requires to compete for scarce resources.

Finally it is important to underline a salient characteristic of coalitions: their dynamic quality. As mentional in discussing factions, coalitions come into being as new resources become available, for they provide a flexible means of exploiting them. Coalitions by their very nature are dynamic, for they are built up out of personal relations, which, as has been repeatedly stressed, are highly fluid. As the relations between the members of a coalition change, so the total configuration of their relations may thus change from a clique to a faction or to some other form of action-set, or vice-versa. Moreover, once some or all of the members achieve the ends for which they originally combined their resources, the coalition changes in character or disappears as its members drop away and withdraw their resources. Thus coalitions are dynamic. In fact, they provide much of the dynamism in social life, for they not only reflect change, they create it, and are continuously subject to it.

The coalition is a basic form of social organization, as basic as the family in that it organizes production, and protection from psychological as well as physical threats. There are other forms of association which also organize protection. These are kinship groups, voluntary associations and other corporate entities including the State. An essential question is therefore: Under which conditions do coalitions thrive? I suggest that predatory and protective alliances and economic coalitions such as Domenico's enterprise predominate where security cannot be guaranteed by the community at large. This is the case in fragmented plural societies or highly stratified societies, such as peasant societies, frontier areas and colonies, where a heterogeneity of values and great differences in relative power exist between social groups. Conversely, we can also ask: Where do corporate structures predominate? I suggest they will be found especially where the community as such can provide security and thus can protect individuals as well as their enterprises. Such protection is accorded in societies with a high level of integration, such as certain small-scale societies and some highly industrialized Western societies. There one finds a greater homogeneity of values and integration of institutions and smaller differences in relative power. This protection permits long-term planning and commitment of resources to an enterprise, whether political or productive. Hence, I suggest, the plethora of corporate groups in North and Western Europe and their paucity in Southern Europe.

With the acceptance of the legitimacy of an overarching set of norms, of a State ideology and the security it provides, the need to make and hold resources available for protection against rivals diminishes: the community protects the enterprise. Defensive or protective coalitions as such are superfluous. Resources thus freed can be invested in political and productive coalitions on a long-term basis. The investment of more resources, plus the guarantee by the community of the right of existence of such productive enterprises, assure that long-term planning by coalition partners is possible. The result is that members interact over a long period and invest more resources in the enterprise. Membership rules are formulated, action is co-ordinated and common behavioural norms and a sense of identity develop. Coalitions become corporate associations. They have acquired a cultural existence apart from the limited purpose of their members.

This analysis appears to be consistent with the ethnographic data for at least Europe. West, Central and Northern Europe have many voluntary associations and corporate groups. Business enterprises thrive and are apparently becoming larger as the State guarantees and regulates their rights. The extreme South of Europe is noted for its lack of voluntary associations. This phenomenon has been studied fairly systematically for Italy. Whereas in North and Central Italy there are many corporate associations which organize productive and other activities, such corporate associations are conspicuously absent in the South. There small coalitions, in which kinsmen play a predominant part, organize productive activities and provide protection.[35] In both Western Europe and in North and Central Italy there is a higher degree of integration and a greater participation of individuals in the Nation-State. People there regard themselves as citizens of the State, not merely as its subjects, as do people in the South of Italy. They regard the State as something to which they contribute, in which they participate, not as something apart from themselves, something that is imposed by others. In the North there is a greater interdependence of people on each other, and smaller differentials in their relative power. There, because the rule of law is accepted, the State can guarantee the interests and values of the entrepreneurs, in particular, and the members of the community at large, in general making possible the development of corporate associations. Coalitions predominate where this security is not found.[36] Such lack of security is not only characteristic for Southern Italy and Sicily, but is also found in large anonymous corporations. There, as Eric Wolf reminds us, persons for psychological protection form coalitions to counterbalance the formal demands of the organization, to render life within it more acceptable and more meaningful, and to try and make unpredictable situations more predictable.

8

Conflict as Process

The coalitions that people build to further their own interests are often short lived. Sometimes however they assume such organizational and ritual trappings that they become an accepted part of the social and cultural scenery. Most of the social organizations which we regard as permanent, such as clubs, churches, businesses and political parties began as coalitions. The development of the festa factions in Malta, to which reference has been made several times, illustrates the process by which institutions evolve from leader-follower coalitions and continue to change. The further analysis of this development provides insights into the course of such transformations and highlights certain patterns in the dynamic processes by which the social institutions, of which we form part, are modified.

But first some additional background information on Malta is necessary.

VILLAGE AND PARTITI IN MALTA

1. *The setting*

Malta's history has been greatly influenced by its small size and strategic location in the centre of the Mediterranean; for centuries it has been run as an island fortress.[1] All govern-

ment services are administered from Valletta by civil servants; there are no mayors, headmen, or councillors who
represent or administer the individual villages. The parliament is composed of elected members representing fairly
large districts. In the absence of secular authorities at the
village level, parish priests emerged as the traditional spokes-
men in both religious and secular affairs for the fervently
Roman Catholic population.

Though it is somewhat smaller than most Maltese villages,
the central features of Hal-Farrug are much the same as
those of its larger neighbours. Authority is distributed between the parish priest, the police, and a host of elected and
appointed office holders representing the interests of the
many formal and informal associations and groups in the
community. These persons form a circle around the parish
priest. Until parliamentary democracy was introduced, only
the parish priest and the police were able to back up their
commands with sanctions which compel respect, if not
obedience. Today the representatives of the political party in
power also form part of the local power elite.

Seven different parish priests have been assigned to the
village since the end of the war. Most were transferred after
running afoul of the village's many conflicting groups.

The people of Farrug occasionally remarked that there are
too many clubs and societies for the size of the village.[2] There
are two brass band clubs, a football club, and committees of
the two leading political parties. There are also two sections
of Catholic Action, a male branch of an ascetic lay society
and three confraternities (devotional brotherhoods), dedicated
to the Blessed Sacrament, the Holy Rosary, and St. Joseph.
Farrug seen as a village has no head, it owns no property, its
inhabitants never meet as a village. But seen as a parish it
has a formal leader in the parish priest, and it owns important
property: the parish church. The only time most of the village
meets as a group is in some religious or political context: for
worship, devotional processions and certain feasts or to listen

to an election speech. The most important occasion is the
annual *festa* of the patron saint. These festas provide the
chief public entertainment of the countryside, and the good
name of a village depends upon its ability to celebrate a
lavish feast. Thus most of the issues and decisions which
affect the village as a group have to do with religious matters.
These are usually decided by the parish priest and the clique
surrounding him (which includes the canvassers of the conservative Nationalist Party). They form the local establishment.

The oldest division in Farrug is that between the followers
or *partit*, of St. Martin, the patron saint of the village, and the
partit which supports St. Joseph. The latter is a secondary
saint as regards his official position in the parish, but one who
has come to assume an importance almost equal to that of the
titular saint in the social life of the community. A more recent
cleavage is that between the supporters of the Nationalist
Party and the Malta Labour Party.

2. *Partiti*

Each partit in Farrug has its own band club, the officers of
which are the leaders of the partit. The band clubs each have
elaborate premises, and arrange the organizational aspects of
the external feast of their patron saint. They are the nuclei of
the partiti. The religious confraternities are also aligned with
the partiti: the older confraternities of the Blessed Sacrament
and the Holy Rosary support St. Martin, while that of St.
Joseph celebrates the feast of its namesake. Several of the
partiti leaders are also officers of their respective confraternities. In addition to the formal members of its band club and
confraternities, each festa partit has a rank and file of men,
women and children who are not members of either, but who
still support the partit against its rival.

The festa partiti compete with each other over almost every
aspect of their festas, from the decoration of the streets and

the adornment of the statues to the number of guest bands and the quantity and quality of fireworks. Even the exact number of communicants, the number and size of candles on the altars and the amount of light bulbs illuminating the facade of the church enter into the competition. During 1960, the year I lived in the village, St. Martin's supporters spent over £1,400 on the centenary celebration of their patron, while their rivals spent almost £600 on the annual festa of St. Joseph. Most of the money was spent on illuminating the streets and the church, on guest bands and on raw materials for the fireworks, which were made in the village by the partisans.

The members of the partiti now rarely change sides, although this often occurred in the generation or so following their establishment, nearly a century ago. Today a person is either born into a partit, or he marries into it. Children normally support the feast of their parents, and an outsider marrying into the village generally supports that of his spouse. Children of mixed marriages support the feast of their favourite parent: boys normally follow their father and girls their mother. Marriages between members of rival partiti are regarded as undesirable, although they occasionally do take place. Thus 72 per cent of the marriages contracted within the village were intra-partit marriages. The high incidence of intra-partit marriages is probably due more to the class orientation of the partiti than their ritual rivalry. Like, in terms of status and power, tend to marry like.

Though each partit claims that it is larger than its opponent, the band clubs each have a membership of about eighty men, and I found that the village was fairly evenly divided between the two. 48 per cent of the men and women supported St. Martin, 42 per cent St. Joseph, and 10 per cent were uncommitted. Of those uncommitted, 63 per cent were outsiders who had married into the village.

There is strong correlation between occupational class and partit affiliation. In general, supporters of the titular saint

P

have more prestigeful occupations than their rivals.[3] As shown in the table below, 83 per cent of the village's professional and white-collar workers belong to the St. Martin partit, while only 38 per cent of those engaged in agriculture do so. In contrast 62 per cent of the village's full-time farmers are in the St. Joseph partit, while only 17 per cent of the professional and white-collar workers are.

Table 8.1 : Partit Affiliation and Occupational Class in Farrug : 1960

	Number	Percentage of Lab. Force	St. Martin	St. Joseph
			%	%
Professional and clerical	12	4	83	17
Service and skilled	115	39	55	45
Semi- and unskilled	124	42	48	52
Agricultural	45	15	38	62
Total	296	100		

We may also note that there is no territorial division between the partiti. There is a tendency, however, for more St. Martin supporters to live in the better residential area near the church, and for St. Joseph supporters to live in the less desirable sections of the village. This is a reflection of their occupational class, and their relative prestige and influence. Social mobility does not involve a change of partit, though it is often linked to a change of residence.

3. *Development of the partiti*

Some time after the events described in chapter 7 took place (pp. 192–4) each partit formed its own social club. According to St. Martin's supporters, their club grew out of a pre-existing band club, but that of their rivals was not established until after the first world war. They thus consider that they have seniority. St. Joseph partisans deny this. They maintain that both clubs came into being when the pre-existing club split around the turn of the century. Consequently they have equal seniority. Both clubs claim that the records crucial to the question of seniority were destroyed by enemy action during the last war. There is thus no documentary evidence which can prove or disprove either claim. This makes for deadlock whenever the issue of seniority is raised.

Dun Guzepp ruled the village for over fifty-six years. When he finally died in 1932, at the age of ninety, he was blind and deaf. Through a variety of means at the disposal of a parish priest he had succeeded in wooing or coercing three-fourths of the village into his partit. There are many stories about the old man and the methods he used to recruit supporters. Although many came willingly from the opposition categories, not all did so and genealogies show that the sons of one or two of the elite families joined him. One method he used, according to the accounts, was to make it difficult for people to marry unless they were, or became, members of the confraternity of St. Joseph.

When the old priest died, it was discovered that most of the festal finery of the parish church had been purchased in the name of the confraternity of St. Joseph. St. Martin supporters were in the humiliating position of having to beg their rivals for the use of the parish valuables in order to decorate the church for the feast of the parish patron. Moreover, while the old priest had firmly controlled the celebration of St. Martin within the church, thus limiting it as best he could, he had allowed the lay leaders of the St. Joseph partit a free hand in planning the religious side of their feast.

The burden of redressing the balance between the partiti fell upon the old priest's successors. There were many incidents between these priests and St. Joseph supporters, and on several occasions the priests had to send for police protection. In spite of increased pressure from the Church after 1935 to limit the extent of the secondary celebrations, the St. Joseph partit retained its numerical superiority as well as most of the church decorations during the 'thirties. It was not until 1942 for example that a shrewd parish priest succeeded in bringing the silver altar front out of the St. Joseph strong-room into that of the parish church, where it has remained ever since. Nonetheless, after the war the number of St. Joseph followers began to decline slowly and the St. Martin partit is now slightly larger than its rival. This is in marked contrast to most other villages divided by this type of rivalry, where the secondary partiti are larger than their rivals. This decline can largely be explained by the fact that the leader of the St. Joseph partit, a very capable school-teacher, has not lived in the village since Dun Guzepp's successor persuaded the school authorities in 1932, 'in the interest of peace in the village', to transfer him to another school. His monthly visits are now too infrequent to keep up the high level of activity which younger members need to remain attached to the club.

Most of the details of the competition for power between Dun Guzepp and the local establishment that gave rise to the hostile factions of the partisans of St. Martin and St. Joseph have long since been forgotten. The building materials he introduced to recruit and bind his followers to him (saint, confraternity and band club) provided a complex of structural features which have transformed the factions. Recruitment is now relatively unambiguous. Each partit has frequent meetings, a common ideology and a very definite sense of unity and purpose in its devotion to its patron saint. Moreover, each owns important property in the furnishings of its club, the costly street decorations for the annual festa and the instruments for its brass band. In short, in the ninety years of their existence, the factions have been transformed into ritual corporations.

4. *Why partiti?*

The ritualized conflict between established and opposition interests, between those who wield relatively more power and authority and those over whom they wield it, studied here in one village, is general in Malta. Today there are festa partiti or at least competing band clubs in nineteen of Malta's forty-four villages and towns.[4] Ten are divided by the type of rivalry described above. Another four are divided by rivalry between their constituent parishes. Five more are divided by rival band clubs not related to the cult of saints, though those in one village once were. Finally, weak festa partiti once existed in another seven villages, but as these were not yet aligned with formal associations such as band or social clubs, they were not well enough organized to resist the firm pressure the Church began to exert after 1935.

All festa partiti came into being during the fifty years or so after 1850. This was because a number of new ingredients were added to the inherent conflict between local establishment and opposition interests which has always existed in the villages, as indeed it exists everywhere authority is exercised. The first of these was a growing awareness on the part of persons in what I have called the opposition categories that they shared certain common characteristics. The ideology of a working-class movement, developed in the north of Europe, reached Malta during this period. Industrialization also began in Malta at this time. The workers movement propagated an egalitarian ideology of the brotherhood of all men. This ideology highlighted the unfavourable political and socio-economic position of the mass of the villagers. It also clashed with the ideological basis of the hierarchical structure of the Church, and the acceptance of the *status quo* that is preached as a means of attaining a better life in the next world. This ideological opposition to the established doctrine of the Church must have created dissatisfaction with the *status quo* and placed in sharp perspective the authoritarian power of the parish priest.

The Church attempted in 1870 to structure this movement in accordance with its own interests by declaring St. Joseph, already the patron of the working classes, the patron of the Universal Church. This introduced, or rather underlined, the availability of St. Joseph as a religious symbol for the workers. A working-man's organization could henceforth also be a cult group honouring St. Joseph. There are many signs that the devotion to St. Joseph was strong in Malta during the latter half of the last century. Four new confraternities were dedicated to him after 1850, and he was chosen as the patron of three new parish churches. Moreover, he is the patron of the secondary partiti in four parishes (including Farrug). Besides these, two other parishes had St. Joseph secondary partiti which succumbed to the increased pressure of the Church after 1935. Finally blue, the colour of the banner and ceremonial cape worn by members of the St. Joseph confraternity, is also the colour of most of the secondary partiti irrespective of whether or not St. Joseph is their patron. The colour of all establishment (titular) partiti is red. During demonstrations partisans display loyalty to their respective saints by waving or wearing red or blue flags, umbrellas, scarves, ties and even hair ribbons.

During this period a conception of social organization relatively new to Malta also gained currency, namely voluntary associations for laymen, and in particular, social clubs for 'gentlemen'. After the establishment in Valletta of the exclusive British Union Club in 1826, and the equally exclusive Casino Maltese in 1850, clubs of various kinds began to spring up in many villages. In most cases the introduction of such clubs, as happened in Farrug, gave greater organization to existing village factions by providing a corporate nucleus.

It is striking that everywhere partiti have arisen, they have done so in pairs: one establishment or titular partit, against one opposition or secondary partit. Several titular partiti split into two clubs. But all, with one very recent exception, have merged again. Whether opposition factions became permanent depended largely on whether they had developed the necessary corporate characteristics by the time the Church decided to eliminate them in 1935. All the case histories I collected of factions which did not develop into ritual corporations indicate the same dichotomy between what I have called establishment and opposition, and have involved no more than two factions.[5]

Finally, the striking similarity in the anti-church orientation of the secondary festa partiti, and the relatively low socio-economic status of their members indicate that the factions from which they grew arose out of what I have called the opposition category. By making use of the new ideological and organizational building materials which became available in the second half of the last century, the members were able to gain offices and perform ritual and organizational activities (in connexion with the celebration of feasts) which had hitherto been monopolized by the cliques of village notables surrounding the parish priests. Older informants from Farrug and other divided villages also noted that many young people were among the founders of the secondary partiti. In this we can see the universal resistance of the young to the authority of their elders. By becoming active in the new cults, they were able to assert their independence from the control of the older generation. In short, the secondary partiti grew out of factions which recruited their members from among people disgruntled with established authority. The cultural materials which the original leaders used to gain power and score points off their rivals have transformed the factions into ritual corporations, thus building firmly into the pattern of village ritual life the political conflict between establishment and opposition.

STRUCTURAL ASYMMETRY

Although locked in combat in the same arena, it is an error to regard competing festa partiti as being in balanced opposition, or even in agreement over the rules which regulate and channel their enterprise. They differ in almost every conceivable way: they are unlike in respect to resources, internal organization and strategy.

1. Resources

As already indicated, there is a difference in socio-economic status between the partiti. The members of the titular or establishment partit by and large tend to be professionals, white-collar workers and skilled labourers. The members of the secondary partit are often semi-skilled and unskilled labourers and farmers. Not surprisingly this difference is reflected in the respective influence they can command in their own communities. In Farrug, for example, twenty-three of the thirty key positions in Catholic Action, the football club and the village's Malta Labour Party Committee in 1961 were in the hands of St. Martin's supporters. Moreover, of the forty-one priests born in and resident in the seven villages divided by partiti that I studied closely during the same period, no less than thirty-three (80 per cent) were sons of families supporting the titular partiti, although in all but Farrug the secondary partiti were equal to or larger than the titular partiti.

Congruent with the higher status of its members, the St. Martin partit enjoys a position of pre-eminence as the organizer of the celebration of the official patron saint of the village. As such the partit enjoys a number of privileges, for its position is protected by the formal laws of the Church and by the sympathy which Church officials at all levels show to representatives of titular partiti. Because St. Martin and other titular partiti form part of the establishment of people and institutions holding positions of pre-eminence and power in Maltese society, they can draw on resources which are denied to their opponents. These give them an edge on their competitors in the various disputes in which they engage, and influence in no small measure the strategy the contestants must adopt.

The special resources of the titular partit are varied. To begin with its constituent confraternities and band club, because they were usually founded before those of its rival, enjoy seniority and thus occupy a more favoured place in the jealously guarded order of precedence in the various religious and secular processions.

There are also a number of Church regulations, enforced by the police (who must grant licences for all aspects of the external celebration of a festa) which favour the titular partiti. In 1935 the Church in Malta severely restricted the celebration of secondary saints in an attempt to control the rivalry between festa partiti and to reduce the scale of the secondary celebrations, which everywhere were surpassing the titular festas. Thus St. Joseph supporters, like those of opposition partiti everywhere on the island, were not allowed to decorate streets remote from the church, and were permitted to hold only two brass band programmes, though their rivals in 1960 held nine.[6]

Because of their superior status and influential positions in their profession and the various associations they control, the members of the titular partiti boast between them a more influential network of strategic contacts than do their rivals. They can gain indirect or direct access via their personal networks to important decision makers—such as police officers, members of government departments and, above all, various monsignori at the Archbishop's Curia—who decide the outcome of the various disputes with their rivals.

Finally, it is worth noting that the opinion of the influential city elite is generally opposed to the rivalry between the partiti in so many villages and parishes. They tend to blame the secondary partiti more than the titular partiti for the excesses.

Given their superior resources, it is not surprising that over the years the titular partiti have consolidated their positions and obtained control over a number of the most important symbols and rights. These include the position and participation of the club and the confraternity in church processions and at other functions, the routes over which these processions travel, and the possession of certain symbols and property and their use and display in the parish church. Any attempt to extend or to reduce these rights is resisted by the partit affected, which takes action to protect its interests by trying to influence the Church authorities who must make the final decisions. Not surprisingly the alignment of the symbols important to the people of Farrug is also congruent with the structural positions of the rival partiti. I have summarized a number of these below.

St. Martin	*St. Joseph*
Titular (establishment) partit	Secondary (opposition) partit
Statue stands on right hand (Evangel) side of church	Statue stands on left hand side of church
Main altar dedicated to St. Martin	Side altar dedicated to St. Joseph
Confraternity oldest	Confraternity youngest
Confraternity of Blessed Sacrament walks last in procession (high seniority)	Confraternity of St. Joseph walks first in procession (low seniority)
Partit colour red (banner of confraternity)	Partit colour blue (banner of confraternity)
Symbol star	Symbol eagle[7]

2. *Internal organization*

In their competition for their valued prizes, their unfavourable position *vis-à-vis* the establishment presents opposition partiti with particular problems. They are at a disadvantage; the titular partiti monopolize important resources. Deprived of the official support of the Church and police, it is not surprising that the secondary partit have strengthened their own internal organization to be able to counter the superior resources of their rivals.

Its position in opposition to Church policy has given most

secondary partiti a certain *esprit de corps* and unity of purpose that their rivals often lack. This has made St. Joseph better able to withstand the divisive effects of the political factions which have recently weakened St. Martin. It has also resulted in the emergence of stronger leaders. Secondary partiti are often united around a single professional class leader who can hold the partit together in the face of the attacks of its opponents, and argue intricate points of Canon Law with the Archbishop. As we have observed, St. Joseph has fewer professional class members who have the status and other qualifications necessary for leadership of an association.[8] Consequently competition in a secondary partit for the role of leader does not occur as often, and there is a longer tenure of office. In the partit of the titular saint, with its better-educated members, there are more men with the necessary qualities of leadership, and accordingly there is more competition for office and a high turnover of office holders. The competition both creates and results from internal factions which weaken the group. The president of the St. Joseph Band Club has led the St. Joseph partit more or less continuously since Dun Guzepp died forty years ago. He is also just about the only member of the partit with the educational qualifications and social position required of a leader. The key positions of the St. Martin Band Club, in contrast, constantly pass between about half a dozen educated persons. This divided leadership has weakened the club; and on one occasion it even split in two. The strong leadership and internal unity of the St. Joseph partit, plus the fact that it rarely presents claims that are not well founded, has enabled it to score many successes in spite of its apparently unfavourable position.

3. Strategy

The structural position of each partit in relation to important resources influences the kind of pressure that it can bring to bear upon the Church. As noted, the Church seeks to build up the celebrations of the titular partiti at the expense of the secondary ones. St. Martin thus has access to important resources denied to St. Joseph. Hence St. Martin can negotiate from a strong position: its ultimate sanction is refusal to participate in the feast of the village patron, an event which the Church is anxious to see celebrated with pomp. Secondary partiti, on the other hand, are inherently opposed to the Church in matters of festa policy. They try to increase the scale of their feasts by introducing new rules, while the Church tries to reduce them. St. Joseph thus does not dare to cancel its feast for fear that the Church would accuse it of making trouble and suppress the festa, as it has done to secondary festas in several parishes.

In short, the strategy of the St. Joseph partit is to attack the vested interests and established position of the St. Martin partit. The latter, secure in its most favoured position, is primarily concerned with defending its rights and privileges against the threats of its rival. The establishment partit thus defends the *status quo* while the opposition attacks it.

CONFLICT

As noted, the disputes between the partiti concern matters which affect their precedence and ability to display devotion to their saints. The course which such disputes take is highly formalized. They usually begin when the St. Joseph partit petitions the Parish Priest for a new privilege. St. Martin leaders then try to check their rivals by threatening to cancel their feast. At this point the Parish Priest passes the dispute up to the Archbishop's Curia for judgement. Both sides then use all the influence they can in order to obtain a decision favourable to them. If the decision is favourable to St. Martin, the dispute usually ends quickly, for St. Joseph's partisans cannot threaten to cancel their feast. But if the decision is favourable to St. Joseph and his followers, St. Martin's

partisans refuse to hold their feast for a year or so, or until
they can wring some concession from the Parish Priest or the
Archbishop. After that a new dispute arises over some other
issue, and the process starts over again.

From 1952 to 1954 there was trouble over the right of the
St. Joseph procession to pass along a street over which St.
Martin claimed exclusive rights. When the new Parish Priest
backed St. Joseph, St. Martin followers not only refused to
celebrate their feast, they also exploded a huge home-made
firework under the unfortunate cleric's house. Relations were
restored when the Archbishop transferred the priest (at the
latter's urgent request) and modified the St. Joseph procession
route. In 1956 the St. Martin band club refused to celebrate
its festa because the St. Joseph confraternity had been given
permission to renew two of the bunches of artificial flowers
which stand on the secondary saint's altar. The following
year the St. Joseph band refused to play at the installation
ceremony of the new Parish Priest because the Archbishop
had denied the St. Joseph confraternity permission to hang a
new picture over the altar of its saint. In 1960 the Parish
Priest infuriated St. Joseph followers when he did not allow
the partit to participate in the centenary festa for St. Martin.
The poor man's hands were tied, for St. Martin supporters
refused to have anything to do with the festa if their rivals
took part in it. Moreover, he knew that they only wished to
participate in the centenary in order to sabotage it. Later in
1960 there was also a sharp dispute over which band was to
have precedence at the installation ceremony of the new
Parish Priest (i.e. the right to escort him to his house from the
church). They could not agree, so neither played.[9]

In 1968 St. Martin partisans boycotted the Parish Priest's
fund raising fair because he refused them permission to build
a new niche to house their patron atop his enormous new
pedestal. Moreover, the St. Joseph's partit has been manoeuvring for several years now to obtain permission to build a
beautiful new pedestal for its patron.

So far only the more important clashes between the partiti have been discussed. During the course of a year, numerous fund-raising fairs run by the band clubs are also occasions on which the village divides along festa partit lines. While supporters of the partit running the fair flock to it, their rivals either stage their own fair or, usually, they hire several buses and leave the village for a picnic or a pilgrimage to some shrine of their saint. Rivalry runs highest, of course, during the festas. Then many policemen are required to keep the jeering and abusive rivals—men, women, and children—from coming to blows.

Although most of the disputes at the village level concern small concessions which the Parish Priest or the Archbishop have in their power to bestow upon the secondary saint, the secondary partiti very often challenge specific rules. Thus in the dispute in 1960 over precedence at the installation ceremony of the new Parish Priest, St. Joseph partisans categorically denied their rivals' claim to precedence based on their alleged seniority as well as their past performances as the only functioning band in the village during the preceding five or six years.

It is also interesting to note that the secondary festa partiti have united in an association (which is opposed by the association of titular partiti) to bring pressure on the Archbishop as well as on the Vatican to modify the provisions of the 1935 regulations reducing the scale of secondary celebrations in Malta.

It is a misconception therefore to think that the secondary festa partiti agree with these regulations, with the 'rules of the game', because they see them as legitimate or morally necessary. They do not agree with the rules, but they are obliged to accept them because they are constrained by the police as well as the sanctions of the Church, which can cancel feasts and interdict leaders. Hence I suggest it would be an error to regard this sort of rivalry, as some do, as competition according to an agreed set of rules which express ultimate and publicly accepted values.[10] There is compliance with rules, not because they are regarded as legitimate or are mutually agreed upon, but rather because they are backed by the sanctions of Church and State. These are resources to which the establishment and not the opposition has access. Secondary partiti, both individually, and collectively through their association, seek to change the rules so that they can expand the celebration of their feasts.

PROCESS

There is a process of continual competition between the two festa partiti. Each strives for power and honour. This drive for power causes changes: each side continually seeks to bend, modify and innovate laws and customs that restrict its behaviour in a way which benefits itself rather than its rival. It has been observed that the establishment partit can mobilize greater resources and is supported by a body of laws enforced both by religious and secular authorities. Its primary strategy is defensive: for it appeals to precedent and law and can obtain protection from official bodies such as Church and government. It defends the *status quo*, from which it derives its pre-eminent position. Its philosophy is essentially conservative in the sense of conserving its pre-eminence. In contrast, the opposition partit, given the handicaps under which it must compete and manoeuvre for changes in the restrictions which limit its activities, is forced to use different strategies. Not only is it more apt to place its organizational house in order, it is also more likely to innovate, to develop new techniques, new ideas, new strategies which will help it modify the *status quo* in its favour. Its outlook may be called progressive, in the neutral sense of favouring change or reform.

In every conflict situation there is an asymmetrical relationship between those with more and less power. Those with less power, the opposition, are obliged by the situation to innovate and change things in order to score off their rivals. In every conflict consequently there is a built in dynamism which can lead to change, for the competitors seek more power. Thus the seeds of change are present in every conflict situation. This does not mean of course that the impetus for change is always successful, or that it always comes from the opposition. The establishment may be able to block for extended periods attempts to reduce its superior power. Moreover, new restrictive policies may be thought up and imposed by the establishment, although these will no doubt be provoked by the action of the opposition. This is in fact what took place in Malta. We have seen how the opposition faction in Hal-Farrug by using the building materials available in the environment built the conflict between it and the establishment faction into the cultural scenery of the village. The same happened in other villages. Thus through the action of local opposition factions throughout the island, institutional changes took place. But because the conflict continued to escalate, the Church in 1935 took the measures which have been discussed. I suspect (but at present have no data to prove) that the increase in the scale of the secondary feasts just prior to 1935 was also related to the political conflict which raged at the national level during the 1920s and early 1930s between the Church supported, pro-Italian Nationalist Party and the anti-clerical, pro-English Constitutional Party. In 1933 the British dismissed the Nationalist government for unconstitutionally trying to re-establish the primacy of Italian in the schools and civil service. Following the closure of the Legislative Assembly, the arena at the national level, more political resources were channelled to the still open parish arenas, and the level of opposition to the Church favoured titular *partiti* increased accordingly. In 1935, as noted, the Church took steps to clip the wings of its increasingly active parish level opponents by introducing restrictive new rules. The opposition *partiti* were bitter but they were obliged to obey owing to the resources their rivals controlled. As in most if not all political contests, might is right. (Italians have a saying which summarizes this neatly: *Chi commanda fa la legge.* He who commands makes the law.)

These measures in turn provided fresh fuel for the conflict between establishment and opposition: secondary partiti became increasingly opposed to the restrictive policies of the Church. Their constant opposition to the edicts of the Church regarding these matters accented the anti-clerical tendencies of the secondary partiti. The action of the Church to restrict the conflict, and thus to save the position of the establishment partiti, provided an issue for conflict which further served to erode respect for the authority of the Church and, I suggest, kept alive and thus helped pave the way for the anti-clerical orientation of the Malta Labour Party.[11]

Throughout the ninety years of their existence the power relations between the festa partiti as well as their internal structure has been changing. An important impetus for change is the competition between them. At the same time other processes are taking place in Maltese society which also influence them. The more recent conflict between the Church and the Malta Labour Party has also had repercussions on the level of conflict between festa partiti, as the Labour Party has made a conscious effort to restrict the scale of festivities. It has encouraged its members to boycott the celebration of feasts, which it regards as a waste of time and money that can better be spent upon the development of the country. This has created within the villages a growing category of persons who take no part in the competition. Moreover, many of the younger members of the clergy have also tried to modify the competition. The increasing welfare of Malta, brought about by a boom in the tourist and building sectors of the economy and the growing number of manufacturing industries, is drawing people away from the village. This particularly affects the youth. Young men who formerly played in the band, made fireworks and decorated the streets for the festa now have money in their pockets, often a car at their disposal

Q

and prefer to spend their free time with the increasingly emancipated girls at the cinema or the beach. They no longer spend their free time celebrating the feasts or loafing in the band clubs. Increasingly fewer men are enrolling in the confraternities, which, as we saw, are of critical importance to the partiti. Thus the internal structure of and the relations between the competing groups in Maltese villages are continually changing. This is caused partly by the internal dynamics of such conflict, and partly by the processes taking place in the wider society in which, as it were, these conflicting groups are embedded.

ESTABLISHMENT AND OPPOSITION IN NATIONAL
POLITICS

The organization and conflict between establishment and opposition partiti at the village level strongly resembles the differences between the Malta Labour Party and the Nationalist Party at the national level.

The Nationalist Party of Malta may be viewed as the establishment party, and the Malta Labour Party as the opposition party. The Nationalist Party is the older of the two. It has been in power many more times than its rival and for longer periods. It has been supported by the Church, and it has been the party of the professional classes—the lawyers, doctors, notaries and higher civil servants—who through their networks of occupational relations tie their clients to the party. Its leadership is diffuse. Although it has an official leader, it is a party composed of professional men, each of whom has his own private political machine. Thus one of its organizational problems is the clash between the interest its leading figures have in retaining their patronage based political machines, and the desirability of creating a tight party structure. As the Nationalist Party has had access to government resources for prolonged periods and it has been able to use these for patronage: government jobs, contracts, licences and other concessions have been systematically used to keep the wheels of the many Nationalist political machines well oiled. Both its internal as well as its foreign policy have been markedly conservative. It has supported the Church, been extremely reluctant to effect any major changes or put an end to a number of serious social problems, such as the housing shortage, and in general has let local developments take their own course. Its foreign policy has been to maintain Malta's traditional alliance with the Western powers in NATO through the mediation of Great Britain. In short, both at home and abroad its policy has been to maintain the *status quo.*

The Malta Labour Party in its present form came into being in 1949 as a coalition led by Dom Mintoff, then a former Minister of Public Works and Reconstruction. Almost at once Mintoff began to reorganize the party and established a tightly structured system of village clubs and regional councils. In short, he set about putting the party's organizational house in order and built up the image of the party with himself as its chief symbol. Henceforth allegiance was not to be to individual politicians and their personal machines, but to the party itself and its leader. This was highly beneficial to the party. There were few members of the Labour Party (in contrast to the Nationalist Party) whose occupational status enabled them to recruit voters from their professional clientele. This also meant fewer competing 'big men'. The Labour Party is a workers' party and its ideology reflects this as do its members, most of whom are recruited from among skilled and unskilled workers as well as the young. Moreover the party made a conscious effort to recruit women into its formal organization, and for a number of years there have been two MLP women members of parliament, one of whom is a cabinet minister. There are no Nationalist female members of parliament.

Its ideological basis has been reflected in its internal and external policy. The party has been strongly anti-clerical and reformist. The first period of government under Mintoff between 1955 and 1958 was characterized by a flurry of social legislation, increased and liberalized educational facilities, and a damming of patronage. Its foreign policy has also been highly reformist. After an initial flirtation with a plan to link Malta with Great Britain along the lines of the union with Northern Ireland, it struck out for independence and neutrality from the NATO bloc. This policy has been set forth by the Labour Party since its victory at the polls in June 1971. The policy both domestic and foreign of the Malta Labour Party may be characterized as reformist and socialist, as progressive (in the sense of favouring change) and antiestablishment. This may be contrasted to the conservative laissez-faire policy of the Nationalist Party.[12]

CONCLUSION

At one time I thought the resemblance between the asymmetrical structure and activity of establishment and opposition parties at the national and parish levels in Malta a coincidence. I no longer do so, for the resemblance is too marked and the explanation too similar. I now believe that they are manifestations of a general pattern. All conflict groups, I should like to argue, are always asymmetrical rather than symmetrical or balanced.[13]

In all societies that have been studied there is a competition for scarce and valued resources. These resources may range from yams, beautiful women and livestock, through knowledge, ritual symbols and influential friends, to land, oil wells and share capital. For many reasons some people control more resources than others do. This enables them to influence the actions of others, if need be, against their wishes. They are obeyed because they wield more power. With this they are able to control or occupy all or most of the offices from which authority can be exercised. These persons form the local 'establishment'. Ranged against them are less powerful persons who do not exercise or share in the exercise of authority. These often include those disgruntled with the way in which the 'establishment' administers the resources it controls, the poor, the failures, the oppressed, the weak, the eccentrics, the drop-outs, the social misfits and, often, the young. These form an anti-establishment or 'opposition' category. These are social categories from which coalitions may be recruited.

Now the more powerful rivals of the establishment recruit support from the social category I have labeled the 'opposition'. Often opposition coalitions unite to exercise concerted opposition against the establishment, which in turn is forced to consolidate its position to protect and advance its interests. The result of this manoeuvring is most often two rather than three or more coalitions or alliances. Either the weaker ones coalesce to be able to compete with the strongest, or the strongest is able to subvert the weakest coalition member to achieve a clear dominance over its chief rival. There are many combinations possible but they usually lead to the formation of two competing and asymmetric coalitions. Thus it is that factions and other conflict groups appear most often in pairs.[14]

The resources of the establishment and the opposition and the way in which they use them differ considerably. The establishment defends tradition. It has a vested interest in maintaining the *status quo*. Tradition provides the charter for its existence. It claims to interpret the norms and defend the moral order. Because it controls most of the formal offices, it can often make use of legally sanctioned physical force, public funds, office and ritual to recruit followers and to defend itself. Moreover, because it defines, defends and interprets tradition and the moral order and has more resources at its disposal than its rivals, it is able to monopolize the most important ideological symbols. In short, the establishment will usually be conservative.

The opposition does not have direct access to these resources. It must attack and challenge to obtain them or to modify the use to which the establishment can put its super-ordinate position. Given its unfavourable position regarding the resources the establishment monopolizes, an opposition leader's problem is how to unseat the establishment from its superior position. One way he can do this is by recruiting more followers. Since he does not have access to the resources controlled by the establishment leader, and thus cannot recruit as many followers through patronage, he is more likely to be attracted by new techniques and ideologies, which he may also develop himself, to meet the anti-establishment interests of his potential followers. Besides using new ideologies and symbols to bind his followers to him and his cause, he will also try to fashion his coalition or party into a better, more tightly organized instrument.[15] Only in this way can he hope to win from his strategically less favourable position: an attacking party needs a strong leadership and a streamlined organization. For these reasons the opposition coalition usually becomes the progressive party. This is not only because it seeks to win a surprise victory over its rival through using a new strategy. By merely *being* progressive it challenges the conservatives. For the same reason it adopts ideologies and symbols which are rivals to those adopted by the conservative establishment coalition.[16]

The competing coalitions may become institutionalized through the introduction of various corporate trappings—such as offices, property, permanent symbols, and so on. The long-term processes taking place and the cultural building materials available explain the particular form the conflict between establishment and opposition assumes. But though the rival coalitions may become institutionalized, they are not static: their relations remain dynamic. This dynamism derives from the attempt of the weaker to obtain more power and so topple its opponent. The opposition can only obtain power through change. The impulse to change is thus ever present in conflict situations. The notion that competing political groups are evenly matched or that certain types of conflict inevitably lead to stability and the preservation of the social order is an illusion, a projection of wishful thinking on sociological analysis. It has, I suggest, hampered our understanding of politics as well as of social change. The impetus to change is always present in the unequal relations between those who command more power and their rivals who seek more power, in the asymmetry between establishment and opposition. Since this inequality is present in all societies, the conclusion must be, therefore, that the seeds of change are present in all societies and social equilibrium does not, and cannot, exist.[17]

This final chapter has examined the origins of certain conflicts in Malta, the form rival coalitions assume, the course the rivalry takes and the strategy of the contestants. It demonstrated that these aspects of conflicts form a pattern. This pattern cannot be made intelligible except in the context of the interests and actions of individual participants in the conflict and in conjunction with the long-term processes in which it is embedded. The history of the development of various conflict groups in Malta has thus demonstrated the thesis of this book. Just as Dun Guzepp, motivated partly by a desire for recognition, established a religious brotherhood to honour his namesake with the assistance of those who stood to benefit from his action, and this in turn grew into a party with an unplanned internal dynamism of its own, so people always and everywhere transact with each other to gain the greatest possible benefit for themselves in their quest for scarce and valued ends. This competition modifies their relationships with others. Because these relations form part of a network or a pattern that is also modified, the total configuration has an inherent dynamism. This inherent movement, called social change, is thus generated by people acting in terms of their own interests, whatever they may be.

This self-interested action is more than just an egoistic striving for profit at the expense of others. It is rather the attempt of people who are mutually interdependent to be able to live the kind of lives they wish. Some wish to achieve prestige and fame. Others prefer inconspicuously to wield power. Yet others prefer to be left alone to pursue a quiet life. Many also wish to be able to devote themselves to helping the unfortunate and needy. And some, even today, merely wish for freedom from hunger, want and violence. These goals are not only provided by custom, they are also influenced by circumstance, ability and feasibility. Because people are mutually dependent upon each other, a person's own goals can never be achieved without helping and harming people, for the goals for which he strives—even that of just being left alone—are scarce and valued ends for which he must compete with others. Thus to achieve the freedom to define the situation so that it is most convenient for himself and those on whom he depends, a person must free himself from the constraints which prevent him from doing so. The constraints may be biological, physical or personal. They can consist of personal inability to cope with a situation or the superior power of a rival. They can also consist of the knowledge that the interests of those one loves and on whom one depends will be damaged if the goals are achieved.

In short, everywhere people compete with each other and search for allies to help them achieve their goals. People everywhere are thus engaged in politics, for they compete directly, via friends and friends-of-friends for valued scarce resources, for prizes which form the important goals of their lives. As we saw clearly in the case of the rival festa partiti, but also noticed in the dealings that Pietru, Cecil and others had with the members of the networks of relations of which they form part, the competition between those who have and those who want has a dynamism. Movement and change are inherent in all social relations.

Man, in order to emancipate himself from the constraints of his social, cultural and physical environment, attempts to bring about changes in the balance of power. Other persons, who benefit from the *status quo*, try to prevent such changes.

Change and resistance to it are thus inherently related. The rebellion of children against the regime of their parents, the revolt of students against an authoritarian university system, anti-clericalism, women's liberation, black power, peasant revolutions, as well as the resistance to these of persons and groups who have opposed interests are explainable in the same terms: the drive for freedom to do what one wishes, to be emancipated from the constraints which hamper the attainment of goals. Both social change and resistance to it are processes which display a definite pattern, and both stem from the same motive: a desire for a better life.

This book, by suggesting a framework for analysis of social behaviour which starts with interacting, mutually dependent people, attempts to provide insights into the social processes in which we all participate. Coalitions, groups, classes and institutions are composed of people who, in different ways, are bound to each other. Together they form the constantly shifting network of social relations that we call society.

Notes

Chapter 1: INTRODUCTION

1. Boissevain (1966b: 27–8).
2. Boissevain (1965, 1966a, 1969a, 1970a).
3. For example see Barth (1967); Elias (1970); Gouldner (1970); Harris (1968); Jarvie (1964); and Leach (1954), to mention but a few.
4. By explanation I mean being able to derive a statement describing what is to be explained from another statement (Jarvie 1964: 17).
5. Boissevain (1966a: 21).
6. For example in the case of the conflicting Nuer political sections given later, the members of the *Leng* segment motivated their decision to protect the *Thiang* by moralizing that they could not refuse to help sisters' sons. Because Evans-Pritchard does not comment on this exception to the rule that agnates should unite against outsiders, he implies that the *Leng* really helped the *Thiang* because they were their sisters' sons, and not, for example, because by giving them protection they gained a valuable ally and thus greatly increased their power.
7. This point of view, like most things, is not at all new. In a certain sense it is a continuation of the discussion Emile Durkheim carried on with Herbert Spencer at the turn of the century. Spencer in his *Principles of Sociology* had argued that the co-operation we call society is the product of individuals pursuing their own interests, thus forming a vast system of particular contracts. Durkheim, in *The Division of*

Labour in Society, maintained just the opposite. Co-operation, far from having produced society, necessarily supposes its existence. Individual action must be seen as a reflection of society: 'Because the individual is not sufficient unto himself, it is from society that he receives everything necessary to him, as it is for society that he works. . . He becomes accustomed to . . . regarding himself as part of a whole, the organ of an organism' (Durkheim 1964: 228). Both views are of course baldly overstated. Individuals do not only work for themselves, nor do they work only for others. Groups and institutions influence individual behaviour, just as interacting individuals can produce institutions. Nonetheless, Durkheim's onesided view of the superhuman, mystical force of society prevailed, and the useful complementary view which Spencer had argued was eclipsed, along with the promising theoretical views on social interaction of Simmel.

8. It might even be seen as the sociological equivalent of Zipf's Principle of Least Effort (1949), which is summarized as follows by Colin Cherry (1966: 103):

    'Zipf collected a large body of statistical data, referring principally to language, and attempted to show that this and other human activities are subject to a single overriding law, which he has called the Principle of Least Effort. Man is a goal-seeking organism; the whole of his striving, his manner of organizing tasks, the mental exertion involved—the paths along which he directs his actions, the whole means of attaining his ends, so Zipf would hold, is governed by a single dynamical law. . . Zipf is emphatic that the course of human activities, whether singly or collectively, need not minimize the total *work* required, physical or mental. . . At best we can but predict the *total likely* work involved, as judged by our past experience. Our estimate of the "probable average rate of work required" is what Zipf means by *effort*, and it is this, he says, which we minimize.'

9. Schneider, Schneider and Hansen (1972) give an excellent critique of the concept of informal organization. See also Boissevain (1968).

10. Elias (1970) demonstrates at great length the errors that result from examining individual and society separately. He regards, and I think rightly, the continuing separation of these two concepts as the greatest obstacle to sociological analysis.

11. These have been set out succinctly by Cohen (1968) and Dahrendorf (1959).
12. Cf. Dahrendorf (1959: 163). Cohen also notes that the models are not genuine alternatives: 'to say that a room is half-full is not to deny that it is half-empty' (Cohen 1968: 170).
13. Cuteleiro (1971: 151).
14. Cf. Harris (1968) and Gouldner (1970).
15. Radcliffe-Brown (1952: 11) and Evans-Pritchard (1940: 262).
16. Radcliffe-Brown (1950: 43).
17. Radcliffe-Brown (1952: 192).
18. These same objections have recently been set out forcefully and eloquently by others (cf. Van Velsen 1964 and 1967; Peters 1967; and Kapferer 1969) and would scarcely need repeating if they were receiving the attention they deserve. But there are still social scientists, both old and, alas, young, who continue to believe in the structural-functional model.
19. While 'it does not follow that behaviour always accords with values and may often be found to be in conflict with them, . . . *it always tends to conform to them*' (Evans-Pritchard 1940: 264–5. My italics).
20. Social anthropology, Evans-Pritchard writes: 'studies societies as moral, or symbolic, system and not as natural systems, . . . it is less interested in process than in design, and . . . it therefore seeks patterns and not laws, demonstrates consistency and not necessary relations between social activities, and interprets rather than explains' (Evans-Pritchard 1951a: 62). While he denies that he is interested in explanation, it is quite clear from his writings that he is attempting to do just that. His problem, along with other structuralists, is that design and pattern are processes, and interpretation involves explanation.
21. See the critique by Easton (1959) of attempts by anthropologists to study politics.
22. See Elias (1969: xxviii–xli) for a stimulating expansion of this argument.
23. Evans-Pritchard (1940: 144–5). My attention was drawn to this case by Nicholas (1966: 50–1).
24. Evans-Pritchard (1951: 8–12).
25. Evans-Pritchard (1951: 28). My italics.
26. Leach (1961a: 302).
27. Boissevain (1970b: 83).
28. Leach (1954 and 1961); Jarvie (1964).

29. Bailey (1963, 1969), Banton (1964), Cohen (1965) to mention but a few in addition to those mentioned in note 18.
30. See the contributions to Banton (1966).
31. Srinivas and Béteille (1964: 165); cf. Mitchell (1969: 9).
32. Barth (1966: 5).
33. Barth (1966: 2). Barth, who carried out some graduate work under Firth and Leach, seems to have been more influenced by the latter than he mentions. Though he indicates (1966: v) a certain affinity between his models and Leach's topological model (Leach 1961b), I think the influence is far greater. Compare, for example, the above quotations with the following:

    'The overall process of structural change comes about through the manipulation of these alternatives (inconsistencies in the scheme of values) as a means of social advancement. Every individual of a society, each in his own interest, endeavours to exploit the situation as he perceives it and in so doing the collectivity of individuals alters the structure of society itself' (Leach 1954: 8);
    and further,
    'The social structure which I talk about . . . is, in principle, a statistical notion. . . It is a by-product of the sum of many individual human actions of which the participants are neither wholly conscious nor wholly unaware. It is normal rather than normative . . .' (Leach 1961a: 300).
    Whatever the influence of Leach on Barth, their combined influence on my thinking has been of great importance, as have the insights I gained from Bailey's *Stratagems and Spoils* (1969).
34. I have received research funds from the British Colonial Social Science Research Council (Boissevain 1965a) and from the Canadian Royal Commission for Bilingualism and Biculturalism (Boissevain 1970a).
35. Gluckman (1968) and Paine (1967).
36. Boissevain (1968: 553). The exchange between Mitchell (1963, 1965) and Murdock (1964) over the concept of the kindred provides a similar example.
37. This is something which Kuhn (1970) surprisingly—for it should be obvious to anyone who is a member of a scientific community—grossly undervalues in his discussion of scientific revolutions.

Chapter 2: NETWORKS: INTERACTION AND STRUCTURE

1. In his introduction to *Social Networks in Urban Situations*, Mitchell (1969b) has provided a comprehensive, critical review of the variety of ways the concept of network has been used in sociological writings and other disciplines, especially mathematical graph theory. For this reason no attempt is made here to cover the same ground. As far as possible I shall use the same precise terminology that he and Barnes (1969) propose. Where my usage differs from theirs will be indicated. Whitten and Wolfe (n.d.) also provide an excellent recent review of the methods and problems of network analysis. Readers are strongly recommended to consult these, and the other contributions in Mitchell (1969). These complement the discussion presented here.
2. Cf. Robert Rapoport's perceptive remarks concerning the theoretical importance of the network concept in his review (1958) of Elizabeth Bott's pioneering *Family and Social Network* (1957), the theoretical significance of which was ignored by virtually all other reviewers.
3. Cf. Barth (1966: 4), who derives this notion from Homans (1958), later elaborated in greater detail in Homans (1961). See also Stebbins (1969).
4. This argument is set out in much greater detail in Blau (1964).
5. Barnes (1969).
6. Cf. Firth (1964: 36–7); Mitchell (1969b: 2); Reader (1964: 22).
7. For the notion of *exchange circuit* see Thoden van Velzen (1973), and for that of *partial network* Barnes (1969: 57). In contrast to Barnes (1969: 55–7) I use the term network to designate an actor- or situation-oriented, bounded universe, thus in the sense of a first order zone or a network segment (partial network) the members of which are known. Barnes prefers 'to use the term "network" only when some kind of social field is intended' (1969: 57) which may thus be unbounded. He designated personal (ego-centric) networks as primary or first order stars and zones. While there may be something to say for greater precision in terminology, these terms are too cumbersome to be able to compete with the already established metaphorical use of personal network.
8. Banton (1965: 29).
9. See chapter 8 below and Boissevain (1965a) for a discussion of such conflicts.

10. Kapferer (1969: 212), from whom I have borrowed this concept, defines the term exchange content as 'the overt elements of the transactions between individuals in a situation which constitute their interactions'. These situations will normally be determined by the role relations of the actor.
11. Exceptions are Niemeijer (1973) and Cubitt (1973).
12. Coalitions recruited for the attainment of a specific goal, Mayer (1965). See chapter 7 below.
13. Mitchell is explicit about this bias:
    'The personal network, as used in this symposium, exists situationally in the sense that the observer perceives only those links of the total set of potential links which are activated and being used by the actor at any moment, and which the observer considers significant for the problem he is interested in' (Mitchell 1969b: 26).
14. See Frankenberg (1966, especially chapter 11), for the notion of redundancy, which he derives from communication theory.
15. Mitchell (1969b: 18).
16. Based on Kapferer (1969: 226). The formula for the total number of possible relations is: $N (N-1) \frac{1}{2}$ where N represents the total number of persons. The number of persons is multiplied by $N-1$ to provide the total number of combinations with other persons, but excluding contacts of a person with himself. This is then divided by 2, because, though two persons are involved in each combination, they constitute but one relation.
17. The unwieldy term *degree* is part of the established technical vocabulary of graph theory. I have retained it as a gesture to interdisciplinary co-operation in spite of a strong personal inclination to use a term more readily understandable to the non-specialist. For a recent discussion of the applicability of the concept to sociological network analysis see Niemeijer (1973).
18. For a discussion of the concept of centrality, which derives from Bavelas (1949), the non-mathematical reader is referred to Klein (1956, chapter 4), which is probably the most lucid statement on the subject in the literature.
19. The centrality index of a in Diagram 2.7 is derived as follows:

$$C = \frac{\text{sum of shortest distances from every member to every other member}}{\text{sum of shortest distances from Ego to every other member}} =$$

sum of shortest distances from a (Ego) to every other member
$$= 1+1+1+2 = 5$$
sum of shortest distances from b (Ego) to every other member
$$= 1+1+2+3 = 7$$
sum of shortest distances from c (Ego) to every other member
$$= 1+1+2+3 = 7$$
sum of shortest distances from d (Ego) to every other member
$$= 1+2+2+1 = 6$$
sum of shortest distances from e (Ego) to every other member
$$= 1+2+3+3 = 9$$

sum of shortest distances from a (Ego) to every other member
$$= 1+1+1+2 = 5$$

$$\frac{34}{5} = 6.8$$

Similarly the centrality of $b = 4.8$, $c = 4.8$, $d = 5.8$, and $e = 3.9$.

20. See for example Leavitt (1951).
21. Klein (1956: 56).
22. Flament (1963: 50–2) discusses this index of centrality, which stems originally from Bavelas. He shows that it measures in fact the degree of automorphism of a graph. This result indicates that in fact the centrality of an individual depends on the way his structural position differs from others, while it is difficult to interpret its exact meaning. It seems necessary to develop some other index more easily interpretable in the future.
23. See Thoden van Velzen (1973) for a discussion of compartments.
24. This definition of cluster is based on Niemeijer (1973) who discusses the concept critically and provides a statistical instrument for isolating clusters without the arbitrariness of the method suggested by Barnes (1969: 64–6).
25. Keenan and Brett (1970). Mayer (1963) provides additional fascinating examples. Peter Brett in the *Nova* article also notes that playing widely differing roles can be very taxing and occasionally may lead to great mental stress.
26. Pons (1969: 207).
27. For a discussion of the useful distinction between emotional and instrumental friendship see Wolf (1966: 10–14) and Reina (1959).

Chapter 3: VALUES AND INTERACTION IN A CONFLICT SITUATION

1. This proposition is taken over partly from Kapferer (1969: 243), but amended to take into account the definition of the situation and hence the choice of values, and the moral crises into which some conflicts can plunge people. This last is an important element which has been left out of Kapferer's analysis, as the situation does not arise in the conflict he studied. The importance of a relation is determined not only by *past* investment in it, which can be quantified and which Kapferer discusses, but also by the expectation of *future* help from it. Kapferer does not consider this, nor can it easily be quantified objectively, as it is a subjective evaluation.
2. Kapferer (1969: 181–244).
3. Kapferer (1969: 191–3).
4. Kapferer (1969: 209).
5. Star multiplexity refers to the direct links of Abraham and Donald with the persons in their first order zones. Zone multiplexity refers to the links between these persons, excluding the direct links to Abraham and Donald. The indices for density and multiplexity are based on Kapferer (1969: 223, Table V). I calculated the indices for degree and centrality separately; they apply only to the *multiplex* relations in the cell room.

Chapter 4: ENVIRONMENT AND SOCIAL NETWORK

1. Bott (1957) and Mayer (1963). Bott's attempt to relate conjugal role performance to network structure must be viewed as a significant and badly needed theoretical leap forward in the study of kinship relations. Its significance may perhaps be measured by the fact that it took a decade, and a new generation of sociologists, to be able to put her stimulating hypotheses to work (cf. Udry and Hall 1965; Nelson 1966; Aldous and Straus 1966; and Turner 1967).
2. The nickname 'Red' is derived from the way they smeared their clothes and bodies with red ochre in the traditional manner.

R

3. The 'School' Xhosa are so called because they attended schools at the Christian mission.

4. For recent exceptions, and fortunately these are increasing, see for example Burgess (1960), Rosow (1967), Simpson and McKinney (1966), Townsend (1957 and 1968) and Wolff (1959). Though most attribute the change in network structure and interaction patterns to physical causes, Cumming and Henry (1961) attribute the withdrawal of older people from social life primarily to personality change. They find there is an increasing introversion, a declining response to the influence of norms and declining emotional investment in others. It would seem very difficult to establish a causal priority: change in personality and change in network structure and interaction patterns due to physical causes are interdependent.

5. In a private communication from Peter Storey.

6. I am thus making the *naive assumption* that personality is influenced by genetic factors. To try to understand how genetic influences operate and what aspects of personality they influence and to incorporate them into my analysis would take me too far afield at this stage. Ely Devons and Max Gluckman (1964) argue that such naive assumptions are scientifically necessary.

    'In research, as in other activities gluttony can choke one. Properly applied, the duty of abstention (from studying the problems of others) involves *a rule of disciplined refusal to trespass* on the fields of other' (168).

    While I agree that entering the field of another can lead to indigestion, if not apoplexy, to ignore the problems of others is often not naive, but simply unwise. Unless we make the *attempt* as social anthropologists to become involved in the problems of our sister disciplines and they in ours, even at a very superficial level, we may never learn which of their problems are our problems, and how they have resolved them. The profitable application of graph and communication theory to the social anthropological problems posed by network analysis is a case in point. Had we been more interested in each other's problems it would not have taken almost fifteen years before the problems of quantification were approached systematically, and the woolly concept of network fashioned into an analytical instrument. To speak of *trespassing* in this context I regard as scientifically naive if not immoral. What we need now is more, not less, scientific cross-fertilization. This can only occur if we become aware of each other's problems. If I limit my analysis at this point it is not because I believe that I *should* do so on scientific grounds (as Devons and Gluckman advocate), but because I am not able to advance it any further.

7. My experience has been with larger first order zones, for of course villages of 3,000 are not isolated. Their inhabitants also have contacts outside their place of residence.

8. Though a few geographers have deplored the effect of this criticism on the study of the relation between climate and behaviour (cf. Smith 1937; Tamsma 1964), it is not an isolated case in the development of science. All too often the baby of an idea is thrown out with the bathwater of heavy criticism. Firth's total destruction of the traditional approach to the study of kinship terminology (Firth 1930) had the unfortunate effect of stopping exploration in this interesting field for decades (Leach 1967: 126).

Perhaps such vigorous blasts are necessary to prevent resources from being squandered digging pointless holes deeper. As de Bono has observed, many experts indeed are to be found 'happily at the bottom of the deepest holes, often so deep that it hardly seems worth getting out of them to look around' (de Bono 1967: 29).

Fortunately the interest in the effect of climate on social relations seem to be reviving (cf. Sewell 1966; Sewell, Kates and Phillips 1968; and Miller 1968; not to mention Leach 1954).

9. Van Gennep (1960: 22).

10. Cf. Banton (1965: 109). I also claim inside information on Swedish customs in spite of not having done research there: my wife is Swedish.

11. Weber (1930).

12. See for example Fanfani (1935), among others.

13. Gadourek (1963: 312); Goudsblom (1967: 59ff.).

14. Boissevain (1965: 120–1, 1966b: 30–1); Kenny (1960: 17); and Bax (1970). The picture sketched above does not reflect the latest developments within the Catholic Church following the Second Vatican Council. Greater emphasis is now being placed upon direct communication between man and God and the religious role of the intermediary, whether saint or priest, is stressed less. This reflects and follows from the ever

increasing division of labour and the resulting specialization of social relationships.

15. Jojada Verrips has noted a difference in social behaviour and organization between Gereformeerd and Hervormd Protestants in a Dutch village he recently studied. He relates this to a number of doctrinal differences between the two. The Gereformeerden preach a 'horizontal' doctrine of brotherly love: salvation is obtained by baptism and obedience to the teaching of the Bible. This is criticized as too Catholic by the Hervormden, who advocate a more 'vertical' doctrine. For Hervormden, attention to neighbours comes after assurance that salvation, which has been predetermined, has been obtained. Since this assurance is never obtained, there is little time for one's fellow-man (Verrips: unpublished working paper).

16. For an overview of some of these opinions the reader may consult the rather subjective but witty account of Dutch society by the former Spanish Ambassador to the Netherlands, the Duke De Baena (1966, especially pp. 59–73). The Dutch sociologist Johan Goudsblom (1966: 33) points to the same bluntness of manner and notes that: 'In part this may be ascribed to the heritage of the self-conscious regent élite, which found little occasion to go out of its way in politeness to anybody, but it may have been equally important that this example was reinforced in the lower strata of society by the teachings of Calvinism, instilling a distrust of extravagance and encouraging sobriety.'

17. Lenski (1963) in Detroit found that the intensity of family relations was higher among Catholics than among Protestants, hence they were less mobile geographically, and were therefore less well off than Protestants. There is evidence that the accumulation of wealth and its investment in economic activity is necessarily related to a readiness to sever relations with persons who are not useful economically. Jongmans (1968) observed that the wealthiest persons in the Tunisian village he studied maintained the fewest exchange relations. Though this 'closing of the hands' lost them honour, it did permit them to accumulate capital and employ it as they thought best. Others who wished to maintain both honour and wealth were forced to move elsewhere.

18. Young and Willmott (1957) have given a vivid description of the effects of physical mobility on the structure of social relations.

19. Bott (1957: 107f.) provides some evidence that the density (connectedness in her terms) is correlated with physical and social mobility.
20. Watson (1964) coined the term 'spiralist' to indicate this combination of social, career and residential mobility.
21. Krech *et al.* (1962: 104–6).
22. Banton (1965: 109).
23. Cf. Elias and Scotson (1965).

Chapter 5: AN EXPLORATION OF TWO SOCIAL NETWORKS

1. This chapter was originally presented to a symposium on social networks organized by the Afrika Studiecentrum, Leyden, 16–22 September 1969, and subsequently published in substantially the same form (Boissevain 1973).
2. Rather than wait until I have the time to gather data on a more comparative basis, I have chosen to present most of it here, so that its relevance may be judged and some of the problems associated with it considered before further attempts to collect similar material are made. Although the data do indeed confirm a number of the hypotheses advanced, the sample used is obviously too small for much weight to be attached to this. Nonetheless I hope the findings will provoke further discussion and research.

    At this point it would seem advisable to say a few words about how the research was carried out. I selected Malta because I had already considerable knowledge of the Island and the social customs of the people (Boissevain 1965, 1969). As informants I chose two school teachers. Pietru, with whom I had worked before, is a village teacher, married to a city girl. Cecil, the second informant, is a city teacher, married to a girl from a rural town. I met him the year previous to carrying out the research. Each made out lists of all the people over fourteen he knew. As Pietru knew 1,751 persons and Cecil 648, this task involved considerable work. After all acquaintances had been listed, an information sheet on every person known was filled out first by me and later by Pietru and Cecil. These provided data on the social background, number of shared role relations, frequency of contact, last contact, the actual contents of the relationship and the other acquaintances held in common. Once the data sheets for each of the informants' acquaintances were completed, I asked Cecil and Pietru to sort the forms according to the affective or emotional importance of their acquaintances to themselves. I then discussed the resulting categorization extensively with them. I also gathered detailed biographical information from each informant and collected case histories on a variety of situations in which segments of their networks had been mobilized. These data, which are continually expanding, were typed on some 200 six by eight inch cards. Finally, back in Holland, the data were coded, punched on cards and tabulated.

3. Kapferer (1973) argues this point in greater detail.

Chapter 6: MANIPULATORS: BROKERS AS SOCIAL ENTREPRENEURS

1. 'To the extent that persons take the initiative, and in the pursuit of profit in some discernable form manipulate other persons and resources, they are acting as entrepreneurs' (Barth 1963: 6).
2. See Boissevain (1969b). In making this distinction between brokerage and patronage I am following Adrian Mayer's lead (Mayer 1963, 1966 and 1967).
3. See for example Bott (1957: 140); Bailey (1963: 59ff.); Geertz (1960); Wolf (1956); Blok (1969) and Bax (1970), to mention but a few.
4. Puzo (1969).
5. See Weaver (1949).
6. See Boissevain (1966b).
7. Bailey (1969: 170–1).
8. Southall (1961: 28).
9. See Mayer (1967).
10. For a discussion of the conversion problems of entrepreneurs see Introduction and articles in Barth (1963).
11. Boissevain (1966a: 230–1).
12. Paine has pointed out, however, that the conversion of second order resources into first order resources can also be fraught with problems (Paine 1963).
13. I have borrowed the useful concept of niche from Barth to

refer to 'The position which the entrepreneur occupies in relation to resources, competitors and clients' (Barth 1963: 9).
14. The account of the career of Tadgh O'Sullivan is based on Bax (1970).

Chapter 7: COALITIONS

1. Gamson (1968: 530); see also Neal (1964: 97).
2. *The Shorter Oxford English Dictionary.*
3. Mair (1965: 13). Nadel (1951: 145–90) and Goody (1961: 5–8) also provide illuminating discussions of the concept of corporate groups.
4. Cf. Firth (1964: 60).
5. Boissevain (1971).
6. A clique has also been defined as 'a sub-group within a larger structure whose members prefer to associate with each other on the basis of sheer liking or common interest' (Volkart 1964: 97). This definition is acceptable if we substitute coalition for sub-group and eliminate 'within a larger structure' as redundant, for depending upon the level of abstraction, all coalitions can be placed within larger, encapsulating structures.
7. Mayer (1966: 116, n. 15) makes the same distinction. Loomis and Beegle (1950) examine sociometric cliques that appear to have no common identity and have been isolated on the basis of sociometric techniques.
8. Warner and Lunt (1941), West (1945), Davis, Gardner & Gardner (1965), and Hollingshead (1961), who use the study of cliques as an important research instrument to analyse social classes, provide illuminating studies. Perhaps the most famous study of cliques is the bank wiring observation room described by Roethlesberger and Dickson (1939).
9. Whyte (1948) gives an example of a clique with a leader, while Davis, Gardner & Gardner (1965) and Hollinghead (1961) give descriptions of leaderless cliques. Roethlesberger and Dickson (1939) describe a clique with an emerging leader.
10. This structuring is apparent in the literature on all cliques, and is particularly carefully analysed by Davis, Gardner & Gardner (1965).
11. Cf. Loomis and Beegle (1950: 134).

12. Wolf (1966a: 15–16).
13. Loomis and Beegle (1950: 133).
14. Cf. Gilmore (1964: 280, 281).
15. For an up to date, short annotated bibliography on juvenile gangs, see Keiser (1969: 81–2). For a theoretical treatment of leader-follower teams see Bailey (1969).
16. Whyte (1955). The following discussion of the Nortons is based on pages 3–51.
17. The reader should compare this diagram with that sketched by Whyte (1955: 13), which reflects the relative pecking order of the gang during the late spring and summer of 1937. I personally find Whyte's diagram misleading, for it sets out a hierarchy or chain of command which does not exist. Whyte notes specifically (1955: 258) that when Doc was absent no one initiated action, and the gang remained split in separate groups that had no contact with each other. This perspective is not given in Whyte's diagram.
18. See for example Yablonsky (1967) and Keiser (1969).
19. As for example do Harries-Jones (1969); Mayer (1966); Whitten & Wolfe (n.d.). See also Barnes (1969: 64) for a somewhat different perspective.
20. Thoden van Velzen (1973) provides an excellent illustration of this principle in what he calls a levelling coalition the members of which are target oriented. That is, their common element is dislike of a certain rich farmer. They merge to bring about his downfall through a series of actions. See also chapter 8, n. 16 below.
21. Blehr (1963); Scheams (1964); Trouwborst (1973); J. Schneider (1969); P. Schneider (1972); and Maas (1969: 81–4, 115–16).
22. Firth (1965: 117–31).
23. Blok (1973 and 1974).
24. Firth and contributors (1957) and Lewis (1954) were perhaps the first to pay serious sociological attention to factions, though others, such as Fenton (1955), Linton (1936: 229) and Murdock (1949: 90) pointed to their prevalence without attempting to analyse them in their own right.
25. Nicholas (1965) provides an excellent analytical survey of factions in various parts of the world and India in particular.
26. My thoughts on factions have in particular been stimulated by the discussions of Bailey (1969) and Nicholas (1965; 1966) in addition to the works listed in a previous discussion (Boissevain 1964).

27. Bailey (1969) sees factions as ideal types, composed exclusively of followers tied to the leader by purely transactional relations. I think this poses a needless limitation, for the leader, concerned with expanding his following, recruits followers by any means available. It is also notable that, especially in Indian villages, kinship (i.e. moral) ties appear to form the most important recruitment principle (cf. Epstein 1962; Lewis 1954; Nicholas 1965).
28. Cf. Layendecker (1967).
29. Bailey (1969: 49).
30. Bailey (1969: 46).
31. Bailey (1969: 54–5, 80–2).
32. Cf. Nicholas (1965: 46ff.); Siegel and Beals (1960a and b).
33. Bailey (1969: 52); Nicholas (1965: 57–8).
34. Cf. Epstein (1962: 129, 140, 284, 290); Nicholas (1965).
35. Banfield (1958); Silverman (1968); Schneider (1969); Schneider (1972); and Schneider, Schneider and Hansen (1972) all deal with Italy. Anderson and Anderson (1962) and Wolf (1966: 81–95) note the proliferation of corporate associations in Western and Northern Europe as compared to the extreme South.
36. Cf. Boissevain and Blok (n.d.). Elias (1972) provides a stimulating discussion of state formation and nation building and the attributes of a Nation-State.

Chapter 8: CONFLICT AS PROCESS

1. Further details on Malta, the village on which this study focuses and the various conflicting groups may be found in several other works (Boissevain 1964, 1965, 1969a) to which reference will be made from time to time.
2. Although I use the present tense I am referring to 1968, the last time I studied the village.
3. I have discussed the relation between status and occupation elsewhere (Boissevain 1965a: 49–53; 1969: 44–50).
4. In Malta's sister island Gozo only Rabat, the capital, is so divided. But the little island's eleven villages are divided into two blocs, each of which centres on a partit in Rabat.
5. Cf. Boissevain (1965: 64–6, 70–3, 111).

6. For further details on these regulations see Boissevain (1965: 75f.).
7. Though both the star and the eagle symbolize high levels of excellence, the eagle, no matter how high it flies, can never reach the star. St. Martin supporters taunt their opponents with this whenever the occasion presents itself.
8. For a discussion of the attributes of village leaders, see Boissevain (1965: 49–53).
9. Details of this dispute are given in Boissevain (1965: 88–91).
10. E.g. Bailey (1969: 1, 4, 5 and passim).
11. See Boissevain (1965: 108–11) for a more detailed discussion of this point. For background on national political conflict see Boissevain (1965: 9–14).
12. For a more detailed discussion of the history, structure and operation of Maltese political parties see Boissevain (1965: 7–14, 23–6, 122–33).

   The transformations which take place in an opposition party once it succeeds in replacing its rival at the control of government is fascinating, but lies outside the immediate scope of this chapter. I suggest that the essential and logical inconsistency of this position ultimately leads to an electoral defeat or the abandonment of its own ideological premises. If it remains true to its ideals, it will, in a democratic electoral system, be defeated from time to time and so be able to renew itself. This has happened to the Labour Parties of Great Britain and Malta, for example. The only way that it can remain in power, I suggest, is by adopting the characteristics of the establishment party as sketched above: it must become a machine run on patronage and enter into coalition with powerful—and thus conservative—blocs in society. In other words, its ideological as well as organizational characteristics must change. Certain political movements which unseated colonial powers, such as the Indian Congress Party, provide examples of this. An alternative method of remaining in power is to abolish the opposition through the establishment of a repressive single party state, as happened in Germany and Italy during the 1920s and 1930s and more recently in many communist countries and a number of the newly independent countries in Africa and Asia.
13. This is something to which Lévi-Strauss pointed in his perceptive article 'Les organisations dualistes existent-elles?' (1956). Lévi-Strauss concludes, by different means than I have

used above, that while moieties have always been treated as symmetric—as a consequence of the overheavy reliance upon the notion of social reciprocity derived from Mauss, Radcliffe-Brown and Malinowski, alongside which there is little place for asymmetrical relations—they are in fact all asymmetrical.

14. For a detailed discussion of the logic behind this process the reader is referred to Caplow's elegant treatise on the subject (1968). His discussion provides an important correction to Dahrendorf's dogmatic assertion that given the dichotomous distribution of authority in any given association, there will thus be 'two, and only two, conflict groups' (Dahrendorf 1959: 173).

15. Cf. Bailey (1969: 54–5; 80–4) who gives a penetrating analysis of the management problems of leaders in general and how ways of resolving them can lead to the progressive institutionalization of conflict groups. The reader can easily assume from his analysis that the problems of all leaders are similar, an assumption that is of course implicit in the notion of balanced opposition. Here I have argued, however, that, while opposition and establishment leaders share some of the same problems, they also have fundamentally different problems to solve, have access to different resources and so employ different strategies.

16. Thoden van Velzen (1972) describes 'interest' coalitions formed by wealthy peasants and government experts in Tanzanian villages, and 'levelling' coalitions of anti-establishment elements which combine periodically to attack the resources of the leading members of the rival coalition. He suggests that competition between coalitions of this type is found in all societies. Although they are organizationally less evolved than the 'establishment' and 'opposition' coalitions described for Malta, they are analogous and corroborate much of the analysis presented above. The low level of internal organization in the Tanzanian coalitions, particularly the 'levelling' coalition, compared to the Maltese festa partiti, derives partly from the fact that wealthy peasants of the establishment or 'interest' coalition wield power but have no authority. In contrast, the Maltese establishment festa partiti centre on roles (those of the parish priest and the offices he can bestow) from which considerable authority can be wielded. (For a useful discussion of the distinction between power and authority see Dahrendorf 1959: 165ff.) Such roles

have greater continuity in time than the often temporary command over resources (other than authority roles) from which persons derive power. Hence coalitions which form to contest the exercise of such authority, or to compete for the roles themselves, have a certain continuity. This continuity in turn permits a greater degree of internal organization to develop.

17. The structured relationship I have established between the inherent nature of conflict and change is similar to the model Dahrendorf developed (1959: 157–240). He fails however to explore fully the differing ideological and organizational characteristics of conflict groups as well as the differing strategies of their leaders. These could probably also have been generated by his model. His failure to do so illustrates, I suggest, the disadvantages of a deductive approach. There is in fact no substitute for the raw data of social behaviour as a basis from which and on which to build social theory.

Bibliography

ALDOUS, J., and M. STRAUS, 1966, Social Networks and Conjugal Roles: a Test of Bott's Hypothesis. *Social Forces* 44: 576–80.

ANDERSON, ROBERT T., and GALLATIN ANDERSON, 1962, The Indirect Social Structure of European Village Communities. *American Anthropologist* 64: 1016–27.

BAENA, DUKE DE, 1966, *The Dutch Puzzle*. The Hague: L. J. C. Boucher.

BAILEY, F. G., 1963, *Politics and Social Change: Orissa in 1959*. London: Oxford University Press.

——, 1969, *Stratagems and Spoils: A Social Anthropology of Politics*. Oxford: Basil Blackwell.

BANFIELD, E. C., 1958, *The Moral Basis of a Backward Society*. Glencoe: The Free Press.

BANTON, MICHAEL, 1964, Anthropological Perspectives in Sociology. *The British Journal of Sociology* 15: 95–112.

——, 1965[a], *Roles: An Introduction to the Study of Social Relations*. London: Tavistock Publications.

——, ed., 1965[b], *Political Systems and the Distribution of Power*. London: Tavistock Publications.

——, ed., 1966, *The Social Anthropology of Complex Societies*. London: Tavistock Publications.

BARNES, J. A., 1969, Networks and Political Process. *In* Mitchell (1969[a]: 51–76).

BARTH, FREDRIK, ed., 1963, *The Role of the Entrepreneur in Social Change in Northern Norway*. Bergen: Universitets-forlaget.

——, 1966, *Models of Social Organization*. London: Royal Anthropological Institute.

——, 1967, On the Study of Social Change. *American Anthropologist* 69: 661–9.

BAVELAS, A., 1948, A Mathematical Model of Group Structures. *Applied Anthropology* 7: 16–30.

BAX, MART, 1970, Patronage Irish Style: Irish Politicians as Brokers. *Sociologische Gids* 17: 179–91.

BLAU, PETER M., 1964, *Exchange and Power in Social Life*. New York: John Wiley & Sons.

BLEHR, O., 1963, Action Groups in a Society with Bilateral Kinship: A Case Study from the Faroe Islands. *Ethnology* 2: 269–75.

BLOK, ANTON, 1969, Variations in Patronage. *Sociologische Gids* 16: 365–78.

——, 1973, Coalitions in Sicilian Peasant Society. *In* Boissevain and Mitchell (1973).

——, 1974, *The Mafia of a Sicilian Village, 1860–1960. A Study of Violent Peasant Entrepreneurs*. Oxford: Basil Blackwell.

BOISSEVAIN, JEREMY, 1964, Factions, Parties and Politics in a Maltese Village. *American Anthropologist* 66: 1275–87.

——, 1965, *Saints and Fireworks: Religion and Politics in Rural Malta*. London: Athlone Press.

——, 1966[a], Poverty and Politics in a Sicilian Agro-Town. *International Archives of Ethnography* 50: 198–236.

——, 1966[b], Patronage in Sicily. *Man* (N.S.) 1: 18–33.

——, 1968, The Place of Non-Groups in the Social Sciences. *Man* (N.S.) 3: 542–56.

——, 1969[a], *Hal-Farrug: A Village in Malta*. New York: Holt, Rinehart and Winston.

——, 1969[b], Patrons as Brokers. *Sociologische Gids* 16: 379–386.

——, 1970[a], *The Italians of Montreal: Social adjustment in a plural society*. Ottawa: Royal Commission for Bilingualism and Biculturalism.

——, 1970[b], Fieldwork in Malta. *In* George D. Spindler, ed., *Being an Anthropologist Fieldwork in Eleven Cultures*. New York: Holt, Rinehart and Winston, Inc., pp. 58–84.

——, 1971, Second Thoughts on Quasi-Groups, Categories and Coalitions. *Man* (N.S.) 6: 168–72.

——, 1973, An Exploration of Two First-Order Zones. *In* Boissevain and Mitchell (1973).

BOISSEVAIN, JEREMY, and J. CLYDE MITCHELL, eds., 1973, *Network Analysis: Studies in Human Interaction*. The Hague: Mouton and Co. for the Afrika Studiecentrum.

BOISSEVAIN, JEREMY, and ANTON BLOK, n.d., Mediterranean Folk Cultures, Western. Revised ed. *Encyclopaedia Britannica*. In press.

BOTT, ELIZABETH, 1957, *Family and Social Network*. London: Tavistock Publications.

BURGESS, ERNEST W., ed., 1960, *Aging in Western Societies*. Chicago: University of Chicago Press.

CAPLOW, THEODORE, 1968, *Two Against One: Coalitions in Triads*. Englewood Cliffs, N.J.: Prentice-Hall.

CHERRY, COLIN, 1966, *On Human Communication: A Review, a Survey, and a Criticism*. 2nd ed. Cambridge, Mass.: The M.I.T. Press.

COHEN, ABNER, 1965, *Arab Border-Villages in Israel*. Manchester: Manchester University Press.

COHEN, PERCY S., 1968, *Modern Social Theory*. London: Heinemann.

CUBITT, TESSA, 1973, Network Density Among Urban Families. *In* Boissevain and Mitchell (1973).

CUMMING, ELAINE, and WILLIAM E. HENRY, 1961, *Growing Old: The Process of Disengagement*. New York: Basic Books.

CUTILEIRO, JOSÉ, 1971, *A Portuguese Rural Society*. Oxford: Clarendon Press.

DAHRENDORF, RALF, 1959, *Class and Class Conflict in Industrial Society*. London: Routledge & Kegan Paul, Ltd.

DAVIS, ALLISON, B. BURLEIGH, A. GARDNER and MARY R. GARDNER, 1965, *Deep South: A Social Anthropological Study of Caste and Class*. 2nd ed. Chicago: The University of Chicago Press.

DE BONO, EDWARD, 1967, *The Use of Lateral Thinking*. London: Jonathan Cape.

DEVONS, ELY, and MAX GLUCKMAN, Conclusion: Modes and Consequences of Limiting a Field of Study. *In* Gluckman (1964: 158–261).

DURKHEIM, EMILE, 1961, *Moral Education*. New York: The Free Press.

——, 1964, *The Division of Labour in Society*. Glencoe: The Free Press.

EASTON, DAVID, 1959, Political Anthropology. *In* Bernard J. Siegel, ed., *Biennial Review of Anthropology* 1959. Stanford: Stanford University Press, pp. 210–62.

ELIAS, NORBERT, 1969, *Ueber den Prozess der Zivilisation: Soziogenetische und psychogenetische Untersuchungen*. 2nd ed. Bern/München: Francke Verlag.

——, 1970, *Was ist Soziologie?* München: Juventa Verlag.

——, 1972, Processes of State Formation and Nation Building. *Transactions of the 7th World Congress of Sociology. Varna, September 1970*. Geneva: International Sociological Association.

ELIAS, NORBERT, and JOHN L. SCOTSON, 1965, *The Established and the Outsiders: A Sociological Enquiry into Community Problems*. London: Frank Cass & Co.

EPSTEIN, T. SCARLETT, 1962, *Economic Development and Social Change in South India*. Manchester: University Press.

EVANS-PRITCHARD, E. E., 1940, *The Nuer*. Oxford: The Clarendon Press.

——, 1951ᵃ, *Kinship and Marriage among the Nuer*. Oxford: The Clarendon Press.

——, 1951[b], *Social Anthropology*. London: Cohen & West Ltd.

FANFANI, A., 1935, *Catholicism, Protestantism, and Capitalism*. London: Sheed and Ward.

FENTON, W. N., 1955, Factionalism in American Indian Society. Vienna: *Actes du IVe Congrès international des sciences anthropologiques et ethnologiques, 1953*. Vol. 2: 330–40.

FIRTH, RAYMOND, 1930, Marriage and the Classificatory System of Relationship. *Journal of the Royal Anthropological Institute* 60: 235–68.

——, 1957, Introduction to Symposium on Factions in Indian and Overseas Indian Societies. *British Journal of Sociology* 8: 291–5.

——, 1964, *Essays on Social Organization and Values*. London: The Athlone Press.

——, 1965, *Primitive Polynesian Economy*. 2nd ed. London: Routledge & Kegan Paul.

FLAMENT, CLAUDE, 1963, *Application of Graph Theory to Group Structure*. Englewood Cliffs, N.J.: Prentice-Hall.

FRANKENBERG, RONALD, 1966, *Communities in Britain: Social Life in Town and Country*. Harmondsworth: Penguin Books.

FREEDMAN, MAURICE, ed., 1967, *Social Organization: Essays Presented to Raymond Firth*. London: Frank Cass.

GADOUREK, I., 1963, *Riskante Gewoonten en Zorg voor Eigen Welzijn*. Groningen: J. B. Wolters.

GAMSON, WILLIAM A., 1968, Coalition Formation. *In* Sills (1968: 529–34).

GEERTZ, CLIFFORD, 1960, The Javanese Kijaji: The Changing Role of a Cultural Broker. *Comparative Studies in Society and History* 2: 228–49.

GENNEP, ARNOLD VAN, 1960, *The Rites of Passage*. Chicago: The University of Chicago Press. First published in 1908.

GILMORE, HARLAN W., 1964, Gang. *In* Gould and Kolb (1964: 280–1).

s

GLUCKMAN, MAX, ed., 1964, *Closed Systems and Open Minds: The Limits of Naïvety in Social Anthropology.* Chicago: Aldine Publishing Company.

——, 1968, Psychological, Sociological and Anthropological Explanations of Witchcraft and Gossip: A Clarification. *Man* (N.S.) 3: 20–30.

GOFFMAN, ERVING, 1959, *The Presentation of Self in Everyday Life.* Garden City, N.Y.: Doubleday Anchor Books.

GOODY, J., 1961, The Classification of Double Descent Systems. *Current Anthropology* 2: 2–25.

GOUDSBLOM, JOHAN, 1967. *Dutch Society.* New York: Random House.

GOULD, JULIUS, and WILLIAM L. KOLB, eds., 1964, *A Dictionary of the Social Sciences.* London: Tavistock Publications.

GOULDNER, ALVIN W., 1970, *The Coming Crisis of Western Sociology.* London: Heinemann.

HARRIES-JONES, P., 1969, 'Home-Boy' Ties and Political Organization in a Copperbelt Township. *In* Mitchell (1969ª: 297–347).

HARRIS, MARVIN, 1968, *The Rise of Anthropological Theory.* London: Routledge & Kegan Paul.

HOLLINGSHEAD, A. B., 1961, *Elmtown's Youth.* New York: Science Editions.

HOMANS, GEORGE, C., 1951, *The Human Group.* London: Routledge & Kegan Paul.

——, 1958, Social Behaviour as Exchange. *American Sociological Review* 62: 597–606.

——, 1961, *Social Behaviour: Its Elementary Forms.* London: Routledge & Kegan Paul.

HUNTINGTON, ELLSWORTH, 1924, *Civilization and Climate,* 3rd ed. New Haven: Yale University Press.

JARVIE, I. C., 1964, *The Revolution in Anthropology.* London: Routledge & Kegan Paul.

JONGMANS, D. G., 1968, Meziaa en Horma. *Kroniek van Afrika* 3: 1–34.

KAPFERER, B., 1969, Norms and the Manipulation of Relationships in a Work Context. *In* Mitchell (1969ª: 181–244).

——, 1973, Social Network and Conjugal Role in Urban Zambia: Towards a Reformulation of the Bott Hypothesis. *In* Boissevain and Mitchell (1973).

KEENAN, BRIGID, and PETER BRETT, 1970, The Network Syndrome. *Nova*, January issue, pp. 20–5.

KEISER, R. LINCOLN, 1969, *The Vice Lords: Warriors of the Streets*. New York: Holt, Rinehart and Winston.

KENNY, MICHAEL, 1960, Patterns of Patronage in Spain. *Anthropological Quarterly* 33: 14.23.

KLEIN, JOSEPHINE, 1956, *The study of Groups*. London: Routledge and Kegan Paul.

KRECH, DAVID, RICHARD S. CRUTCHFIELD and EGERTON L. BALLACHEY, 1962, *Individual in Society*. New York: McGraw-Hill.

KUHN, THOMAS S., 1970, *The Structure of Scientific Revolutions*. 2nd ed. International Encyclopedia of Unified Science, vol. 2, no. 2. Chicago: University of Chicago Press.

LAEYENDECKER, LEONARDUS, 1967, *Religie en Conflict: de zogenaamde sekten in sociologisch perspectief*. Meppel: Boom en Zoon.

LEACH, EDMUND R., 1954, *Political Systems of Highland Burma*. London: The London School of Economics and Political Science.

——, 1961ª, *Pul Eliya: A Village in Ceylon*. Cambridge: Cambridge University Press.

——, 1961ᵇ, *Rethinking Anthropology*. London: The Athlone Press.

——, The Language of Kachin Kinship: Reflections on a Tikopia Model. *In* Freedman (1967: 125–52).

LEAVITT, HAROLD J., 1951, Some Effects of Certain Communication Patterns on Group Performance. *Journal of Abnormal and Social Psychology* 46: 38–50. Reprinted *in* Smith (1966: 222–43).

LENSKI, GERHARD, 1963, *The Religious Factor*. New York: Doubleday & Co.

LÉVI-STRAUSS, CLAUDE, 1956, Les Organisations Dualistes Existent-Elles? *Bijdragen tot de taal-, land- en volkenkunde* 112: 99–128. Reprinted as: Do Dual Organizations Exist? *in* C. Lévi-Strauss, *Structural Anthropology*. London: Allen Lane The Penguin Press, 1968, pp. 132–63.

LEWIS, OSCAR, 1954, *Group Dynamics in a North Indian Village: A Study of Factions*. Delhi: Programme Evaluation Organization of the Government of India Planning Commission.

LINTON, RALPH, 1936, *The Study of Man*. New York: D. Appleton-Century Co.

LOOMIS, C. F., and J. BEEGLE, 1950, *Rural Social Systems*. New York: Prentice-Hall.

MAAS, PETER, 1969, *The Canary That Sang: The Valachi Papers*. London: MacGibbon & Kee.

MAIR, LUCY, 1962, *Primitive Government*. Harmondsworth: Penguin Books.

——, 1965, *An Introduction to Social Anthropology*. Oxford: Clarendon Press.

MARKHAM, S. F., 1947, *Climate and the Energy of Nations*. 2nd ed. New York: Oxford University Press.

MAYER, PHILIP, 1963, *Townsmen or Tribesmen: Conservatism and the Process of Urbanization in a South African City*. Cape Town: Oxford University Press.

MAYER, ADRIAN, 1963, Some Political Implications of Community Development in India. *European Journal of Sociology* 4: 86–100.

——, 1966, The Significance of Quasi-Groups in the Study of Complex Societies. *In* Banton (1966: 97–122).

——, 1967, Patrons and Brokers: Rural Leadership in Four Overseas Indian Communities. *In* Freedman (1967: 167–188).

MILLER, WILLIS H., 1968, Santa Ana Winds and Crime. *Professional Geographer* 20: 23–7.

MITCHELL, J. CLYDE, ed., 1969[a], *Social Networks in Urban Situations*. Manchester University Press for the Institute for Social Research, University of Zambia.

——, 1969[b], The Concept and Use of Social Networks. *In* Mitchell (1969[a]: 1–50).

MITCHELL, W. E., 1963, Theoretical Problems in the Concept of Kindred. *American Anthropologist* 65: 343–54.

——, 1965, The Kindred and Baby Bathing in Academe. *American Anthropologist* 67: 977–85.

MONTESQUIEU, CHARLES-LOUIS, 1748, *L'Esprit des Lois*.

MURDOCK, GEORGE P., 1949, *Social Structure*. London: Macmillan.

——, 1964, The Kindred. *American Anthropologist* 66: 129–132.

NADEL, S. F., 1951, *The Foundations of Social Anthropology*. London: Cohen & West.

NEAL, F. W., 1964, Coalition. *In* Gould and Kolb (1964: 97–8).

NELSON, JOEL I., 1966, Clique Contacts and Family Orientations. *American Sociological Review* 31: 663–72.

NICHOLAS, RALPH W., 1965, Factions: A Comparative Analysis. *In* Banton (1965[b]: 21–61).

——, 1966, Segmentary Factional Political Systems. *In* Marc J. Swartz, Victor W. Turner, Arthur Tuden, eds., *Political Anthropology*. Chicago: Aldine Publishing Co., pp. 49–59.

NIEMEIJER, RUDO, 1973, Some Applications of the Notion of Density to Network Analysis. *In* Boissevain and Mitchell (1973).

PAINE, ROBERT, 1963, Entrepreneurial Activity Without Its Profits. *In* Barth (1963: 33–55).

——, 1967, What is Gossip About? An Alternative Hypothesis. *Man* (N.S.) 2: 278–85.

PETERS, E. L., 1967, Some Structural Aspects of the Feud among the Camel-Herding Bedouin of Cyrenaica. *Africa* 37: 261–82.

PONS, VALDO, 1969, *Stanleyville: An African Urban Com-*

262   *Bibliography*

munity under Belgian Administration. London: Oxford University Press for the International African Institute.

PRESSY, SIDNEY L., and RAYMOND G. KUHLEN, 1957, *Psychological Development Through the Life Span*. New York: Harper and Row.

PUZO, MARIO, 1969, *The Godfather*. London: Heinemann.

RADCLIFFE-BROWN, A. R., 1950, Introduction. *In* A. R. Radcliffe-Brown and Daryll Forde, eds., *African Systems of Kinship and Marriage*. London: Oxford University Press, pp. 1–85.

——, 1952, *Structure and Function in Primitive Society*. London: Cohen and West.

RAPOPORT, ROBERT N., 1958, Review of Bott (1957). *Man* 88: 182–3.

READER, D. H., 1964, Models in Social Change with Special Reference to Southern Africa. *African Studies* 23: 11–33.

REINA, RUBEN, 1959, Two Patterns of Friendship in a Guatemalan Community. *American Anthropologist* 61: 44–50.

RIKER, WILLIAM H., 1968, The Study of Coalitions. *In* Sills (1968: 524–9).

ROETHLESBERGER, F. J., and WILLIAM JOHN DICKSON, 1939, *Management and the Worker*. Cambridge, Mass.: Harvard University Press.

ROSOW, IRVING, 1967, *Social Integration of the Aged*. New York: Free Press.

SCHEAMS, DANIEL J., 1964, Kith-Centered Action Groups in an Ilokano Barrio. *Ethnology* 3: 364–8.

SCHNEIDER, JANE, 1969, Family Patrimonies and Economic Behavior in Western Sicily. *Anthropological Quarterly* 42: 109–29.

SCHNEIDER, PETER, 1972, Coalition Formation and Colonialism in Western Sicily. *European Journal of Sociology* 13: 255–67.

SCHNEIDER, PETER, JANE SCHNEIDER and EDWARD HANSEN, 1972, Modernization and Development: The Role of Regional Elites and Non-Corporate Groups in the European Mediterranean. *Comparative Studies in Society and History* 14: 328–50.

SEWELL, W. R. DERRICK, ed., 1966, *Human Dimensions of Weather Modification.* Chicago: University of Chicago Press.

SEWELL, W. R. DERRICK, ROBERT W. KATES and LEE E. PHILLIPS, 1968, Human Response to Weather and Climate. *Geographical Review* 58: 262–80.

SIEGEL, BERNARD J., and ALAN R. BEALS, 1960ᵃ, Pervasive Factionalism. *American Anthropologist* 62: 395–417.

——, 1960ᵇ, Conflict and Factionalist Dispute. *Journal of the Royal Anthropological Institute* 90: 107–17.

SILLS, DAVID L., ed., 1968, *International Encyclopedia of the Social Sciences.* U.S.A.: The Macmillan Co. and the Free Press.

SILVERMAN, SYDEL, 1968, Agricultural Organization, Social Structure, and Values in Italy: Amoral Familism Reconsidered. *American Anthropologist* 70: 1–20.

SIMPSON, IDA HARPER, and JOHN MCKINNINEY, eds., 1966, *Social Aspects of Aging.* Durham: Duke University Press.

SMITH, ALFRED G., ed., 1966, *Communication and Culture: Readings in the Codes of Human Interaction.* New York: Holt, Rinehart and Winston.

SMITH, J. RUSSEL, 1937, Climate. *In* E.R.A. Seligmann, ed., *Encylopaedia of the Social Sciences.* New York: Macmillan, vol. II, pp. 556–61.

SOUTHALL, AIDEN, 1961, Introductory Summary. *In* A. Southall, ed., *Social Change in Modern Africa.* London: Oxford University Press, pp. 1–66.

SRINIVAS, M. N., and ANDRÉ BETEILLE, 1964, Networks in Indian Social Structure. *Man* 64: 165–8.

STAËL, MADAME DE, 1800, *De Littérature considérée dans ses rapports avec les institutions sociales.*

STEBBINS, ROBERT A., 1969, On Linking Barth and Homans: A Theoretical Note. *Man* (N.S.) 4: 432–7.

TAINE, HIPPOLYTE, 1865, *La Philosophie de l'art.*

264 *Bibliography*

TAMSMA, R., 1964, Aspecten van aride gebieden. *Tijdschrift van het Kon. Ned. Aardrijkskundig Genootschap* 81: 142–171.

THODEN VAN VELZEN, H. U. E., 1973, Coalitions and Network Analysis. *In* Boissevain and Mitchell (1972).

TOWNSEND, PETER, 1957, *The Family Life of Old People: An Inquiry in East London.* London: Routledge & Kegan Paul.

——, 1968, *Old People in Three Industrial Societies.* London: Routledge & Kegan Paul.

TROUWBORST, ALBERT A., 1973, Two types of Partial Networks in Burundi. *In* Boissevain and Mitchell (1973).

TURNER, CHRISTOPHER, 1967, Conjugal Roles and Social Networks. *Human Relations* 20: 121–30.

UDRY, J. R., and M. HALL, 1965, Marital Role Segregation and Social Networks in Middle-Class, Middle-Aged Couples. *Journal of Marriage and Family Living* 27: 392–5.

VAN VELSEN, J., 1964, *The Politics of Kinship.* Manchester: Manchester University Press.

VOLKART, EDMUND, H., 1964, Clique. *In* Gould and Kolb (1964: 97).

WARNER, W. L., and P. S. LUNT, 1941, *The Social Life of a Modern Community.* New Haven: Yale University Press.

WATSON, W., 1964, Social Mobility and Social Class in Industrial Communities. *In* Gluckman (1964: 129–57).

WEAVER, WARREN, 1949, The Mathematics of Communication. *Scientific American* 181: 11–15. Reprinted *in* Smith (1966: 15–24).

WEBER, M., 1930, *The Protestant Ethic and the Spirit of Capitalism.* New York: Scribners.

WEST, JAMES, 1945, *Plainville U.S.A.* New York: Columbia University Press.

WHITTEN, NORMAN E. Jr., and ALVIN W. WOLFE, n.d., Network Analysis. *In* John J. Honigmann, ed., *The Handbook of Social and Cultural Anthropology.* Chicago: Rand-McNally. In press.

WHYTE, WILLIAM FOOTE, 1948, *Human Relations in the Restaurant Industry*. New York: McGraw-Hill.

——, 1955, *Street Corner Society*, 2nd ed. Chicago: University of Chicago Press.

WOLF, ERIC R., 1956, Aspects of Group Relations in a Complex Society: Mexico. *American Anthropologist* 58: 1065–1077.

——, 1966[a], Kinship, Friendship, and Patron-Client Relations in Complex Societies. *In* Banton (1966: 1–22).

——, 1966[b], *Peasants*. Englewood Cliffs, New Jersey: Prentice-Hall.

WOLFF, KURT, 1959, *The Biological, Sociological and Psychological Aspects of Aging*. Springfield, Ill.: Thomas.

YABLONSKY, LEWIS, 1967, *The Violent Gang*. Harmondsworth: Penguin Books.

YOUNG, MICHAEL, and PETER WILLMOTT, 1957, *Family and Kinship in East London*. Harmondsworth: Penguin Books.

ZIPF, G. K., 1949, *Human Behavior and the Principle of Least Effort*. Cambridge, Mass.: Addison-Wesley Publishing Co., Inc.

Index

Corporate characteristics. *See* Group (corporate); Institutionalization of coalitions; Organization, formal (corporate)

Costs, social and material, 25, 89, 95, 158, 161. *See also* Investment in relationships; Resources

Credit, 4, 149, 152–3, 159–64, 167–9, 197

Cubitt, T., 239 n. 11

Cultural factors affecting network, 83, 94, 97, 157. *See also* Ideology; Religion

Cultural gap, 148, 155

Cumming, E., 242 n. 4

Cutileiro, J., 236 n. 13

Dahrendorf, R., 236 n. 11, n. 12, 251 n. 14, n. 16, 252 n. 17

Davis, A., 247 n. 8–10

de Bono, E., 243 n. 8

Debt relationship, 85, 159–61, 163–5, 168–9. *See also* Credit

Degree (degree of connexion), 35, 40, 45, 60, 63, 90–1, 122, 239 n. 17, 241 n. 5

Density (adjacency) definition and measurement of, 37, 39, 112, 239 n. 16, 241 n. 5; discussion of, as structural characteristic of networks and coalitions, 35, 37–40, 60, 63, 112–13, 118, 173, 191, 195, 200–2; influences on, 67, 69–74, 77–8, 84–8, 121–3, 141, 196, 202, 245 n. 19; influence of, on behaviour, 84, 90–3, 122–4, 144; relationship of, with other

characteristics of network, 37, 40–5, 77, 85–6, 202

Development of social patterns, 5–6, 13, 19. *See also* Change

Devons, E., 242–3 n. 6

Dickson, W. J., 247 n. 8, n. 9

Differentiation, social. *See* Specialization, internal

Directional flow of interaction, 26, 28, 33–5, 45, 176, 202, 251 n. 13

Division of labour. *See* Specialization, internal

Doc's gang. *See* Whyte, W. F.

Domenico and Edoardo, case of, 188–91, 203

Duration of coalition, 170–2, 174, 189, 190–1, 195–6, 198–9, 202, 204, 206, 251–2 n. 16; of interaction, 4–5, 34–5, 45, 48, 93, 95, 98, 141–6

Durkheim, E., 9, 234–5 n. 7

Dynamism of relationships. *See* Change

Easton, D., 236 n. 21

Economic development, 74–5, 83, 203–5, 213, 225

Edoardo and Domenico, case of, 188–91, 203

Education, 228; affecting network structure and behaviour, 83, 86–7, 89, 155, 165–6, 175, 177, 219; composition of networks and coalitions in terms of, 108–9, 118–119, 121, 174, 219

Effective zone of network. *See* Zones of network, intimacy

Effort, Zipf's principle of least, 235 n. 8

T

203, 206, 233, 234–5 n. 7.
See also Activity fields
Institutionalization of coalitions, 170, 172, 191, 195, 197–199, 202–6, 212, 214–15, 251 n. 15, 251–2 n. 16
Instrumental relationship. *See* Transactional relationship
Integration model of society. *See* Structural-functionalism
Interactional characteristics of network (content of network), 27–8, 35, 37–8, 45–6, 59, 66, 84, 97, 146, 153, 173, 179, 242 n. 4, 245 n. 2. *See also* Directional flow; Duration of interaction; Frequency of interaction; Multiplexity; Redundancy; Transactional content
Interactional content. *See* Multiplexity; Transactional content
Interconnection of network. *See* Density
Interest, broker's, 158, 161
Interest coalition, 251 n. 16
Interest, common, of coalition. *See* Goal-orientedness of coalition
Interests, conflicting. *See* Conflict; Conflict groups; Establishment and opposition
Interests, individual, 4, 6–8, 12, 19, 27, 170, 172–3, 206, 231–233, 234–5 n. 7, 235 n. 8, 237 n. 33
Interests, vested. *See* Establishment and opposition
Interference. *See* Noise
Interlinkage, 44–5
Intermediary. *See* Brokerage

Intimacy of relationship. *See* Zones of network, intimacy; Multiplexity; Transactional content
Intimacy zone of network. *See* Zones of network, intimacy
Investment in relationships, 5, 33–4, 47, 69, 83, 87, 93, 95, 133, 140, 157, 161, 180, 183–184, 196, 241 n. 1, 242 n. 4. *See also* Interactional characteristics of network; Resources
Ireland, politics and brokerage in, 166–9
Italy
climate and network in, 75–6; role of state in, 10, 204–5, 249 n. 35, 250 n. 12. *See also* Sicily

Jarvie, I. C., 18, 22, 234 n. 3, n. 4, 236 n. 28
Jongmans, D. G., 244 n. 17

Kapferer, B., 33, 50, 53, 59, 62, 72, 236 n. 18, 239 n. 10, n. 16, 241 n. 1–5, 246 n. 3
Kates, R. W., 243 n. 8
Keenan, B., 240 n. 25
Keiser, R. L., 248 n. 15, n. 18
Kenny, M., 243 n. 14
Kinship and affinity
affecting network and behaviour, 83–4, 89–90, 122–4, 244 n. 17; composition of networks and coalitions in terms of, 15–17, 69, 83–4, 89, 94, 98, 112, 115, 117–23, 126–7, 133–135, 138–41, 145–6, 148, 150–153, 180, 187–9, 192, 204, 209, 234 n. 6, 37 n. 36, 241